W9-BTO-903

Seats

NEW YORK
THIRD EDITION

6/12

Seats
NEW YORK
THIRD EDITION

180 Seating Plans to
New York Metro Area
Theatres, Concert Halls
& Sports Stadiums

www.worldseats.com

Jodé Susan Millman

New York

Limelight Editions
An Imprint of Hal Leonard Corporation
7777 West Bluemound Road
Milwaukee, WI 53213

Trade Book Division Editorial Offices
19 West 21st Street, New York, NY 10010

Third edition published by Limelight Editions in 2008

First edition published in 1998 by Applause Theatre & Cinema Books.
Second edition published in 2002 by Applause Theatre & Cinema Books.

Printed in the United States of America

Cover and title page photo: Nate Shepard
Interior photographs: Jodé Susan Millman
Stadium renderings courtesy of the New York Yankees and the New York Mets

Book design by Jodé Susan Millman and Ethan Kaplan
Graphic design by Emily Flynn

Assistant Editor: Pamela Keenan
Contributing Editors: Megan Flynn, Charles Schneider, and Aaron Lefkove

The Library of Congress has cataloged the second Applause edition as follows:

Millman, Jodé Susan
    Seats New York: 150 seating plans to New York metro area theatres,
    concert halls & sports stadiums / Jodé Susan Millman.
    Rev. ed. of: Seats / Sandy Millman. New York: Applause.
     p. cm.
    Includes index.
1. Theaters—New York Metropolitan Area—Charts, diagrams, etc.
2. Sports facilities—New York Metropolitan Area—Charts, diagrams, etc.
I. Title.

PN2277.N5 M44 2002
792'.097471 21   2003267651

Limelight ISBN: 978-0-87910-354-5

www.limelighteditions.com

The information contained within this edition of *Seats: New York* has been provided by the participating venues, organizations, governmental agencies, and public information sources. Every effort has been made to ensure the accuracy of the information presented herein; however, neither the author nor the publisher can accept responsibility for any errors, omissions, or changes in this guide.

Contents

Seating Plans

Broadway Theatres

Off-Broadway Theatres

Concert Halls

Stadiums

Theatre District Maps

Introduction

I'll admit it. The first time I ever saw a book of theater seating plans, I got out my collection of theater ticket stubs, grabbed my yellow Magic Marker highlighter, went to the book, and colored in every seat I'd occupied.

As Evita sings, "Remember, I was very young then."

Now, no one is expecting you to do the same, but you should find *Seats: New York* a most useful guide.

Notice that when you buy a ticket at a Broadway box office, the theater's seating plan is many feet away from where you purchase your ticket. There's a reason for this: the person who just sold you that ticket doesn't want you to see precisely where your seat is. He or she is afraid you might not like it when you see it in context with the other seats, and then you'll ask him for another. Or another. Or another.

But if you come to the box office armed with a copy of *Seats: New York* in your hand, you can, to use a phrase from yore, confound your enemies (the box office staff) and astound your friends (the ones for whom you agreed to pick up tickets).

Seats: New York will save you from potential embarrassment, too. Many theatergoers who've bought four tickets in Row H have gone home, immediately called their friends, and bragged, "We're all in the eighth row!" Alas, when they arrive at the theater, they've found that they're actually in the 11th row. Oh, those sneaky A, AA, and AAAs that some theaters have! With *Seats: New York*, you'll know where you stand — er, sit — before you get in the theater, and won't have made erroneous introductions in advance.

And sometimes it's fun just to peruse the pages, to see how many different theaters there are, and reminisce about the shows you saw there. Maybe you won't go so far as to grab a yellow Magic Marker highlighter, but you will be glad on many occasions that you grabbed this copy of *Seats: New York*.

— Peter Filichia

Peter Filichia is a theater critic for The Star-Ledger in Newark, New Jersey, and a columnist for theatermania.com

Acknowledgments

The theatre scene in New York was always vibrant, but now it is off the charts. Both Broadway and Off-Broadway have blossomed, bringing new venues and productions to the attention of the world. New York has three new sports stadiums and several new concert halls and auditoriums. It was a difficult, if not overwhelming, task to track down the venues and information for our 3rd Edition, but my wonderful and dedicated staff met the challenge. For that I am extremely grateful, and they deserve endless kudos.

My assistant editor, Pamela Keenan, deserves a dozen roses and curtain calls for her patience, persistence, and perseverance.

My art director, Emily Flynn, has earned a Drama Desk Award for outstanding performance in a leading role.

Thanks, once again, to the Center for the Performing Arts, Dexter High School, Dexter, Michigan, for allowing us access to the spectacular facility pictured on the cover.

Thanks to all of the facilities and organizations that provided us with special photographs and access, especially the New York Yankees and the New York Mets.

Thanks to my publisher, Limelight Editions; Clare Cerullo; Marybeth Keating; and, especially, Michael Messina for his continued assistance, guidance, and support of this project.

Thanks to Theatermania and Peter Filichia for joining the *Seats* cast.

Thanks to all of the theatre administration and box office personnel who assisted us with this project and exercised great patience with our stream of questions.

Special thanks to my children, Max and Ben, for their support and helping me retain my sense of humor and perspective on this project.

Very special thanks to my husband, Mike Harris, for his extraordinary love, patience, and enabling of this project and my love of New York theatre; and in celebration of our attaining and sharing twenty-five years of marriage, I lovingly dedicate this book.

Key to the Seating Plans

Theatre Seat Prices

Most Expensive

Least expensive

Stadium Seat Prices

Most Expensive

Least expensive

 Subways/Trains

 Buses

 Automobile directions

 Parking

 Theatre location on the Seats Theatre District Map

 Theatres that are completely wheelchair accessible

Theatres offering assisted hearing devices

Getting to Your Seats

Subways and Buses

MTA subways and buses connect you to all theatres, concert halls, sports stadiums, and events around New York City with a base fare of $2.00 no matter how far you ride.

The Subway and buses you need to get you to your destination are indicated on each *Seats* seating plan. Our *Seats* Theatre District maps highlight the important MTA transportation stops in the Midtown, Westside, and Downtown Theatre Districts.

SUBWAY TIPS

As the Theatre District is located in the Times Square area, here are some subway lines that will get you to Times Square/42nd Street: N, Q, R, S, W, 1, 2, 3, 7, 9

Still confused about taking the NYC subway? Create your own subway route, travel times, and sites along the way at *www.stophop.com* or *www.subwaynavigator.com*

BUS TIPS

As the Theatre District is located in the Times Square area, here are some quick and easy bus transportation tips for getting you to Times Square/42nd Street:

M6	Broadway/6th Avenue
M7	Columbus/Amsterdam Avenues
M10	Central Park West
M20	7th/8th Avenues
M27	49th/50th Streets Crosstown
M42	42nd Street Crosstown
M104	Broadway

All MTA buses are user-friendly because they lower themselves to curbside for easy entrance and are equipped with wheelchair lifts. Also, children under 44" tall ride the buses for free! For fares, use your MetroCard or pay as you go, but remember you need exact change or tokens for the buses, and don't forget to ask for your transfers.

MetroCard

The MetroCard is the smart and convenient way to travel around New York City. The card allows you to take the subway, hop the buses, and transfer between buses and subways (and is good for two hours from the time you pay your fare). The basic fare is $2.00, but the more you ride, the cheaper your trips!

A super-buy is the Fun Pass, which gives you a day of unlimited subway and local bus rides for $7.50.

There are many other riding options, so select the card that fits your needs. MetroCards are available at all subway stations, MetroCard merchants, vending machines, and tourist information centers.

Also, seniors and people with disabilities who have proper identification are eligible for reduced fares on all MTA services. For more information, maps, and schedules, call (212) METROCARD (within NYC) or 1-800-METROCARD (outside NYC), or visit *www.mta.info*.

Taxi

One of the most convenient, yet most frustrating, ways around town is by taxicab. Hailing a cab is no easy task, so here are a few tips:

> **TAXI TIPS**
> - Look for the yellow medallion cabs with the center roof light on. These cabs are empty and are looking for fares.
> - If the center light is off and the end lights are on, the cab is off duty. These drivers will not stop for you.
> - If the entire set of top lights is off, the cab is occupied.

Sometimes it is better to use alternate transportation or in nice weather, just hoof it!

The taxi directions you need to get you to your destination are indicated in brackets [ ] near the venue address on each *Seats* seating plan.

Parking

The parking facilities convenient to your destination are indicated on each *Seats* seating plan. For additional parking locations in the five NYC boroughs, log on to *www.parkingcarma.com*, *www.parking.com*, *www.gmcparking.com*, *www.parkfast.com*, or *www.iconparking.com*. (Icon and Edison Parkfast offer online coupons for their MSG and Broadway lots.) Also, check with your Off-Broadway box office for special discounts with local lots.

Limousine and Car Services

A show-stopping way to get to and from your theatre or sporting event is to splurge and hire a car or limousine service. These services often cost more than a taxi, and the fee depends upon your specific request and the event. For a special treat, make sure to plan ahead by checking your local phone book or contacting NYC Coach Limo International at (877) 669-5734, *www.nycitycoachlimo.com*, or New York Limo Reserve at (877) 666-0011, *www.newyorklimoreserve.com*.

Getting to Your Seats

BAMbus

For events at the Brooklyn Academy of Music, ride the BAMbus for only $5.00, round-trip. The bus departs from Manhattan's Whitney Museum at Altria, 120 Park Avenue, one hour before performances in the Howard Gilman Opera House or the Harvey Theater. Call (718) 636-4100 for reservations at least 24 hours in advance or visit *www.bam.org* for more information.

Disability Services

Access Ticket Information

Each *Seats* seating plan indicates whether the theatre is wheelchair accessible or offers assisted listening devices. Before you order your tickets, check the theatre's *Seats* seating plan for the location of the wheelchair seating. When ordering tickets, be sure to request wheelchair and companion seating or inquire as to other available disability services for your event.

Performances for the Hearing Impaired and Deaf
Theatre Development Fund: (212) 221-0013

Performances for the Partially Sighted and Blind
HAI (Hospital Audiences Inc.), (212) 575-7663

Telecharge Access Ticket Information
(212) 239-6222 or (800) 872-8997
TDD/TTY: (212) 239-2820 or
TDD/TTY: (888) 889-8587

To order accessible seating locations for wheelchairs or transfer arm locations.

Assistive Listening System
Sound Associates at (212) 582-7678 to reserve in advance. Driver's license or ID with printed address required as a deposit.

Open Electronic Captioning, Sign Language Interpreters, Preferred Seating and "Talking Hands"
Theatre Development Fund: (212) 221-0885, *www.tdf.org*

Facility Disability Services
Lincoln Center: (212) 799-3100 ext. 2204
Madison Square Garden: (212) 465-6034
Radio City: (212) 465-6115

Access a Ride
If your disability makes you unable to travel by subway or bus, the MTA offers a shared ride, door-to-door para-transit service, 24 hours a day, seven days a week. For applications, call (718) 393-4999 or visit *www.mta.info*.

Discounts for Wheelchair Guests/Companions

Available in person or by calling the box offices of the following Nederlander theatres:

Brooks Atkinson: (212) 719-4099
Gershwin: (212) 586-6510
Lunt-Fontanne: (212) 573-9200
Marquis: (212) 382-0100
Minskoff: (212) 869-0550
Nederlander: (212) 921-8000
Neil Simon: (212) 575-9200
Palace: (212) 730-8200

How to Use *Seats* to Snag the Seats You Want

The following are a few ticket tips when ordering your tickets in person, by phone or on the Web:

1. Locate the page of the theatre offering your production in *Seats*.
2. Based upon your budget and the theatre seating plan, select the best seats in the house for you.
3. To help insure that you acquire the seats you want, it is *always* best to order seats over the phone. It is worth the wait on hold.
4. It is well known that ticket vendors sell seats in the back of the house first. *Therefore, don't be shy; request the specific seats within your price range. You may be pleasantly surprised!*
5. Confirm your price and seat location with the customer service representative before you complete your purchase. Ticket sales are final and non-refundable.
6. Congratulations on getting *your* seats!

Audience Etiquette

PLEASE DO:

- Arrive before curtain time. Theater doors open one half hour prior to the performance.
- Be courteous and silent, so that all members of the audience can enjoy a memorable experience.
- Enter swiftly, sit down and be quiet. Latecomers will be seated at the discretion of the management.
- Remove your hat so as not to block the view.
- Share the armrest or keep arms folded during the performance to avoid turf wars.
- Turn off all pagers and cell phones prior to entering the theater.
- Unwrap candy or cough drops before the curtain.

PLEASE DO NOT:

- Make calls or answer the phone from your seat.
- Should the phone ring/vibrate, please proceed outside or to the lobby to answer the call.
- Check mail on your glaring BlackBerry or phone during the show. Theatres are a no-text zone.
- Bring outside food into the theater.
- Smoke in the theater; patrons may go outside during intermission.
- Use recording devices, including still cameras in the theater.

Counterfeit Tickets

Buyers beware! Do not purchase tickets sold on the street. Tickets not purchased from the theatre box office, legitimate ticket brokers, or TKTS may be counterfeit and the theatre will not honor your ticket.

Children

Check with your theater to determine whether children under the age of five are admitted and whether the production is appropriate for your children.

Theatre Schedules

Mondays are mostly dark, but a few shows do have Monday evening performances. Many shows on Tuesdays start early, so check your tickets or with the theatre for curtain times.

Security

Some venues may require the checking or searching of oversized purses, backpacks, briefcases, and bags. If you carry such items, plan to arrive early, as you may be required to proceed to baggage check.

Prices and Views

When ordering your ticket, it is recommended that you select rows behind or next to the highest price seats and enjoy virtually the same view. Be sure to ask the box office if your seats have an obstructed or partial view.

Our *Seats* seating plans do not note obstructed views or changes warranted by specific productions.

Buying Your Seats by Phone

Ticketmaster
www.ticketmaster.com
Local telephone numbers for Ticketmaster outlets:
New York: (212) 307-7171
Long Island: (631) 888-9000
Westchester: (845) 454-3388

Telecharge
(212) 239-6200, *www.telecharge.com*

Ticket Central
(212) -279-4200, *www.ticketcentral.org*

Ticket Web
(800) 965-4827, *www.ticketweb.com*

Theatermania
(212) 352-3101, *www.theatermania.com*

Smarttix.com
(212) 868-4444, *www.smarttix.com*

Other Helpful Numbers
AMEX Gold Card: (800) NOW-AMEX
Broadway Inner Circle: (212) 307-4599
Broadway Premium: (212) 220-0500
Broadway Performing Arts: (212) 307-4100
Disney on Broadway: (212) 307-4747
MSG Hotline: (212) 307-5554
NBA: (800) 4NBA-TIX
MSG/Radio City Hotline: (212) 307-1000
Spanish Language: (212) 307-4757
U.S. Open: (866) 673-6849
WNBA Hotline: (877) WNBA-TIX
Yankees Hotline: (212) 307-1212

Anatomy of a Ticket

ASTJGY	ST. JAMES THEATRE	ASTJGY061108D
061108D	246 WEST 44TH STREET	961447756423
	G Y P S Y	
$117.00		$117.00 *
TA	2:00 PM WED	TAAMEX TA
032808	JUN 11, 2008	
ORCHO	XAWEB1770-0328-S108N	ORCHO
	*INCLUDES $2.00 FACILITY FEE	
H 18	Jane Doe	H 18

Base Ticket	Facility Fee	Extra Charges:
Price $115	(Included) $2	Handling Fee $2.50
		(box office or e-mail)
		Telecharge Fee $6.75
		Mailing: $4 standard mail,
		$19 two-day delivery

Buying Your Seats Online

Thanks to the Web, the box office is now right on your desktop. And the *Seats* seating plans give you the web addresses of all your favorites venues.

Whether you order your tickets on-line or by phone, here is a glossary of terms to help you understand the ticketing system:

Face value: This is the price that is determined and charged for your ticket by the promoter, venue, or artist.

Facility charge: A fee that is collected on behalf of the venue (however, not all venues charge a facility charge).

Convenience charge: A fee that varies from event to event, and supports your access to web, phone, and kiosk services virtually 24 hours a day.

Handling fee: This is the charge for filling your ticket order, maintaining it on the system, and arranging for shipping.

Delivery fees: Telecharge: free email tickets and will call. Standard mail is a flat fee. Ticketmaster: free standard mail and will call; nominal charge for email tickets. Expedited Delivery (both): sliding scale fee based on how quickly you want your tickets.

Will-Call: Your tickets are available to be picked up at the venue box office, on the day of the event, starting one hour before the curtain time. For security purposes, the original purchasing credit card and a valid ID will be used to confirm your name on the will-call list.

Where Else Can You Buy Your Seats?

Box Offices

The box office telephone numbers you need to purchase your seats are indicated on each *Seats* seating plan.

Box office hours are customarily:
Monday–Saturday: 10 a.m.–8 p.m.
Sunday: Noon–6 p.m.

To avoid additional fees, buy your tickets in person and in advance at the venue's box office. However, purchasing tickets at the box office often adds a charge, since most places use a computer ticket brokering system.

The Broadway Concierge and Ticket Center
In the heart of Times Square, at 1560 Broadway, between 46th and 47th Streets, the Broadway Ticket Center offers information on Broadway in six languages, and tickets to every Broadway and many Off-Broadway shows under one roof. Located inside the Times Square Information Center, the hours of operation are Monday to Saturday, 9 a.m.–7 p.m.; Sunday, 10a.m.–6 p.m. Visit *www.broadwayconciergeandticketcenter.com* for complete show listings.

Ticket Brokers

If you want premium or sold-out seats or want to impress your client or family, perhaps a ticket service can help. You will most likely pay more than the original face value of the ticket, based upon the supply and your demand— but you will have those tickets in your hand!

When you purchase tickets on the secondary market from a brokerage service, make sure that the ticket broker is recognized by the NATB, the trade group of legitimate ticket brokers. Members are required to adhere to a strict code of ethics to protect consumers. Before you buy, check their membership directory at *www.natb.org* for a reputable ticket broker in your area.

Ticket Auctions

Ticketmaster and Telecharge
Going … going … gone. Both Telecharge.com Marketplace and Ticketmaster.com have entered the ticket auction market to compete with brokers and scalpers for the highest price a ticket will bear. The venues, promoters, and performers will decide on an event-by-event basis whether to participate in online auctions. For details, check out *www.telecharge.com* and *www.ticketmaster.com*.

TicketExchange
Ticket holders will no longer be stuck with those extra tickets, thanks to this forum for buying and selling tickets online. Ticket holders can post the extra tickets and fans can view these tickets safely and securely. For more information, check out *www.ticketmaster.com*.

EBay
If luck is your lady tonight, try a ticket auction at *www.ebay.com*. You may find a great theatre bargain, get tickets at just the right price, or spend more than you wanted for that special night on the town. You will never

know until you try and try again. For your information, EBay maintains a very strict ticket resale policy to promote lawful ticket sales, so whether you are buying or selling theatre tickets, be sure to read the fine print.

Broadway Cares / Equity Fights AIDS

BC / EFA is the nation's leading not-for-profit AIDS fundraising organization. Join in their special online auctions while helping out a good cause. Don't miss their Annual Flea Market and Grand Auction in September where Broadway costumes, autographs, and scripts could be yours. Visit *www.broadwaycares.org* or call (212) 840-0770.

Priority Seating

AMEX Gold Card Events

As an exclusive benefit of the American Express Gold Card Service for their Gold, Platinum, or Centurion Card, members can purchase the most sought-after seats to sporting and entertainment events—in advance of public sale—when they use their card. And should you be unable to attend your performance, you are covered by AMEX's Event Ticket Protection Plan. Look for the American Express logo in the theatre advertisement: call (800) 448-TIKS or go to *www.americanexpress.com*.

VISA Signature Events

Not to be out done by AMEX, Visa has teamed up with Broadway.com to bring their cardholders preferred service, cancellation insurance, and special packages. To learn more, visit *www.broadway.com* or *www.visa.com/signature*.

StubHub.com

Don't miss out on the chance to see the latest show or to root for your favorite home team. StubHub is an online marketplace for the easy and secure buying and selling of tickets to sporting events, the theatre, and concerts. Registered users can search for seats and manage their transactions online. (866) STUBHUB or *www.stubhub.com*.

TicketsNow.com

With TicketsNow.com, you have your own personal web ticket broker searching for premium seating and tickets to sold-out events. For extra security, TicketsNow.com requires a signature on all deliveries. Therefore, all deliveries are made using an express courier service. For more information, check them out on the Web at *www.ticketsnow.com* or call (800) 927-2770.

Craigslist.com

Buy, sell, and swap tickets at this online marketplace. Listings are absolutely free, and they work (*www.craigslist.com*).

Discount Seats

Many venues offer largely discounted tickets to students, seniors, or any people willing to stand through a show. Check with your theatre to see if you are eligible for these discount tickets:

Student rush offers students discounted tickets when they present a student ID. Usually tickets are available on the night of the show, and are limited to one per student. Find listings at *www.talkinbroadway.com*.

Senior discount means that you must present government-issued identification indicating your senior status. While eligible age varies with each theatre, generally 62 is the magic number.

Obstructed view seats are when you are not able to see the entire stage from your seat. This means that you might be sitting near a pole, under a mezzanine, or far off to the side.

Standing room only (SRO) tickets are available at the box office on the day of the performance when the show is sold out. At prices around $20.00, it may be worth it to wear your sneakers and enjoy the show. For show availability, prices, and purchase times check your favorite show's website or box office, or visit *www.talkinbroadway.com*.

Preview discounts are offered when, before opening to the general public, productions present previews to fine-tune the show before opening night. Many of the larger theatres reduce their prices for the previews, so ticket bargains are to be had before the production opens and the reviews come out.

Lotteries

To continue the buzz, many popular shows have ticket lotteries before each performance. You must sign up at the box office three hours before show time; you must be present at the drawing (which is usually 2½ hours before show time), and you must pay cash. Hey, when a Broadway show costs you only $20.00, a lottery may just be the ticket.

Starving Artist Ticket

One of the best kept secrets in New York is the Starving Artist Ticket. Most of the top shows reserve seats, usually in the first three rows, for people who love theatre but cannot afford the regular prices. The tickets are $20.00, so do your research by calling the theatre directly and asking them about the Starving Artist Tickets, and these ticket bargains may be yours.

Online Discount

See the *Seats* Top Ten Discount Sites on the Web section for great ticket bargains to Broadway and beyond.

Ticket Concierge

Theatre Subscriptions

Many theatres operate as not-for-profit organizations that offer innovative series of events for members and subscribers. Not only do these special theatergoers receive super discounts, priority seating, and informative newsletters, but they may be invited to attend post-performance discussions with actors from the shows, pre- or post-theatre cocktail parties, and gala events. Just contact your favorite theatre, support the arts, and save!

Ticket Clubs

Audience Rewards

(866) 313-9635, *www.audiencerewards.com*
Welcome to the Theatergoers Frequent Buyers Club. Enrollment is free and you earn reward points when you purchase tickets to participating shows through an authorized outlet. Search listings and redeem points for theater tickets, show merchandise, and memorabilia.

Hit Show Club

(212) 581-4211, *www.hitshowclub.com*
This free service distributes the original two-fer coupons, which can be redeemed for one or two tickets at one-third or more off the regular ticket price with no service charge. Redeem coupons at the box office (at least one hour before the performance), by phone, or by mail.

Audience Extras

(212) 686-1966, *www.audienceextras.com*
For an $115.00 membership fee, receive one or two complimentary tickets to as many shows as you can see in one year! Simply pay a $3.00 reservation service charge per ticket and attend the best of over 1000 Broadway, Off-Broadway, and fringe productions, dance showcases, concerts, and sporting events.

Audience Project

(212) 564-1142, *www.dramaleague.org*
Sponsored by the Drama League, for a mere $85.00 membership fee, you can attend over 100 discounted performances each year on Broadway, Off–Broadway and across the country. Members can attend workshops, panels, open rehearsals, backstage tours, and other theatrical events.

House Seats

Sold-Out Show Tickets

Even if a show is sold out to the general public, prime house seats are held by the theatre at every performance for the producers, the creative teams and the stars. If, on the day of the show, the house seats remain unclaimed, the VIP seats are sold to the general public at full price. House seats can go on sale as soon as the box office opens or as late as one hour before the curtain, so contact the individual theatres for details—and good luck.

Standby/Cancellation Tickets

Some theatres recycle unclaimed tickets right before show time, and others may drastically reduce prices at the very last minute to fill the house. Those in the know line up early for these abandoned treasures.

Volunteer Your Time

A great and fulfilling way to catch the show for free is to volunteer your time to your favorite theatre. By contacting your theater, both of you will benefit and have a great time doing it.

What's Playing Where

Publications
To find out what's playing and where, several publication list plays, dance, cabaret, music, and theatrical events. *New York Magazine*, *The New Yorker*, *Where*, and *Time Out* magazines offer excellent monthly listings of the performing arts. The Sunday Arts and Leisure section of *The New York Times* presents the most comprehensive picture of the current arts and entertainment scene in the New York metropolitan area.

The Broadway Line
(888) BROADWAY
"The Official Hotline for Show Information and Tickets" is Broadway's first toll-free, interactive telephone hotline. Using the interactive menus, search for Broadway shows by title, location, or genre. Information such as show synopses, performance schedules, student discounts, and ticketing are available at your fingertips. For more information, check out *www.livebroadway.com*.

NYC's Official Visitor Information Center
(212) 484-1222, *www.nycvisit.com*
810 7th Avenue, between 52nd and 53rd Streets
Planning a trip to the Big Apple? Visit the city's official tourism website for the most up to date information for a fun-filled visit to New York City. Find discount theater coupons and information on special theater related celebrations.

Hotel Concierges

When you are staying at a hotel, the concierge can be your best ticket friend, as they may have access to "sold out" shows or sporting events. Stop by the desk with any requests for tickets, restaurant reservations, directions, or any additional requests to make your stay more enjoyable.

Back Stage Tours

Apollo Theater
(212) 531-5337
Monday, Tuesday, Thursday and Friday at 11 a.m., 1 p.m., and 3 p.m.
Weekends at 11 a.m. and 1 p.m.

Carnegie Hall
(212) 903-9765
Monday–Friday at 11:30 a.m., 2 p.m., and 3 p.m.
Saturday at 11:30 a.m. and 12:30 p.m.
Sunday at 12:30 p.m.

Lincoln Center
(212) 875-5350; Accessible tours (212) 875-5374
Daily at 10:30 a.m., 12:30 p.m., 2:30 p.m., and 4:30 p.m.

Madison Square Garden
(212) 307-7171
Daily on the half hour from 11 a.m.–3 p.m.

Metropolitan Opera House
(212) 729-7020, *www.operaed.org*
In season, weekdays at 3:30 p.m.
Sundays at 10:30 a.m.

Radio City Music Hall
(212) 307-7171
Daily from 11 a.m.–3 p.m.

Yankee Stadium
(718) 579-4594, *newyork.yankees.mlb.com*
Check website for dates and times

Theatre Development Fund

1501 Broadway, 21st Floor, New York, N.Y., 10036
(212) 221-0885, *www.tdf.org*

The Theatre Development Fund (TDF) is the largest not-for-profit service organization for the performing arts in the United States. While TDF is best known for its operation of the TKTS discount ticket booths, it also sponsors the TDF voucher programs, offers memberships for ticket discounts, and is committed to lowering the barriers of access to all theatergoers.

TDF Membership

Dedicated theatergoers receive offers of up to 70% off of the full ticket price to hundreds of live productions each year. Membership is restricted to students, teachers, union members, retired persons, performing arts professionals, the clergy, and members of the Armed Services. Apply online at *www.tdf.org*. There is a small annual fee for those eligible individuals.

Vouchers

Experience the exciting world of emerging Off-Off-Broadway music, theatre, and dance with TDF vouchers, which are open tickets of admission good for one year. The single voucher is $9.00 and the four-pack can be purchased for $36.00 online at *www.tdf.org*, and are accepted as payment in full when presented to the box office. Voucher holders will receive a quarterly newsletter of participating theatres, or check the TDF website for events accepting the vouchers.

Theatre Access Program (TAP)

TDF is proud to provide access to the NYC performing arts to individuals with physical disabilities. Through free membership, TAP offers ticket discounts for those who are hard of hearing, deaf, blind, partially sighted, medically unable to climb stairs, require aisle seats, or use wheelchairs. TAP also provides preferred seating, special sign-language interpreted, and open-captioned performances of Broadway and Off-Broadway productions. For information about the TDF/TAP offers and programs, call (212) 221-1103 or visit *www.tdf.org*.

TDF Show Search

At the TDF Show Search online at *www.tdf.org*, you are one click away from a world of theater that allows you to search the NYC boroughs as well as the national and international scenes for theatrical events and ticketing organizations.

TKTS

If you are looking for the best day of performance Broadway and Off-Broadway seats at the best price, the TKTS booths at Times Square and South Street Seaport are the places to go. Tickets are either 25% or 50% off the ticket price (plus a $4.00 per ticket service charge). Changes in show availabilities can occur hourly, so watch the big board posted outside the ticket windows. Even though you may stand in a long line, the wait will be well worth it!

To plan ahead, a listing of shows sold at the TKTS booths is available at *www.tdf.org*. You can also purchase TKTS gift certificates on the Web, at the booths, or at (212) 221-0885, ext. 246.

Locations and Hours
Times Square
Duffy Square, 47th Street and Broadway, but temporarily at the Marriott Marquis Hotel, 1535 Broadway, between 45th and 46th Streets.

Monday–Saturday evening tickets: 3 p.m.–8 p.m.
Wednesday and Saturday matinees: 10 a.m.–2 p.m.
Sunday Matinees and evenings: 11 a.m.–close

Subway transportation to TKTS: 1, 2, 3, 4, 5, 6, N, R, W, A, C to Times Square.

TKTS TIPS:
- Try to get to TKTS at 2 p.m. to be first on line for the popular shows.
- Tickets are made available throughout the day, so the shortest lines will be after 7 p.m., but your selections may be limited. However, some shows not on sale earlier in the day may release seats just prior to curtain time.
- The stand remains open until curtain time, so even if you wait until the very last minute, you can dash to the theatre without missing a beat of the overture.

South Street Seaport*
Front and John Streets, at the rear of the Resnick/Prudential Building, 199 Water Street.

Monday–Saturday evening tickets: 11 a.m.–6 p.m.
Sun. evening: Closed during winter.

* Note: matinee tickets must be purchased the day before.

Subway transportation to South Street Seaport: J, M, Z, 2, 3, 4, 5 to Fulton Street A, C to Broadway-Nassau.

Take Bus M15 downtown on Second Avenue to the Seaport.

Seats for Kids

Broadway Classroom
Presented by Theatre Direct International, this program offers discount tickets to Broadway shows, Theatre District workshops, and educational events and materials for students and educators. Call (800) 334-8457 or visit *www.broadwayclassroom.com*.

High 5 Tickets to the Arts
Adolescents (ages 13–18) get a big break on culture with this special program designed to increase the attendance of middle and high school students at art events. Tickets to over 1000 events and museums in and around New York City can be purchased for $5.00 without a service fee from all local Ticketmaster outlets. Visit *www.high5tix.org* or call the High 5 Hotline at (212) HI5-TKTS or (212) 445-8587 for schedules and information.

Kids Night on Broadway
This annual February event lets kids go free to the theatre when an adult purchases a ticket. Also, with each adult full-priced meal, receive a kid's meal free at participating restaurants. Some restrictions apply; go to *www.kidsnightonbroadway.com* for details.

School Theatre Ticket Program
Schools, camps, or organizations can obtain discount coupons to musicals and plays on and off Broadway or at Lincoln Center, and for other events in New York City, through this program. For more information, visit *www.schooltix.com* or call (212) 354-4722.

Student Rush Tickets
On the day of the performance, most theaters offer front-row orchestra seats for $20.00 to students presenting valid student identification. Policies vary from theatre to theatre, but the limit is usually one ticket per student and cash is the preferred currency at the box office. Purchase times are restricted, so check your favorite show's website, its box office, or *www.talkinbroadway.com* for rush ticket information.

Wednesday Matinee Workshops
Student groups should inquire whether their selected theatre offers interactive workshops prior to a production. Workshops have included backstage theatre tours, meet and greets with the actors, and topical discussions about the play's themes. The programs are usually free and participants are selected on a first come, first served basis. So don't forget to ask.

Seats Top 10 Discount Websites

Check out these terrific portals to ticket, hotel, and restaurant discounts as well as the insider's buzz on and off the boards of the Great White Way!

www.broadwaybox.com: Free Broadway, Off-Broadway, and event discount codes, which can save you up to 50%, are at your fingertips. Redeem the codes over the phone, online, or at the box office for incredible savings.

www.ilovenytheater.com: The Broadway League presents the best of Broadway, hotels, travel, and restaurants, along with a free newsletter and Broadway Fan Club to keep you up to date on Broadway's current and future happenings.

www.nytheatre.com: This site offers terrific theatre listings and show reviews as well as "virtual coupons" good for ticket discounts, and student and senior discounts.

www.nytimes.com: Log on to *The New York Times* Ticketwatch, an insider's email service offering discount tickets to the hottest shows on Broadway.

www.offbroadwayonline.com: Cool customers flock to "The official website of Off Broadway," which serves over 400 not-for-profit theatres and organizations. The site not only lets you search for productions by neighborhood and type, but offers tickets, discounts, and shows accepting TDF vouchers.

www.playbill.com: Home of the Playbill Online Club, where members enjoy the opportunity to receive discount tickets as well as exclusive travel and dining discounts and offers. Members receive email updates announcing savings and specials.

www.seasonofsavings.com: Discounts on Broadway tickets and Times Square hotel and parking await the avid theatergoer at a "Season of Savings."

www.theatredirect.com: Group tickets (10 or more) at discount prices are available on the Web or at (800) BROADWAY.

www.theatermania.com: Join the free TM Insider Club for access to their Broadway, Off-Broadway, Off-Off-Broadway, and performing arts ticket discounts around NYC and the country.

www.worldseats.com: Visit *Seats*' official website offering updated and bonus New York and Chicago seating plans, where to buy *Seats: New York* and *Seats: Chicago*, an author biography, *Seats* news and reviews, and, of course, all the theatre-savvy sites to guide you to the best seats in the house!

Four Seasons of Free Seats

Spring

Circus Animal Walk

What: Step right up and watch as the elephants and horses of the Ringling Brothers Barnum & Bailey Circus parade through the Queens-Midtown Tunnel to Madison Square Garden.
When: Mid-March, 12:00 a.m.
Where: 34th–35th Streets and 2nd Avenue
Info: *www.ringling.com*

Fleet Week New York City

What: Welcome the fleet at one of the largest celebration events of the year as nearly two dozen U.S. Navy, Coast Guard, and international ships from around the world dock in the Big Apple and lower their gangplanks for free public tours. Other highlights include the Parade of Ships, a sunset parade, demonstrations, and free Navy Band and USO shows.
When: The week up to and including Memorial Day
Where: Pier 86 at 46th Street, Pier 88 at 48th Street, and all along the West Side Highway
Info: *www.fleetweek.navy.mil*

Lower East Side Festival of the Arts

What: The Theater for the New City celebrates the rich artistic, cultural, and ethnic diversity of Manhattan's Lower East Side with dozens performing groups from the neighborhood and loads of activities for the whole family.
When: May
Where: 155 First Avenue
Info: (212) 254-1109, *www.theaterforthenewcity.net*

Good Morning America Concert Series

What: This free concert series, broadcast live on the popular *Good Morning America*, has featured the likes of Carrie Underwood, Jennifer Lopez, Santana, and John Mayer. Set the alarm clock early if you're going: Viewers are advised to arrive at the Times Square studio by 7 a.m.
When: May through November
Where: May–August: Bryant Park (41st and 6th Avenue); August–November: GMA Times Square studio (43rd Street and 7th Ave.)
Info: *http://abcnews.go.com/GMA, www.bryantpark.org*

New York Philharmonic Memorial Day Concert

What: The nation's oldest symphony orchestra celebrates spring with a free concert at St. John the Divine, one of the largest and most spectacular Gothic cathedrals in the world.

When: Memorial Day, 8 p.m.

Where: The Church of St. John the Divine, 1047 Amsterdam Avenue

Info: (212) 662-2133, *www.newyorkphilharmonic.org*

Random Acts One-Act Play Festival

What: Do you have a short attention span? Are you the sort of person who craves novelty? If so, this is the festival for you. Some of the world's finest aspiring actors, playwrights, and directors showcase their talents within the abbreviated confines of the single-act play.

When: February–April

Where: The New School for Drama, 151 Bank Street

Info: (212) 279-4200, *www.drama.newschool.edu*

Toyota Concert Series on the Today Show

What: For more than a decade, the *Today Show* has been bringing the biggest names in music, including Bruce Springsteen, Maroon 5, Martina McBride, and Josh Groban, to rock the Plaza. Viewing is on a first-come, first-served basis, so get there early.

Where: Outside *Today*'s Window on the World Studio, located at 49th Street and Rockefeller Plaza

When: April through the fall. *Today* runs from 7 a.m.–11 a.m., Monday through Friday.

Info: *www.todayshow.com*

Upper West Fest

What: Proving that New York's Upper West Side remains a vital cultural destination, Symphony Space, in conjunction with more than 20 cultural and arts organizations, presents a colorful array of performances and exhibitions. Catch a flick at the NY Yiddish Film Festival, enjoy a concert by renowned Lincoln Center Jazz musicians, or check out the rockin' moms at Mamapalooza in Riverside Park.

When: May

Where: Upper West Side

Info: *www.upperwestfest.com*

Wall to Wall

What: Symphony Space presents an annual gift to New York City with a free, 12-hour musical marathon celebrating the works of a preeminent composer with selections from the artist's best-loved music. Past honorees have represented all musical genres, including classical, jazz, pop, and Broadway.

When: May
Where: The Peter Jay Sharpe Theatre, 2537 Broadway at 95th Street
Info: (212) 864-5400, *www.symphonyspace.org*

Summer

BAM Rhythm and Blues Festival
What: The Brooklyn Academy of music hosts a bevy of jazz, soul, pop, reggae, and doo-wop all-stars at this free, summerlong outdoor concert series.
When: June–August, Thursday's
Where: The Metrotech Center Commons, Downtown Brooklyn
Info: (718) 636-4100, *www.bam.org*

Battery Dance Company Downtown Dance Festival
What: As the summer draws to a close, experience free professional live dance in Lower Manhattan. Whether the choreography is ballet, jazz, tap, or ethnic, the festival's rhythms and patterns of dance are as diverse as the ages and backgrounds of the audience enjoying this outdoor festival. Go downtown and experience the grandeur of dance set against the backdrop of the harbor and the Statue of Liberty.
When: August
Where: Battery Park
Info: (212) 219-3910, *www.batterydanceco.com*

Broadway Under The Stars
What: Relax under the stars on Central Park's lush Great Lawn as the Great White Way's biggest stars kick off the summer performing choice selections from the smash hits of the Broadway season.
When: June
Where: Central Park, Great Lawn
Info: *www.livebroadway.com*

Brooklyn Hip-Hop Festival
What: The BHF has outgrown its humble neighborhood beginnings as a block party to become one of Brooklyn's most anticipated events of the summer, offering incendiary live performances, a stellar lineup of DJs, and an accompanying film series.
When: June
Where: Empire-Fulton Ferry State Park, Brooklyn
Info: (718) 802-0603, *www.brooklynbodega.com*, *www.broooklynbridgepark.org*

HBO Bryant Park Summer Film Festival

What: Spend a warm summer Monday evening picnicking with fellow film buffs behind the New York Public Library. A different classic is screened every week, and there isn't a bad seat in the house, but be warned: The lawn fills up fast, so arrive early and stake your spot!

When: June–August; lawn opens at 5p.m., films start at dusk

Where: Bryant Park, between 40th and 42nd Streets

Info: *www.bryantpark.org*

Celebrate Brooklyn!

What: Enjoy world-class jazz, classical, reggae, rock and roll, and international musical artists at the band shell or on the lawn all summer long at one of New York's longest-running free summer outdoor performing arts festivals.

When: June–August

Where: Prospect Park Band Shell, Brooklyn

Info: (718) 855-7882, *www.briconline.org*

Central Park SummerStage

What: Central Park's Rumsey Playfield buzzes with the hottest rock, pop, and world music. Dance, spoken word, theatrical, and opera performances round out the diverse summerlong program.

When: June–August

Where: Central Park West between 69th and 72nd Streets

Info: (212) 360-2777, *www.summerstage.org*

Charlie Parker Jazz Festival

What: The neighborhoods of Harlem and the Lower East Side celebrate the end of summer as they welcome home the sounds of jazz inspired by their local hero, Charlie Parker. Nationally renown jazz masters release their velvety tones and percussive rhythms in two free concerts.

When: Late August

Where: Marcus Garvey Park, 124th Street and Mt. Morris Park; Tompkins Square Park, East 8th Street, between Avenues A and B

Info: *www.cityparksfoundation.org*

CityParks Concerts, Dance, and Theater

What: City Parks around the five boroughs are not just for summer time picnics and softball. They also play host to a series of over 100 free programs as diverse as the city itself. Highlights have included the Classical Theater of Harlem, Hip-Hop hall of famers, and Dance Out! Presented in conjunction with The Joyce Theater.

When: July–August

Where: City parks throughout the five boroughs

Info: (212) 360-8290, *www.cityparksfoundation.org*

Hudson River Flicks for Grown-Ups

What: Blockbuster films are screened on Wednesday nights at the Hudson River's Pier 54 on the West Side. This is a popular event, so get there early.
When: July–August, Wednesdays at 8:30 p.m.
Where: Hudson River Park Pier 54 at West 14th Street
Info: *www.hudsonriverpark.org*

Hudson River Flicks for Kids

What: Fun, fantasy, and family-friendly adventure are the focus of this Friday-night film series on New York's West Side. Bring the blankets, the picnic basket, and the kids to Pier 46 on the Hudson River.
When: July–August
Where: Pier 46 at Christopher Street
Info: *www.hudsonriverpark.org*

Lincoln Center Out Of Doors

What: Face it: August was meant to be spent out of doors, and Lincoln Center aims to help the whole family do just that, with a diverse program of free music and dance performances and special events, all held in the facility's stunning, tree-lined plazas.
When: August
Where: Lincoln Center Plaza
Info: (212) 875-5108, *www.lincolncenter.org*

Fourth of July Fireworks Spectacular

What: Is that the sun setting in the east? No, but Macy's annual July 4th fireworks extravaganza is so fiery and brilliant, viewers might be forgiven for suspecting the switch! Four barges stationed on the East River between 23rd and 42nd Streets set off the largest display of fireworks in America.
When: July 4th, 9:00 p.m.
Where: For best viewing, try the southbound lanes of the FDR between 14th and 42nd Streets.
Info: (212) 494-4495,
www.macys.com/campaign/fireworks/index.jsp

Met in the Parks

What: The cast of the Metropolitan Opera step off the stage and into the grass with this free, three-week open-air series. Lucky viewers can expect to see two full operas, performed in various parks throughout the tristate region.
When: June–July
Where: Various parks across NYC, New Jersey, and Connecticut
Info: (212) 362-6000, *www.metoperafamily.org*

Mostly Mozart

What: A New York summertime favorite for over 40 years, the Mostly Mozart festival treats fans to a special free outdoor concert, held every year at the end of the season.
When: July–August
Where: Damrosch Park, 62nd Street at Amsterdam Avenue
Info: (212) 875-5399, *www.lincolncenter.org*

Movies with a View

What: You may have a hard time focusing on the free films here, as Brooklyn Bridge Park provides one of the most spectacular views in all of New York City. Other perks include DJ music before the movies and free bike valet service.
When: July–August, Thursday nights 8:30 p.m.
Where: Empire-Fulton Ferry State Park, Brooklyn
Info: *www.brooklynbridgepark.org*

New York Philharmonic Concerts in the Park

What: City parks from Central Park to New Jersey play host to free concerts featuring the New York Philharmonic, with special guest artists. Each concert reaches a crescendo with a pyrotechnical display sure the please the entire family.
When: Late June to Mid-July
Where: Various parks around the five boroughs
Info: (212) 875-5709, *www.nyphil.org*

Naumburg Orchestral Concerts

What: The Naumburg concert series, dedicated to showcasing promising new talent and promoting the works of young composers, is the oldest of its kind in the U.S. Concertgoers can thrill to the knowledge that they are seeing stars on the rise.
Where: The Naumburg Band Shell, Central Park, 72nd Street at mid-park
When: Several Tuesdays, June–August
Info: (718) 340-3018, *www.naumbergconcerts.org*

New York Grand Opera

What: Visitors to Central Park in July shouldn't be surprised to hear the occasional aria wafting through the trees: That's the month when the New York Grand Opera brings opera's most-beloved classics to the great outdoors.
When: July
Where: The Naumberg Band Shell, Central Park
Info: (212) 245-8837, *www.newyorkgrandopera.org*

New York Philharmonic Open Rehearsals

What: Grab a cup of java and head to Avery Fisher Hall to hear musical masters tune up and fine tune selected programs, from Schubert to Beethoven.

When: May–June: 9:45 a.m.

Where: Avery Fisher Hall, Lincoln Center, Plaza, corner of Columbus Avenue and 65th Street

Info: (212) 875-5656, *www.nyphil.org*

River Rocks

What: Make your way through Manhattan's trendy Meatpacking District to find famous-name artists from all walks of rock performing against the breathtaking backdrop of the Hudson River.

When: June–August

Where: Hudson River Park Pier 54 at West 14th Street

Info: *www.hudsonriverpark.org*

River to River Festival

What: Each summer the River to River festival brings more than 500 free music, dance and cultural events to Lower Manhattan. Even if you're a Wall Street banker who doesn't get out of the office till 9, there's still a pretty good chance you can zone out with Sonic Youth or release your inner animal at the Bang on a Can marathon.

When: June–August

Where: Downtown venues, such as South Street Seaport, Battery Park, and the World Financial Center

Info: *www.rivertorivernyc.com*

Shakespeare in Central Park

What: Each summer, the screen and stage's biggest and brightest stars light up the lawns of Central Park. The Public Theater presents popular free performances at this open-air amphitheater just south of the Great Lawn. The reserved seating tickets, two per patron, are free and are good for the day of issue only.

When: June–August

Where: The Delacorte Theater, West 81st Street at Central Park West

Info: (212) 539-8662, *www.publictheater.org*

Stars in the Alley

What: The stars of Broadway's most popular musicals and plays celebrate the end of the season with a free outdoor concert in legendary Shubert Alley. Fans can vote online for their favorite play and musical.

When: June

Where: Shubert Alley, between 44th and 45th Streets, between 8th Avenue and Broadway

Info: *www.starsinthealley.com*

Summer on the Hudson

What: Pier 1 presents their picks for the best of old and new classics, from Hitchcock to *Caddyshack*. Movies are Wednesdays at 8:30 p.m. and seating on the pier is limited, so get there early with lawn chair in tow.
When: July–August, Wednesdays at 8:30 p.m.
Where: Riverside Park South, Pier 1 at 70th Street
Info: *www.nycparks.org*

Tribeca Drive-Ins

What: The Tribeca Film Festival takes it to the streets with free cinema under the stars at two glorious NYC locations. Movie lovers of all ages can enjoy cult and classic films, kooky contests, and an eclectic lineup of guest performers.
When: Late April
Where: World Financial Center Plaza, 220 Vesey Street, and Rockefeller Plaza
Info: *www.tribecafilmfestival.org*

Fall

Broadway on Broadway

What: The brightest stars of the Great White Way's biggest musicals converge in the heart of the city for a free live performance previewing the upcoming theater season. Watch out for confetti showers and fans dressed as their favorite Broadway characters!
When: September
Where: Times Square
Info: *www.livebroadway.com*

CultureFest

What: Head downtown to Battery Park, where more than 125 cultural organizations congregate for two days of music, dance, art, and food. Dozens of cultures that make NYC the magnificent melting pot that it is are represented, and there are loads of hands-on activities for kids and adults alike.
When: October
Where: State Street and Battery Place, Lower Manhattan
Info: *www.nycvisit.com*

Macy's Thanksgiving Parade

What: Fabulous floats, marching bands, and super-sized, eye-popping balloons of favorite cartoon characters glide by at the world's most famous Thanksgiving Day parade. Celebrities ride on floats down the parade route and perform at the official viewing area in front of Macy's at Herald Square, but the area is very crowded and restricted. To snag the best parade viewing spot along the main route, plan to arrive by 7 a.m. with your lawn chairs and blankets.

When: Thanksgiving Day at, 9:00 a.m.
Where: South from 77th Street and Central Park West, onto Broadway at Columbus Circle, and down to 34th street at Herald Square
Info: *www.macyparade.com*

New York's Village Halloween Parade

What: Absolutely anything goes at this Big Apple tradition! New York's Village Halloween Parade is the largest Halloween celebration in the world. Featuring puppets, marchers and marching bands, floats, cars, and the people of New York, the only nighttime parade in the city gets wilder every year.

When: Halloween night, 7:00 p.m.
Where: Greenwich Village, along 6th Avenue between Spring Street and 23rd Street
Info: *www.halloween-nyc.com*

92nd Street Y Street Festival

What: Not your average Manhattan street fair, the 92nd Street Y Street Festival boasts dance performances, pony rides, live music and, recently, an International Way area, featuring representatives from tourist offices from countries as diverse and far-flung as Austria, China, and Tanzania. Represent!

When: September
Where: Lexington Avenue between 79th and 94th Streets
Info: (212) 415-5500, *www.92y.org*

Winter

Central Park Winter Jam

What: Let it snow! Come take part in Central Park's annual Winter Jam by watching ice sculpture demonstrations and local snowboarders or participating in winter activities.

When: February
Where: Central Park, Naumburg Band Shell and Mall Concert Ground, mid-park from 66th to 72nd Streets
Info: *www.nycgovparks.org*

Christmas at Rockefeller Center

What: Ring in the holiday season in NYC with the lighting of the Rockefeller Center Christmas tree. The ceremony takes place during the first week of December as the highlight of a free two-hour extravaganza featuring

today's hottest musical stars and, of course, the Radio City Rockettes. Can't make it? Don't worry: The tree's lights continue to blaze through the week after New Year's.
When: The first week of December to one week after New Year's Day
Where: Rockefeller Center on Fifth Avenue between 49th and 50th Streets
Info: *www.thetreenyc.com, www.rockefellercenter.com*

New Year's Eve at Times Square

What: Join a crowd of thousands from all over the globe at the Crossroads of the World to revel in the streets and welcome in the new year with the famous Waterford Crystal ball-drop at the stroke of midnight.
When: New Year's Eve
Where: Times Square, 42nd to 47th Streets
Info: *www.timessquarenyc.org*

Year-Round

Carnegie Hall Neighborhood Concert Series

What: These intimate neighborhood concerts offer a chance to catch Carnegie Hall-quality musicians performing classical, Latin, jazz, tango, doo-wop, blue-grass, Brazilian, African, Indian, and Caribbean music and more at a street-corner price!
When: Year-round
Where: Across the five NYC boroughs
Info: *www.carnegiehall.org* for schedules and details

Free Tour of Grand Central Station

What: Historians lead this free award-winning "grand tour" of the Grand Central neighborhood. Explore the architecture and social history of this landmark-rich area and see the city through new eyes.
When: Every Friday at 12:30 p.m.
Where: Sculpture Court of the Whitney Museum at Altria,
42nd Street and Park Avenue
Info: (212) 883-2420, *www.grandcentralpartnership.org*

Free Tour of Times Square

What: The Times Square Alliance's free walking tour, a "Times Square Exposé," offers visitors a behind-the-scenes look at NYC's most fabled district.
When: Every Friday at 12:00 p.m.
Where: Times Square Information Center, 7th Avenue (between 46th and 47th Streets)
Info: *www.timessquarenyc.org*

Memberfest

What: Every Tuesday night at 7 p.m., the members of the Ensemble Studio Theatre gather to present projects in development, providing viewers with an intimate glimpse into the exciting world of playwriting and production as it happens. Admission is free.

When: Weekly on Tuesday nights

Where: Ensemble Studio Theatre, 549 West 52nd Street

Info: (212) 247-4982, *www.ensemblestudiotheatre.org*

Merce Cunningham Dance Company Experiments in the Studio

What: This series, founded to celebrate original American music and the unique relationship enjoyed by choreographer Merce Cunningham and composer John Cage, features new and innovative American music. Each performance is followed by a question-and-answer session with the composer and choreographer.

When: Mondays, 8:30 p.m. (about once per month)

Where: Merce Cunningham Studio, 55 Bethune Street

Info: (212) 255-8240, *www.merce.org*

The Movado Hour

What: Got an hour to spare? Why not enjoy a free chamber music concert presented in an intimate salon setting. Seating is limited at this series, so make sure to call in advance for reservations.

Where: Baryshnikov Arts Center, 37 Arts, 450 West 37th Street

Info: (917) 934-4966, *www.baryshnikovdancefoundation.org*

TV Show Tapings

What: Every day, live studio TV programs, like *The Late Show with David Letterman*, *Late Night with Conan O'Brien*, *The View*, *Live with Regis & Kelly*, and *SNL* are shot in the city. Free audience tickets are available in advance by mail, or on standby.

When: Check show's website for taping schedule and requirements.

Info: *www.nycvisit.com*; for MTV's *TRL* and *Last Call* tickets: *www.1iota.com*

Almost Free Seats

Festivals

Savor the flavor of New York City's neighborhoods through a variety of theater, comedy, and dance festivals presented year-round. These entertainment bargains prove that there is always something fun to do without breaking the bank.

All Points West Music & Arts Festival

What: Rock out with the greatest cutting-edge musicians of today, such as Radiohead, Jack Johnson, The Roots, and Cat Power, at this three-day green-leaning festival on the New Jersey banks of the Hudson, just a guitar pick's throw from the Statue of Liberty.

When: August

Where: Liberty State Park, New Jersey

Info: *www.apwfestival.com* for schedules, tickets, and "green" transportation directions

The Annual New Year's Day Marathon Reading

What: Over 100 writers and other artists share the spotlight at this unique gathering (which continues into the "wee hours"). Participants have included actor-novelist Eric Bogosian, spoken-word pioneer Maggie Estep, poet-novelist-essayist Wayne Koestenbaum, and downtown legend Eileen Myles, and literary musicians Lenny Kaye, Patti Smith, Steve Earle, Philip Glass, and many others.

When: New Year's Day

Where: The Poetry Project, St. Marks Church, 131 East 10th Street

Info: (212) 674-0910, *www.poetryproject.com*

The Broadway Flea Market and Grand Auction

What: Broadway and daytime television fans flock to this annual extravaganza for autographs, memorabilia, and the chance to take home a piece of theater history. Since all proceeds benefit Broadway Cares/Equity fights Aids, sharing the photo spotlight with your favorite soap or Broadway star will not only be thrilling, but will help a great cause. The day is capped with a Grand Auction, where the highest bidder could be the next walk-on th brighte the Greta White Way.

When: September

Where: Shubert Alley and West 44th Street

Info: (212) 840-0770, *www.broadwaycares.org*

Culturemart

What: HERE presents its annual festival showcasing works in development by its resident artists. Genres range from cabaret to dance to, recently, "a multimedia meditation on architectural absence."

When: January

Where: HERE, 145 Sixth Avenue

Info: (212) 352-3101, *www.here.org*

First Chance Music Development Workshops

What: Help write an opera! This series, presented by American Opera Project, features works in progress by young composers and librettists, many of whom see their work performed here for the first time. A Q&A session following each performance is meant to help the creators hone their projects, so don't be afraid to speak up!

When: January

Where: South Oxford Space, 138 South Oxford Street, Brooklyn and the Rose Building at Lincoln Center, 70 Lincoln Center Plaza, between 65th and 66th Streets.

Info: (718) 398-4024, *www.operaprojects.org*

Flamenco Festival

What: This hotly anticipated festival celebrating Spain's flamenco arts has exploded in popularity and size over the past few years. Fiery dancers, smoldering singers, and lightning-fingered guitarists heat up New York's stages in the dead of winter.

When: February

Where: Various venues in Midtown

Info: (212) 545-7536, *www.flamencofestival.org*, *www.worldmusicinstitute.org*

Fortnight

What: The Barrow Street Theatre's two-week mini-festival is a bright spot in chilly January. Genres represented nightly include improv, standup, music, spoken word, and, most tantalizing of all, "category-defying performance."

When: January

Where: Barrow Street Theatre, 27 Barrow Street

Info: (212) 239-6200, *www.barrowstreettheatre.com*

FRIGID Festival

What: Trek to NYC's colorful East Village to see Horse Trade Theatre Group's winter event, featuring some 30 productions from all over the country. The unique festival is committed to fringe performance and to independent artists: Visiting companies take home 100% of their box office, so support the arts and catch as many performances as you can!

When: February–March
Where: The Kraine Theater and The Red Room, 85 East 4th Street, and Under St. Marks, 94 St. Marks Place
Info: (212) 777-6088, *www.frigidnewyork.info*

Fresh Fruit Festival

What: The annual (and always festive) international lesbian, gay, bisexual, and transgender cultural and arts festival draws performers from locations as diverse as Staten Island and Mauii, and hosts events guranteed to shake even the shyest banana from its peel!
When: July
Where: Various venues around New York City
Info: *www.freshfruitfestival.com*

Gilbert and Sullivan Fest

What: The New York Gilbert & Sullivan Players present a twice-yearly festival featuring classic works by arguably the most beloved librettist and composer of all time. A free kids' night spawns a new generation of fans.
When: January and June
Where: City Center, 130 West 56th Street
Info: (212) 769-1000, *www.nygasp.org*; for tickets, City Tix at (212) 581-1212, *www.nycitycenter.org*

Hip-Hop Theater Festival

What: This vibrant festival focuses aims to get young people into the theater with plays and dance performances showcasing hip-hop.
When: September–October
Where: Various NYC venues
Info: (718) 497-4282, *www.hiphoptheaterfest.org*

Ice Factory

What: The Soho Think Tank's Obie Award–winning festival has been proclaimed one of the hippest by *Time Out New York*. Seven new theater pieces will each receive a weeklong run at the Ohio Theatre.
When: July–Mid-August
Where: Ohio Theatre, 66 Wooster Street
Info: (212) 868-4444, *www.smarttix.com*

Jazz Improv Live!

What: Jazz stars from all over the world descend upon Midtown Manhattan for four days of panels, workshops, and, of course, white-hot performances.
When: October
Where: Manhattan Center Grand Ballroom, New Yorker Hotel
Info: (215) 885-0670, *www.jazzimprov.com/live*

Ladies Night on Broadway

What: Grab your gal pals and leave the guys at home! One crisp, fall night each October on Broadway is dedicated to the ladies, who can enjoy discounted shows, meals, and parking all night long.

When: October

Where: Use the website's promotional code at participating Broadway shows and restaurants.

Info: (888) BROADWAY, *www.ladiesnightonbroadway.com*

LeftOut Festival

What: Gay solo performance steps into the spotlight at Stage Left Studio with this series of cabaret, stand-up, monologue, and spoken-word acts, each featuring only one player.

When: April

Where: Stage Left Studio, 438 West 37th Street

Info: (212) 868-4444, *www.leftoutfestival.com*

JVC Jazz Festival

What: Jazz heats up the town for two weeks as the hottest musical talent around blows the roofs off of the premier concert halls, clubs, parks and museums in NYC. Turn up the air conditioning and get jazzy at a world-class event.

When: Mid to late June

Where: Various venues around NYC

Info: (646) 862-0458, *www.festivalnetwork.com*

Lincoln Center Festival

What: The world's most renowned performers in the fields of dance, theater, music, and opera converge upon one of NYC's most storied institutions for this annual summer festival. Highlights have included the Goran Bregovic Wedding & Funeral Band peforming Serbian Gypsy music, and Alan Cumming performing in the National Theatre of Scotland's *The Bacchae*.

When: July

Where: Lincoln Center, 70 Lincoln Center Plaza

Info: (212) 721-6500, *www.lincolncenter.org*

Long Island Guitar Festival

What: Electric, acoustic, six-string, twelve-string: Guitars of all kinds will be stroked, strummed, and perhaps occasionally shattered at this annual festival featuring master classes, workshops, and performances by emerging artists and living legends.

When: March

Where: Tilles Center, Long Island University, Brookville, NY

Info: (516) 299-3100, *www.liu.edu/gfest*

Marathon

What: Running isn't necessary when you attend The Ensemble Studio Theater's annual festival of new one-act plays. For more than 30 years, this Marathon has produced ground-breaking, stimulating productions by such noted playwrights as Neil LaBute and Lewis Black. Experiencing five plays in one evening will leave you breathless and exhilarated, without any physical exertion.

When: May–June

Where: Ensemble Theater Studio Mainstage, 549 West 52nd Street, 2nd Floor

Info: Theatermania, (212) 352-3101, *www.ensemblestudiotheater.org*

Midsummer Night Swing!

What: Every season, New York's hottest outdoor dance party turns up the heat on Lincoln Center's Josie Robertson Plaza. Smoking dance bands play everything from salsa to swing, two-step, disco, and more during these sizzling summer nights.

When: July

Where: Lincoln Center, 70 Lincoln Center Plaza

Info: (212) 934-4966, *www.lincolncenter.org*

Midtown International Theater Festival

What: Whether your theater taste runs to comedy, drama, or musical, this month long festival of eclectic staged plays wil keep you coming back for more. From a one-woman show about nannies, mothers, and children to a rock opera about Cleopatra, the MTIF's Off-Off Broadway showcase sure keeps the city cool during the dog days of summer.

When: Mid-July to Mid-August

Where: Various venues in the West 30's

Info: *www.midtownfestival.org, www.ticketcentral.com*

New York City Tap Festival

What: That clacking sound you hear is hundreds of tap dancers gathering for the annual tap-dance festival known affectionately as "Tap City." Take a master class, participate in a workshop, or catch one of the premiere performances that stud the event.

When: July

Where: Symphony Space, Peter Norton Theater, 2537 Broadway, and various venues.

Info: (646) 230-9576, *www.atdf.org/tapcity*

New York Clown Theater Festival

What: The clown jewel of theater festivals may be held in Brooklyn's trendy Williamsburg, but the appeal of the pie fight remains purely universal. Workshops, performances, and the Clown Olympics, in which participants compete in such arenas as slapstick and "eccentric dance," round out the event.

When: September
Where: The Brick Theater, 575 Metropolitan Avenue, Brooklyn
Info: (718) 907-6189, *www.bricktheater.com*

New York Festival of Song

What: Whether it's a brash '60s tune by the Beatles, a 17th-century ballad played on a lute, or a brand-new work by a young American composer, you're likely to hear it at NYFOS, where the song (apologies to Led Zeppelin) never remains the same.

When: October–May
Where: Carnegie Hall, West 57th Street
Info: 646-230-8380, *www.nyfos.org*; Carnegie Charge (212) 247-7800

New York Film Festival

What: Brought to you by the Lincoln Center Film Society, which introduced American audiences to François Truffaut, Jean Godard, and Pedro Almodóvar, among others, the NYFF screens groundbreaking works by established filmmakers and new talent from around the world.

When: September–October
Where: Carnegie Hall, West 57th Street
Info: (212) 875-5050, *www.filmlinc.org*; tickets also available at CenterCharge (212) 721-6500

New York Guitar Festival

What: Before there was Guitar Hero, there was . . . well, the guitar hero! The NYGF plays proud host to an array of the world's best guitarists spanning multiple genres. Past performers have included Pepe Romero, The Assad Duo, Vernon Reid, Andy Summers, Daniel Lanois, Jorma Kaukonen, Bill Frisell, Sonny Landreth, Cindy Cashdollar, Taj Mahal, Leo Kottke, and surprise guests Bruce Springsteen and Emmylou Harris. Bonus: Many of the concerts are free!

When: January–February
Where: Past venues have included: Carnegie Hall, The 92nd Street Y, Merkin Concert Hall, Joe's Pub, and the World Financial Center Winter Garden.
Info: *www.newyorkguitarfestival.org*

New York International Fringe Festival

What: Subvert the dominant paradigm! Each summer, his huge, hotly anticipated multi-arts festival brings filmmakers, artists, musicians, and performers of all stripes together to thrill audiences with the rawness and unpredictability that can only accompany new, untested work. In plainer English: This is the festival that brought you *Urinetown*.

When: August
Where: Various venues in Soho and Greenwich Village
Info: (212) 279-4488, *www.fringenyc.org*

New York Musical Theatre Festival

What: Each year the NYMF attracts a young, energized crowd to Midtown Manhattan with full productions of more than two dozen new musicals and tons of special events, including readings, workshops, concerts, parties, seminars, and master classes. In the festival's first three years, seven shows made the leap to Off-Broadway, including *Altar Boyz* and *Gutenberg! The Musical*.

When: Mid-September–October
Where: Various venues
Info: (212) 664-0979, *www.nymf.org*

New York Stage and Film Powerhouse Program

What: Ready to get out of town? Hop aboard the Metro-North and check out one of the many stellar performances that make up Powerhouse Theater's eight-week festival for the creative development of new works by artists such as Eric Bogosian, Eve Ensler, Mark Linn-Baker, David Strathairn, and Duncan Sheik.

When: June–August
Where: Powerhouse Theater, Vassar College, Poughkeepsie, NY
Info: June–August (845) 437-7021, September–May (212) 736-4240, *www.newyorkstageandfilm.org, www. powerhouse.vassar.edu*

New York Times Arts & Leisure Week

What: Providing a much-needed respite from January's bleakness and bluster, the *New York Times* brings together its finest journalists and some of the most celebrated talent and thinkers from the worlds of art, film, theater, music, television, literature, media, and politics for a thrilling week of interviews, screenings, and discussions.

When: January
Where: The TimesCenter, 242 West 41st Street
Info: (888) NYT-1870, *www.artsandleisureweek.com*

Seaport Summer Theatre Festival

What: Having made its debut in the summer of 2007 to much acclaim, this festival returns with three eclectic performances running repertory-style throughout the month of August. Past performances included Shakespeare's *Twelfth Night*, *Snapshots '07*, a one-act series of world premieres by Clay McLeod Chapman, and the Late Night Comedy series, showcasing emerging and well-known comics.

When: August

Where: S-P-A-C-E Gallery and Performance Space, South Street Seaport, 207 A Front Street

Info: (212) 393-9191, *www.southstreetseaport.com;* for tickets (212) 868-4444, *www.smarttix.com*

Summer Play Festival

What: The Public Theater's got you covered for hot fun in the summertime for only $10.00 a ticket. You never know when you will catch a rising star, like past participant Quira Alegria Hudes, who hit it big with *In the Heights*. So, test out innovative works by emerging playwrights, directors, and producers at the SPF without breaking the bank.

When: July

Where: The Public Theater, 425 Lafayette Street

Info: (212) 279-4040, *www.spfnyc.org*, *www.publictheater.org*

Tribeca Film Festival

What: If you love movies, head downtown to a festival phenomenon that's taking the film industry by storm. Attend premieres, showings, family festivals, and outdoor free screenings designed to entertain, educate, and inspire.

When: April–May

Where: Various venues

Info: (646) 502-5296, *www.tribecafilmfestival.org*

Tropfest@Tribeca Film Festival

What: Juried short films (each under seven minutes long) from around the world will entertain, delight, and intrigue at the one-day, late-September, absolutely free Tropfest.

When: September; music starts at 5 p.m., red carpet at 6 p.m., films at 8 p.m.

Where: World Financial Plaza, Vesey Street

Info: *www.tribecafilmfestival.org*

Under the Radar Festival

What: The best and brightest in new theater from across the country and around the world converge upon New York for this annual event. The 12-day festival spotlights emerging talent and boasts performances by masters in the field.

When: January

Where: The Public Theater, 425 Lafayette Street and various venues around town

Info: (212) 967-7555, *www.publictheater.org*

Vision Festival

What: Since 1996, the Vision Festival has been bringing the bleeding edge of avant-garde and free jazz to the Lower East Side. Experimental dance, film, and art round out the multicultural experience.

When: January–April, June

Where: The Living Theatre, 21 Clinton Street, and CSV Cultural Center, Suffolk Street

Info: (212) 696-6681, *www.visionfestival.org*

92nd Street Y Harkness Dance Festival at the Ailey Citigroup Theater

What: Innovative choreography and a wide variety of styles of contemporary dance are on display during this five-week extravaganza featuring companies from around the world.

When: February–March

Where: Ailey Citigroup Theater, Joan Weill Center for Dance, 405 West 55th Street

Info: (212) 415-5500, *www.92y.org*

Almost Free Seats

Music/Cabaret

BAMcafé at The Brooklyn Academy of Music
30 Lafayette Avenue, Brooklyn, NY 11271
(718) 636-4139, *www.bam.org*

Birdland
315 West 44th Street, New York, NY 10036
(212) 581-3080, *www.birdlandjazz.com*

The Bitter End
147 Bleecker Street, New York, NY 10012
(212) 673-7030, *www.bitterend.com*

Blue Note
131 West 3rd Street, New York, NY 10012
(212) 475-8592, *www.bluenote.net/newyork*

**Broadway Baby Bistro/ Songbook Theatre
at The Broadway Comedy Club**
318 West 53rd Street, New York, NY 10019
(212) 757-5808, *www.broadwaybabybistro.com*

Cafe Carlyle at the Carlyle Hotel
35 East 76th Street, New York, NY 10021
(212) 744-1600, *www.thecarlyle.com*

Cafe Wha
115 MacDougall Street, New York, NY 10012
(212) 254-3706, *www.cafewha.com*

Canal Room
285 West Broadway, New York, NY 10013
(212) 941-8100, *www.canalroom.com*

The Carnegie Club
156 West 56th Street, New York, NY 10019
(212) 957-9676, *www.hospitalityholdings.com*

China Club
268 West 47th Street, New York, NY 10036
(212) 398-3800, *www.chinaclubnyc.com*

**Dizzy's Club Coca-Cola at Rose Hall
at Lincoln Center**
33 West 60th Street, New York, NY 10023
(212) 258-9595, *www.jalc.org/venues/dccc*

Don't Tell Mama
343 West 46th Street, New York, NY 10036
(212) 757-0788, *www.donttellmamanyc.com*

Feinstein's at the Loews Regency
540 Park Avenue, New York, NY 10065
(212) 339-4095, *www.feinsteinsattheregency.com*

Hank's Saloon
46 3rd Avenue, Brooklyn, NY 11217
(718) 625-8003, *www.hankssaloon.com/hankssaloon*

Highline Ballroom
431 West 16th Street, New York, NY 10011
(212) 414-5994, *www.highlineballroom.com*

Jazz Standard
116 East 27th Street, New York, NY 10016
(212) 576-2232, *www.jazzstandard.net*

Iridium Jazz Club
1650 Broadway, New York, NY 10019
(212) 582-2121, *www.iridiumjazzclub.com*

Joe's Pub at the Public Theater
425 Lafayette Street, New York, NY 10003
(212) 539-8778, *www.joespub.com*

Kenny's Castaways
157 Bleecker Street, New York, NY 10012
(212) 979-9762, *www.kennyscastaways.net*

Knitting Factory
74 Leonard Street, New York, NY 10013
(212) 219-3132, *www.knittingfactory.com*

Lenox Lounge and Zebra Room
288 Malcolm X Boulevard, New York, NY 10027
(212) 427-0253, *www.lenoxlounge.com*

The Living Room
154 Ludlow Street, New York, NY 10002
(212) 533-7235, www.livingroomny.com

Maxwell's
1039 Washington Street, Hoboken, NJ 07030
(201) 798-0406, *www.maxwellsnj.com*

Mercury Lounge
217 East Houston Street, New York, NY 10002
(212) 260-4700, *www.mercuryloungenyc.com*

Metropolitan Room
34 West 22nd Street, New York, NY 10010
(212) 206-0440, *www.metropolitanroom.com*

Oak Room at the Algonquin Hotel
59 West 44th Street, New York, NY 10036
(212) 419-9331, *www.algonquinhotel.com*

Reprise Room at Dillons
245 West 54th Street, New York, NY 10019
(212) 307-9797, *www.dillonslounge.com*

Rockwood Music Hall
196 Allen Street, New York, NY 10002
(212) 477-4155, *www.rockwoodmusichall.com*

Rodeo Bar
375 3rd Avenue, New York, NY 10016
(212) 683-6500, *www.rodeobar.com*

Smalls
183 West 10th Street, New York, NY 10014
(212) 675-7369, *www.smallsjazzclub.com*

Smoke
2751 Broadway, New York, NY 10025
(212) 864-6662, *www.smokejazz.com*

Sweet Rhythm
88 Seventh Avenue South, New York, NY 10014
(212) 255-3626, *www.sweetrhythmny.com*

Uptown Jazz Lounge at Minton's Playhouse
208 West 118th Street, New York, NY 10026
(212) 864-8364, *www.uptownatmintons.com*

Village Vanguard
178 17th Avenue South, New York, NY 10014
(212) 255-4037, *www.villagevanguard.net*

Zinc Bar
90 West Houston Street, New York, NY 10012
(212) 477-8337, *www.zincbar.com*

Theaters/Black Boxes

3LD Art and Technology Center
80 Greenwich Street, New York, NY 10006
(212) 645-0374, *www.3leggeddog.org*

13th Street Repertory Theatre
50 West 13th Street, New York, NY 10011
(212) 675-6677, *www.13thstreetrep.org*

14th Street Y Theater
344 East 14th Street, New York, NY 10003
(212) 780-0800, *www.14streety.org*

29th Street Rep Theatre at Altered Stages
212 West 29th Street, New York, NY 10001
(212) 868-4444, (212) 465-0575, *www.29thstreetrep.com*

Abrons Art Center
466 Grand Street, New York, NY 10002
(212) 598-0400, *www.henrystreet.org*

Access Theatre
380 Broadway, New York, NY 10013
(212) 996-1047, *www.acccesstheater.com*

Actor's Temple Theatre
339 West 42nd Street, New York, NY 10036
(212) 245-6945, *www.theactorstemple.org*

Algonquin Theater
123 East 24th Street, New York, NY 10010
(212) 730-4664, *www.algonquinproductions.org*

Arclight Theatre
152 West 71st, New York, NY
(212) 213-5786

Ars Nova
511 West 54th Street, New York, NY 10019
(212) 868-4444, *www.arsnovanyc.com*

Bank Street Theatre
155 Bank Street, New York, NY 10014
(212) 868-4444

The Brick Theater
575 Metropolitan Avenue, Brooklyn, NY 11211
(718) 907-6189, *www.bricktheater.com*

Center Stage New York
48 West 21st Street, New York, NY 10010
(212) 929-2228, *www.centerstageny.com*

Clemente Solo Velez Cultural Center
107 Suffolk Street, New York, NY 10002
(212) 260-4080, *www.csvcenter.com*

Connelly Theater
220 East 4th Street, New York, NY 10009
(212) 982-2287

Daryl Roth Theatre
101 East 15th Street, New York, NY 10003
(212) 375-1110, *www.darylroththeatre.com*

Dixon Place
258 Bowery, New York, NY 10012
(212) 219-0736, *www.dixonplace.org*

Dorothy Strelsin at Abingdon Arts Complex
312 West 36th Street, New York, NY 10019
(212) 868-2055, *www.abingdontheatre.org*

The Flea Theater
14 White Street, New York, NY 10013
(212) 226-2407, *www.theflea.org*

Galapagos Art Space
70 North 6th Street, Brooklyn, NY 11211
(718) 782-5188, *www.galapagosartspace.com*

The Gene Frankel Theatre
24 Bond Street, New York, NY 10012
(212) 613-3107, *www.genefrankel.com*

Gloria Maddox Theater at T. Schreiber Studio
151 West 26th Street, New York, NY 10001
(212) 352-3101, *www.tschreiber.org*

HERE Arts Center
145 6th Avenue, New York, NY 10013
(212) 352-3101, *www.here.org*

Jean Cocteau Bouwerie Lane Theater
3300 Bowery, New York, NY 10012
(212) 677-0060, *www.jeancocteaurep.org*

Joyce Soho
155 Mercer Street, New York, NY 10012
(212) 242-8800, *www.joyce.org*

Kraine Theatre and The Red Room
85 East 4th Street, New York, NY 10003
(212) 777-6088, *www.horsetrade.info*

LaMama, E.T.C.
74A East 4th Street, New York, NY 10003
(212) 475-7710, *www.lamama.org*

Lamb's Theatre
130 West 44th Street, New York, NY 10036
(212) 575-0300, *www.lambstheatre.org*

Laurie Beecham Theater at The West Bank Café
407 West 42nd Street, New York, NY 10036
(212) 695-6909, *www.westbankcafe.com*

The Living Theatre
21 Clinton Street, New York, NY 10002
(212) 792-8050, *www.livingtheatre.org*

Looking Glass Theatre
422 West 57th Street, New York, NY 10019
(212) 307-9467, *www.lookingglasstheatrenyc.com*

Manhattan Children's Theatre
52 White Street, New York, NY 10013
(212) 226-4085, *www.manhatttanchildrenstheatre.org*

Metropolitan Playhouse
220 West 4th Street, New York, NY 10009
(212) 995-5302, *www.metropolitanplayhouse.org*

Manhattan Repertory Theater
303 West 42nd Street, New York, NY
(646) 239-6588, *www.manhattanrep.com*

Manhattan Theatre Source
117 MacDougall Street, New York, NY10011
(212) 501-4751, *www.theatresource.org*

National Black Theatre
2301 Fifth Avenue, Harlem, NY 10035
(212) 722-3800, *www.nationalblacktheatre.org*

Ohio Theatre
66 Wooster Street, New York, NY 10012
(212) 966-4844, *www.sohothinktank.org*

Ontological Theater at St. Marks Church
131 East 10th Street, New York, NY 10003
(212) 420-1916, *www.ontological.com*

Performance Space 122
150 First Avenue, New York, NY 10009
(212) 477-5288, *www.ps122.org*

The Producer's Club Theatres
358 West 44th Street, New York, NY 10036
(212) 315-4743, *www.producersclubtheatres.com*

Rattlestick Playwrights Theater
224 Waverly Place, New York, NY 10014
(212) 627-2556, *www.rattlestick.org*

Rockwood Music Hall
196 Allen Street, New York, NY 10002
(212) 477-4155, *www.rockwoodmusichall.com*

The Sage Theater
711 7th Avenue, New York, NY 10036
(212) 302-6665, *www.sagetheater.us*

Stanley H. Kaplan Penthouse at Lincoln Center
165 West 65th Street, New York, NY 10023
(212) 875-5400, *www.lincolncenter.org*

TADA! Youth Theater
15 West 28th Street, New York, NY 10001
(212) 252-1619, *www.tadatheater.com*

Theater for the New City
155 1st Avenue, New York, NY 10003
(212) 254-1109, *www.theaterforthenewcity.net*

The Rubin Museum Theater
150 West 17th Street, New York, NY 10011
(212) 620-5000 ext. 344, *www.rmanyc.org*

Theater Three
311 West 43rd Street, New York, NY 10036
(212) 279-4200

Triad
58 West 72nd Street, New York, NY 10023
(212) 362-2590, *www.triadnyc.com*

The Village Theater
158 Bleecker Street, New York, NY 10012
(212) 307-4100

Urban Stages
259 West 30th Street, New York, NY 10017
(212) 868-4444, *www.urbanstages.org*

Under St. Marks
94 St. Marks Place, New York, NY 10009
(212) 777-6088, *www.horsetrade.info*

The Wild Project
195 East 3rd Street, New York, NY 10009
(212) 228-1195, *www.thewildproject.com*

Wings Theater
154 Christopher Street, New York, NY 10014
(212) 627-2961, *www.wingstheater.com*

WorkShop Theater
312 West 36th Street, New York, NY 10018
(212) 695-4173, *www.workshoptheater.org*

COMEDY

Broadway Comedy Club
318 West 53rd Street, New York, NY 10019
(212) 757-2323, *www.broadwaycomedyclub.com*

Carolines on Broadway
1626 Broadway, New York, NY 10019
(212) 757-4100, *www.carolines.com*

Comic Strip Live
1568 2nd Avenue, New York, NY 10028
(212) 861-9386, *www.comicstriplive.com*

Comix
353 West 14th Street, New York, NY 10014
(212) 524-2500, *www.comixny.com*

Dangerfield's
1118 1st Avenue, New York, NY 10065
(646) 404-3393, *www.dangerfields.com*

Gotham Comedy Club
208 West 23rd Street, New York, NY 10011
(212) 367-9000, *www.gothamcomedyclub.com*

Joe Franklin's Comedy Club
713 8th Avenue, New York, NY 10036
(212) 977-0025

The Laugh Factory
303 West 42nd Street, New York NY 10036
(212) 586-7829, *www.laughfactory.com*

The People's Improv Theater
154 West 29th Street, New York, NY 10001
(212) 563-7488, *www.thepit-nyc.com*

Upright Citizen's Brigade Theatre
307 West 26th Street, New York, NY 10001
(212) 366-9176, *www.ucbtheatre.com*

Large Halls

John Birks Gillespie Auditorium at Baha'i Center
53 East 11th Street, New York, NY 10003
(212) 674-8998, *www.bahainyc.org*

Baruch Performing Arts Center at Baruch College
Engelman Recital Hall
Rose Nagelberg Theater
55 Lexington Avenue, New York, NY 10010
(646) 312-4085, *www.baruch.cuny.edu/bpac/*

Bowery Ballroom
6 Delancey Street, New York, NY 10002
(212) 533-2111, *www.boweryballroom.com*

Brooklyn College Center for the Performing Arts
2900 Campus Road, Brooklyn, NY 11210
(718) 951-4500, *www.brooklyncenteronline.org*

CAMI Hall at Columbia Artist Management, Inc.
165 West 57th Street, New York, NY 10019
(212) 841-9650

Cooper Union Great Hall
7 East 7th Street, New York, NY 10003
(212) 353-4195, *www.cooper.edu*

Dorothy and Lewis B. Cullman Center at
New York Public Library for the Performing Arts
40 Lincoln Center Plaza, New York, NY 10023
(212) 870-1630, *www.lincolncenter.org; www.nypl.org*

Grand Ballroom at the Manhattan Center
311 West 34th Street, New York, NY 10001
(212) 279-7740, *www.mcstudios.com*

Haft Auditorium at F.I.T.
227 West 27th Street, New York, NY 10001
(212) 217-4585, *www.fitnyc.edu*

Hammerstein Ballroom
311 West 34th Street, New York, NY 10001
(212) 485-1534, *www.mcstudios.com*

Hudson Theatre at the Millennium Hotel
145 West 44th Street, New York, NY 10036
(212) 768-4400, *www.millenniumhotels.com*

Fillmore New York at Irving Plaza
17 Irving Plaza, New York, NY 10003
(212) 777-6800, *www.irvingplaza.com*

**LaGuardia Concert Hall at Fiorello
LaGuardia High School**
100 Amsterdam Avenue, New York, NY 10023
(212) 496-0700 ext. 2208, *www.laguardiahs.org*

**Leonard Davis Center for the Performing Arts
Aaron Davis Hall / Harlem Stage / The Gatehouse**
150 Covenant Avenue, Bronx, New York 10031
(212) 281-9240, *www.harlemstage.org,*
www.aarondavishall.org

**Mainstage Theater at Laguardia
Performing Arts Center**
31-10 Thomson Avenue, Long Island City, NY 11101
(718) 482-5151, *www.laguardiaperformingarts.org*

Music Hall of Williamsburg
66 North 6th Street, Brooklyn, NY 11211
(212) 260-4700, *www.musichallofwilliamsburg.com*

**Peter B. Lewis Theater at Solomon R.
Guggenheim Museum**
1071 5th Avenue, New York, NY 10128
(212) 423-3587, *www.guggenheim.org*

Roseland Ballroom
239 West 57th Street, New York, NY 10019
(212) 777-6800, *www.roselandballroom.com*

Terminal 5
610 West 56th Street, New York, NY 10019
(212) 260-4700, *www.terminal5nyc.com*

Union Hall
702 Union Street, Brooklyn, NY 11215
(718) 638-4400, *www.unionhallny.com*

Webster Hall
125 East 11th Street, New York. NY 10003
(212) 353-1600, *www.websterhall.com*

World Financial Center Winter Garden Theater
220 Vesey Street, New York, NY 10281
(212) 945-5050, *www.worldfinancialcenter.com*

Outdoor/ Sports Facilities

Bargemusic
Fulton Ferry Landing, Brooklyn, NY 11201
(718) 624-2083, *www.bargemusic.org*

Damrosh Park at Lincoln Center
175 West 62nd Street, New York, NY 10023
(212) 307-4100, *www.lincolncenter.org,*
www.bigapplecircus.org

Delacorte Theater at Central Park
81 Central Park West, New York, NY 10023
(212) 539-8500, (212)-539-8750, *www.publictheater.org*

Keyspan Park: The Brooklyn Cyclones
1094 Surf Avenue, Brooklyn, NY 11224
(718) 507 TIXX, *www.brooklyncyclones.com*

Randall's Island Park on Manhattan East River
New York, NY 10035
(212) 408-0100, *www.nycgovparks.org/parks/*
randallsislandpark;www.ticketmaster.com

The Richmond County Bank Ballpark at St. George:
The Staten Island Yankees
75 Richmond Terrace, Staten Island, NY 10301
(718) 723-5763, *www.siyanks.com*

Spiegeltent at Fulton Fish Market
Pier 17, South Street Seaport, South Street, New York,
NY 10038
(646) 775-2880 ext. 202, *www.spiegelworld.com*

Offbeat Seats

Awards

Drama Desk Awards

The Drama Desk Award recognizes shows produced on Broadway, Off-Broadway, Off-Off-Broadway, and by legitimate not-for-profit theaters. These awards have proven to be the first step towards stardom for Edward Albee, Wendy Wasserstein, George C. Scott, Stacy Keach, and Dustin Hoffman. Off-Broadway productions such as *Driving Miss Daisy*, *Steel Magnolias*, and *The Boys in the Band* were propelled to international recognition based on their wins. The Drama Desk Awards ceremony is held annually at the LaGuardia High School Concert Hall at Lincoln Center. For tickets, call TheaterMania at (212) 352-3101 or visit *www.dramadesk.com.*

Drama League Awards

The Drama League Awards honor distinguished productions and performances both on Broadway and Off-Broadway, in addition to recognizing achieve-ments in theatre, musical theatre, and directing. Each May, the awards are presented at the Annual Awards Luncheon with performers, directors, producers, and Drama League members in attendance. Called "a won-derful, notoriously swanky affair" by Playbill magazine, the Luncheon is generally acknowledged in the theatre community as the most enjoyable event in the awards season. Make plans to attend the next Annual Awards Luncheon. For more information or to attend the Awards Luncheon, call (212) 244-9494, ext. 5 or visit *www.dramaleague.org.*

Lucille Lortel Awards

The Lucille Lortel Awards recognize excellence in New York Off-Broadway theatre. The awards are named for Lucille Lortel, an actress and theater producer. Past recipi-ents include *Spring Awakening* and *In the Heights*, which later opened on Broadway; and Kevin Kline for a lifetime achievement award. For information, *visit www.lortel.org.*

Obie Awards

The Obie Awards, or Off-Broadway Theater Awards, are annual prizes bestowed by *The Village Voice* newspaper to Off-Broadway theater artists in New York City. Similar to the Tony Awards for mainstream Broadway productions, the Obies cover Off-Broadway and Off-Off-Broadway productions. Past recipients include Dustin Hoffman, Meryl Streep, William Hurt, Morgan Freeman, Mos Def, Amy Irving, Kevin Kline, Nathan Lane, Olympia Dukakis, Robert Duvall, Kevin Bacon, Alec Baldwin, Kathy Bates, James Earl Jones, Felicity Huffman, and Harvey Fierstein. The ceremony is held in New York City. For information, visit *www.villagevoice.com/obies*.

Outer Critics Circle Awards

The Outer Critics Circle Awards are presented annually for theatrical achievements both on and Off-Broadway. The awards are decided upon by theater critics who review for newspapers, national publications, and other media outlets outside of New York City. The nominees are announced each April. The presentation of awards is made in late May at Sardi's Restaurant in New York City and precedes the Tony Awards by about two weeks. Visit *www.outercritics.org* for information.

Antoinette Perry Awards

The Antoinette Perry Awards for Excellence in Theatre, known as the Tony Awards, recognize achievement in live American theatre and are presented by the American Theatre Wing and The Broadway League at an annual ceremony at Radio City Music Hall. The awards are for Broadway productions and performances, as well as Special Tony Awards and the Regional Theatre Tony Award, and the Tony Honors for Excellence in the Theatre. Nominations are announced in May and the ceremony is broadcast on CBS in June. To be a part of the three-hour telecast audience, call (212) 307-4544 or *visit www.tonyawards.com*.

Theatre World Awards

Six lucky actors and actresses making their performing debuts in Broadway and Off-Broadway productions are honored annually since 1944 with the Theatre World Janus Award. Peter Filichia leads a committee of New York area theater critics in choosing the winners, recognizing outstanding talent. Harry Connick Jr. and Christina Applegate have joined the ranks of past winners which includes Alan Alda, Audra McDonald, and Antonio Banderas. The awards are presented at a ceremony each spring where past and present winners unite to celebrate. For more information on the awards or Theatre World publications, visit *www.theatreworld.org* or *www.applausepub.com*.

broadway theatres

302 West 45th Street // New York, NY [between 8th & 9th Avenues]

Telecharge: (212) 239-6000 // Group Sales: (212) 239-6262

[www.jujamcym.com]

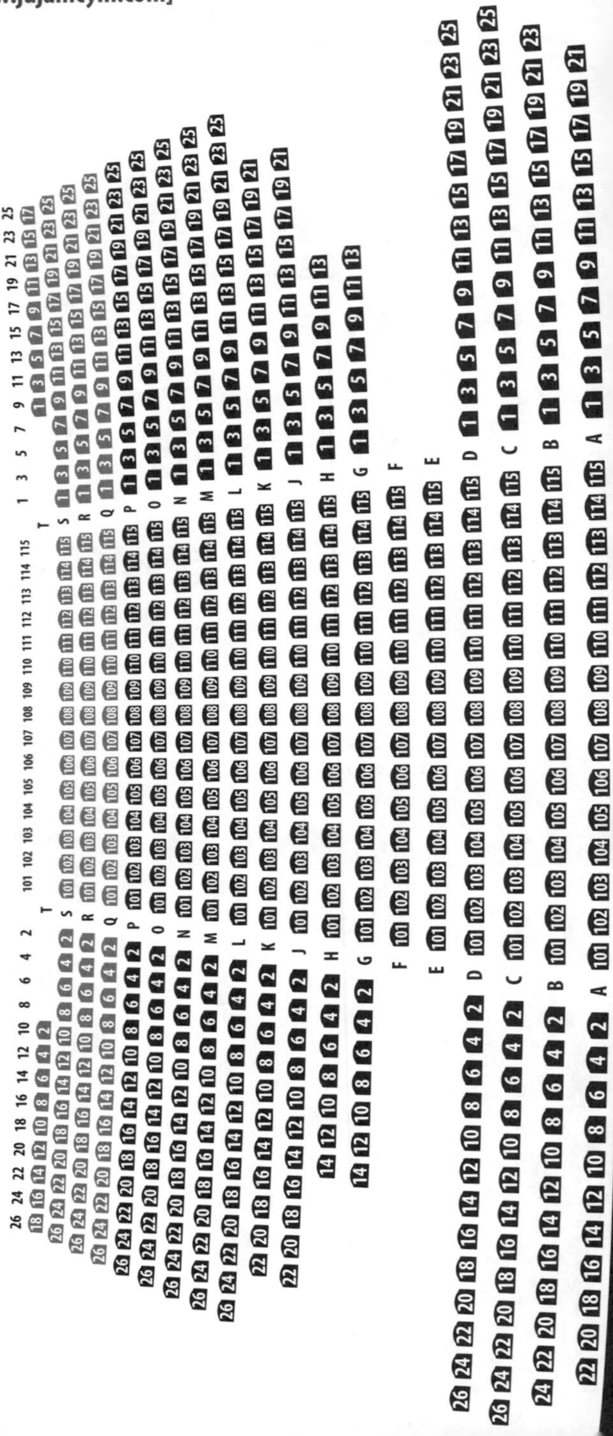

A,C,E to 42nd St. & 8th Ave.

333 West 46th: 333 West 46th St. [bet. 8th & 9th Aves.]
Astor: 1515 Broadway [bet. 43rd & 44th Sts.]

M6, M7, M10, M11, M42, M104   Midtown Map #28

Premium Broadway Inner Circle Tickets: (212) 563-2929

Orchestra

$$$$
$$$

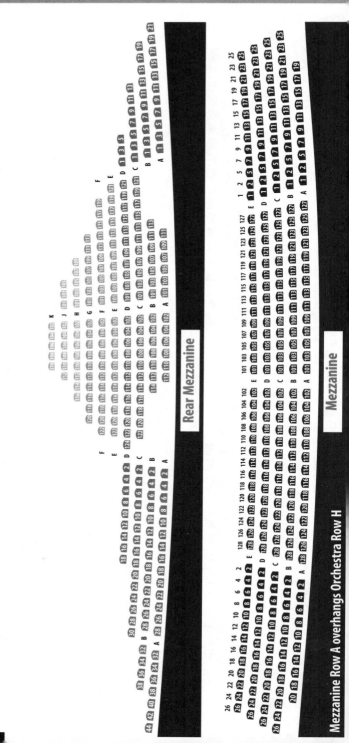

Rear Mezzanine

Mezzanine

Mezzanine Row A overhangs Orchestra Row H

1, 9 to 50th St. // N, R to 49th St.

GMC: 225 W. 49th St. [bet. Broadway & 8th Ave.]
Astor: 1515 Broadway [bet. 43rd & 44th Sts.]

M6, M7, M10, M27, M50, M104

Midtown Map #7

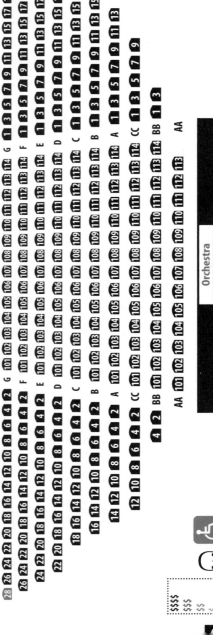

Orchestra

$$$$
$$$
$$
$

227 West 42nd Street // **New York, NY** [between 7th & 8th Avenue]
Box Office: (212) 719-1300 // Group Sales: (212) 719-9393

[www.roundabouttheatre.org]

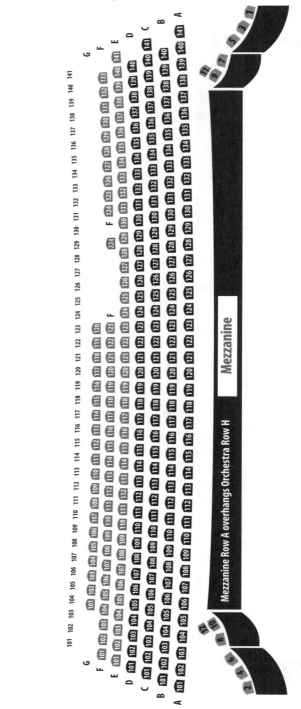

Mezzanine

Mezzanine Row A overhangs Orchestra Row H

to 42nd St. & 7th Ave. | Astor: 1515 Broadway [bet. 43rd & 44th Sts.]

M6, M7, M10, M42, M104 | Midtown Map #37

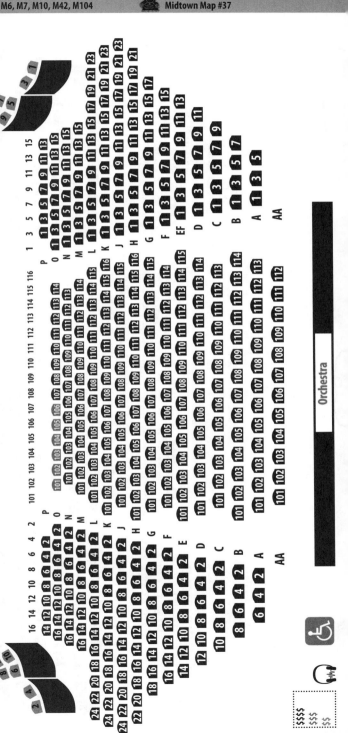

Orchestra

Rear section (odd numbers):

1 3 5 7 9 11 13 15 17 19 — Q
1 3 5 7 9 11 13 15 17 19
1 3 5 7 9 11 13 15 17 19
1 3 5 7 9 11 13 15 17 19
1 3 5 7 9 11 13 15 17 19
1 3 5 7 9 11 13 15 17 19
1 3 5 7 9 11
1 3 5 7 9 11
1 3 5 7 9 11 — F
1 3 5 7 9 11 13 15 17 19 — E
1 3 5 7 9 11 13 15 17 19 — D
1 3 5 7 9 11 13 15 17 19 — C
1 3 5 7 9 11 13 15 17 19 — B
1 3 5 7 9 11 13 15 17 19 — A

Center section (100-series):

101 102 103 104 105 106 107 108 109 110 111 112 113 114

Rows: P, O, N, M, L, K, J, H, G (upper) / F, E, D, C, B, A (lower)
115 116 117 118 (partial on P/O rows)

Left section (even numbers):

20 18 16 14 12 10 8 6 4 2 — Q
20 18 16 14 12 10 8 6 4 2
20 18 16 14 12 10 8 6 4 2
20 18 16 14 12 10 8 6 4 2
20 18 16 14 12 10 8 6 4 2
12 10 8 6 4 2
12 10 8 6 4 2
12 10 8 6 4 2
20 18 16 14 12 10 8 6 4 2 — F
20 18 16 14 12 10 8 6 4 2 — E
20 18 16 14 12 10 8 6 4 2 — D
20 18 16 14 12 10 8 6 4 2 — C
20 18 16 14 12 10 8 6 4 2 — B
20 18 16 14 12 10 8 6 4 2 — A

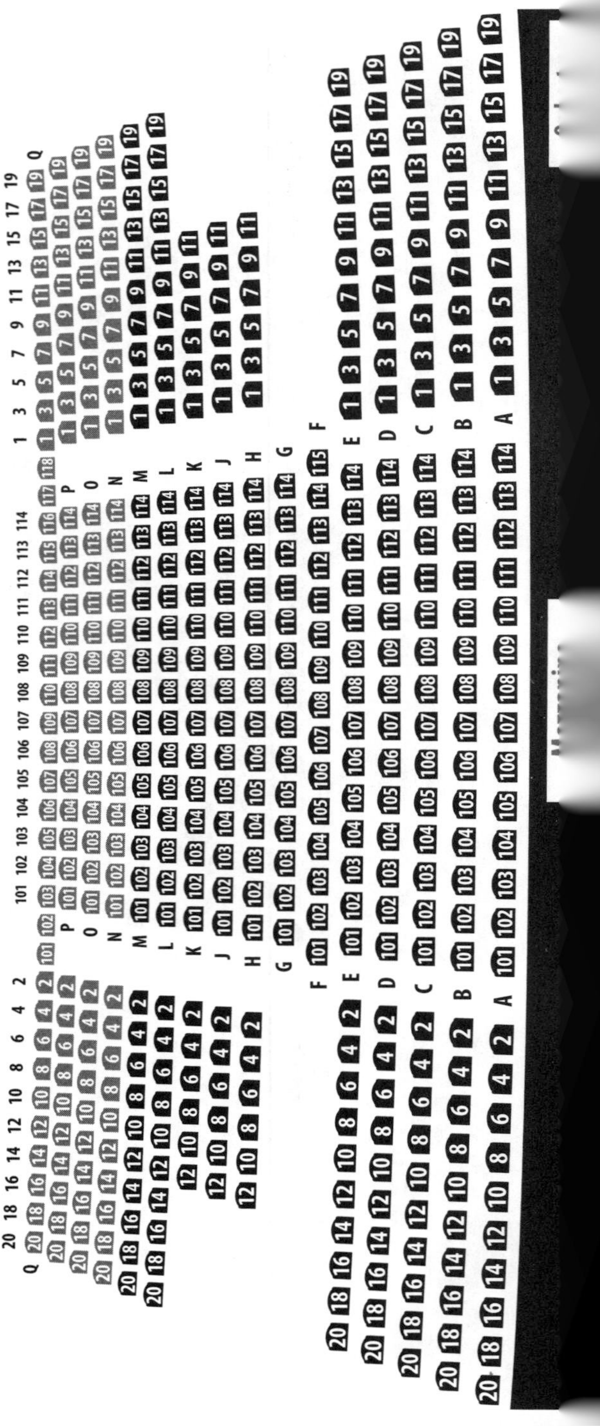

Premium Broadway Inner Circle Tickets: (212) 563-2929

111 West 44th Street // **New York, NY** [between Broadway & 6th Avenue]

Telecharge: (212) 239-6200 // Group Sales: (212) 302-7000

[www.shubertorganization.com]

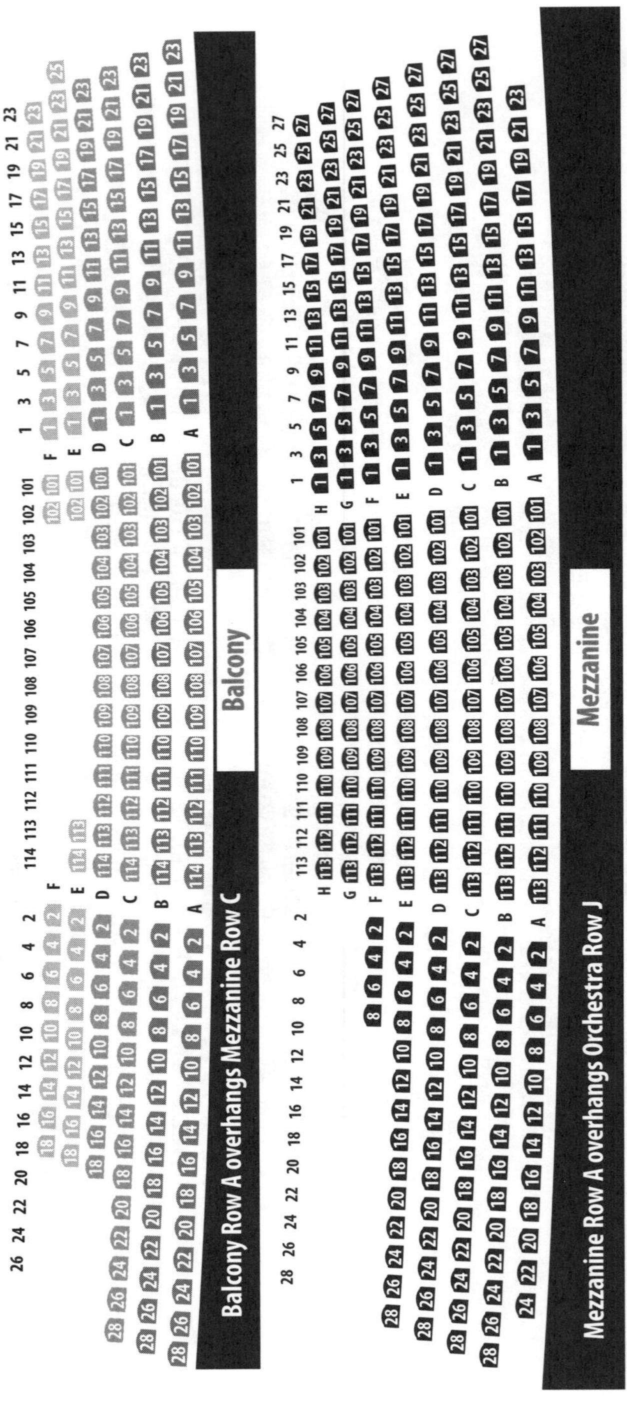

Balcony

Balcony Row A overhangs Mezzanine Row C

Mezzanine

Mezzanine Row A overhangs Orchestra Row J

B, D, F, Q to 42nd St. & 7th Ave. — Astor: 1515 Broadway [bet. 43rd & 44th Sts.]

M5, M6, M7, M10, M42, M104 — Midtown Map #30

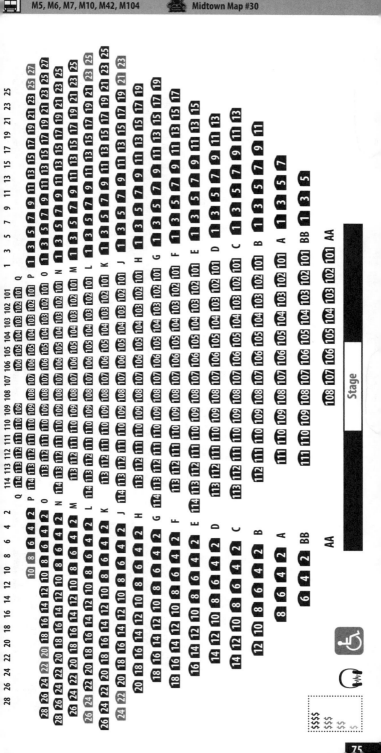

Stage

$$$$
$$$
$$
$

242 West 45th Street // New York, NY [between Broadway & 8th Avenue]

Telecharge: (212) 239-6200 // Group Sales: (212) 239-6262

[www.shubertorganization.com]

Balcony Row A overhangs Mezzanine Row C
Rear Mezzanine
Mezzanine Row A overhangs Orchestra Row I
Front Mezzanine

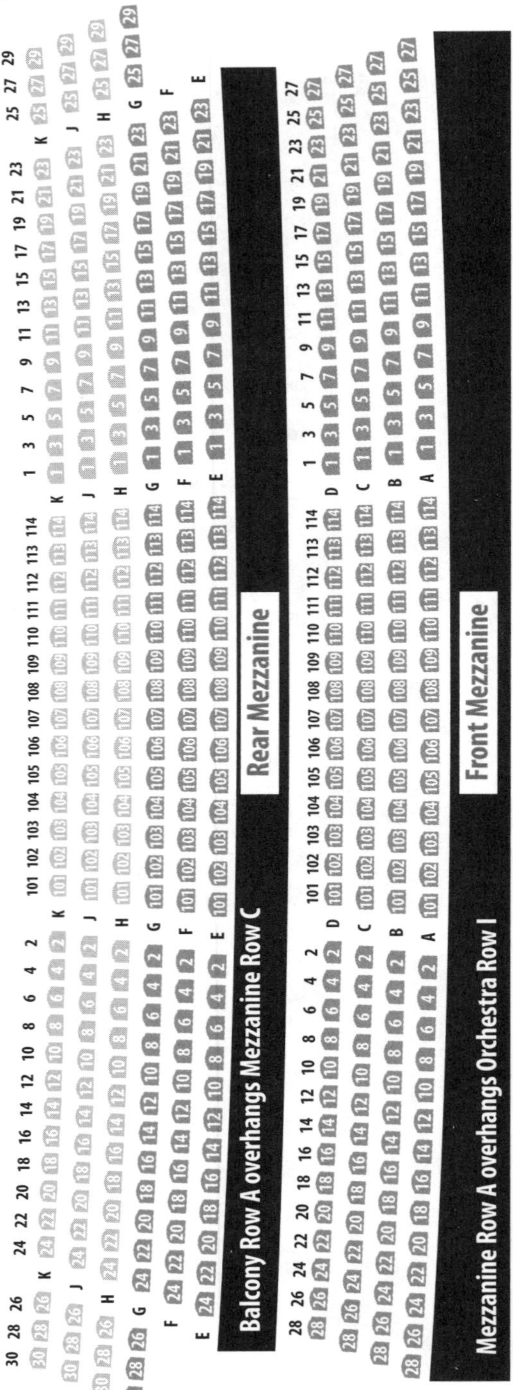

1, 2, 3, 7, 9, N, R, S to 42nd St. & 7th Ave.
A, C, E to 42nd St. & 8th Ave.

M6, M7, M10, M42, M104

Mir6: 139 West 45th St. [bet. 6th & 7th Aves.
Astor: 1515 Broadway [bet. 43rd & 44th Sts.]

Midtown Map #24

Orchestra

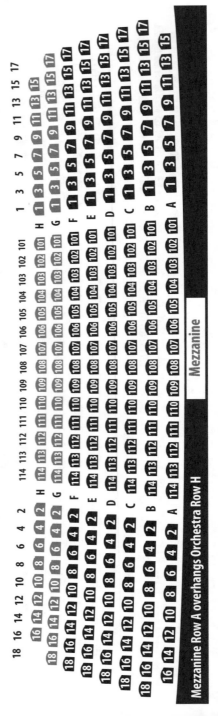

Mezzanine

Mezzanine Row A overhangs Orchestra Row H

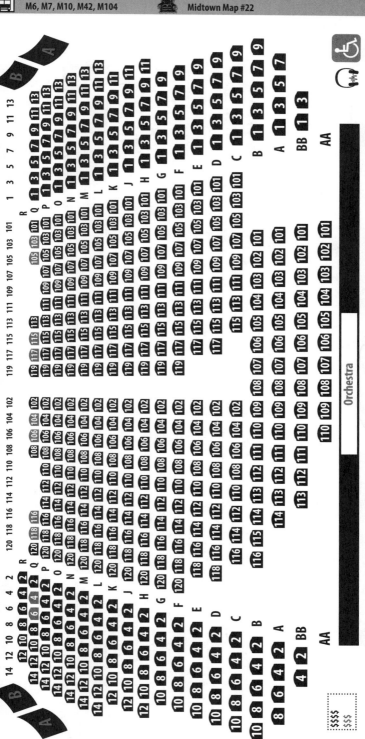

Orchestra

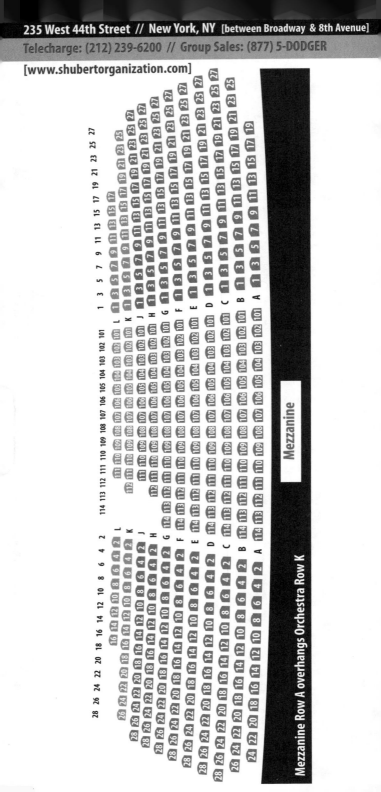

235 West 44th Street // New York, NY [between Broadway & 8th Avenue]
Telecharge: (212) 239-6200 // Group Sales: (877) 5-DODGER

[www.shubertorganization.com]

Mezzanine

Mezzanine Row A overhangs Orchestra Row K

4, 5, 6, 9 @ 42nd St. & 7th Ave.

Kinney: 100 W. 44th [bet. 6th & 7th Aves.]
Astor: 1515 Broadway [bet. 43rd & 44th Sts.]

M6, M7, M10, M42, M104

Midtown Map #26

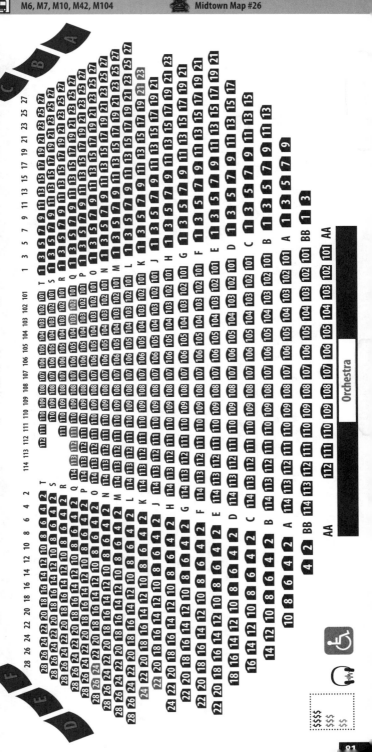

Orchestra

Rear Mezzanine

Mezzanine Row A overhangs Orchestra Row

1, 9, C, E to 50th Street | Command. 216 W. 54th [bet. Broadway & 7th Ave.]

52nd/Broadway: 1675 Broadway [bet. 52nd & 53rd Sts.]

M6, M7, M10, M27, M50, M104 | Midtown Map #1

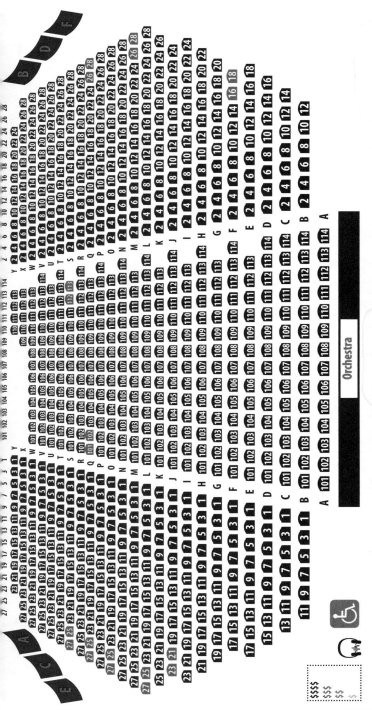

Orchestra

$$$$
$$$
$$
$

256 West 47th Street // New York, NY [between Broadway & 8th Avenue]

Ticketmaster: (212) 307-4100 // Group Sales: (212) 840-3909

[www.nederlander.com] [brooksatkinsontheater.org]

Rear Mezzanine
Front Mezzanine
Mezzanine Row AA overhangs Orchestra Row K

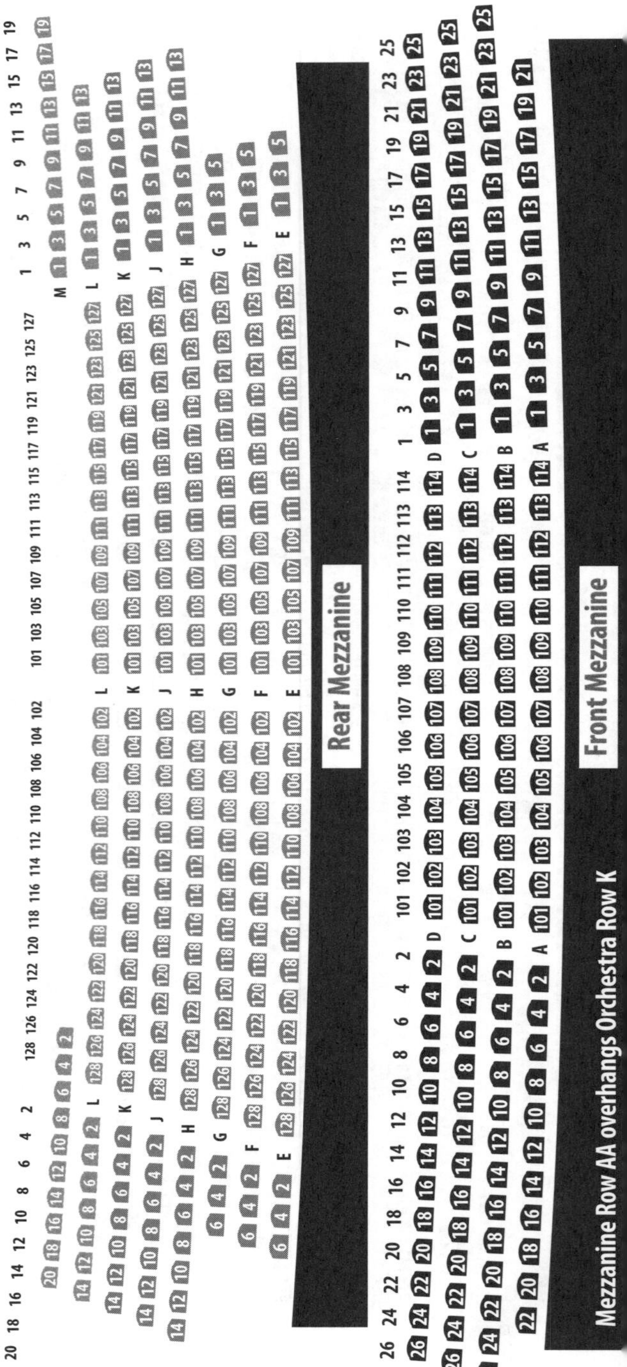

Kinney: 253 W. 47th St. [bet. Broadway & 8th Ave.]

M6, M7, M42   Midtown Map #13

Orchestra

$$$$
$$$
$$

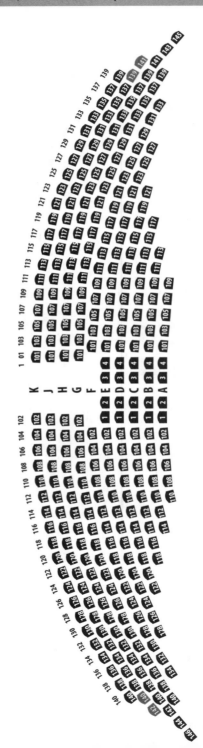

B, D, E to 7th Ave. & 53rd St.   52 Broadway: 1675 Broadway [at 52nd St.]

M6, M7, M10, M27, M50, M104   Midtown Map #5

Balcony

Balcony Row A overhangs Mezzanine Row B

Mezzanine

Mezzanine Row A overhangs Orchestra Row J

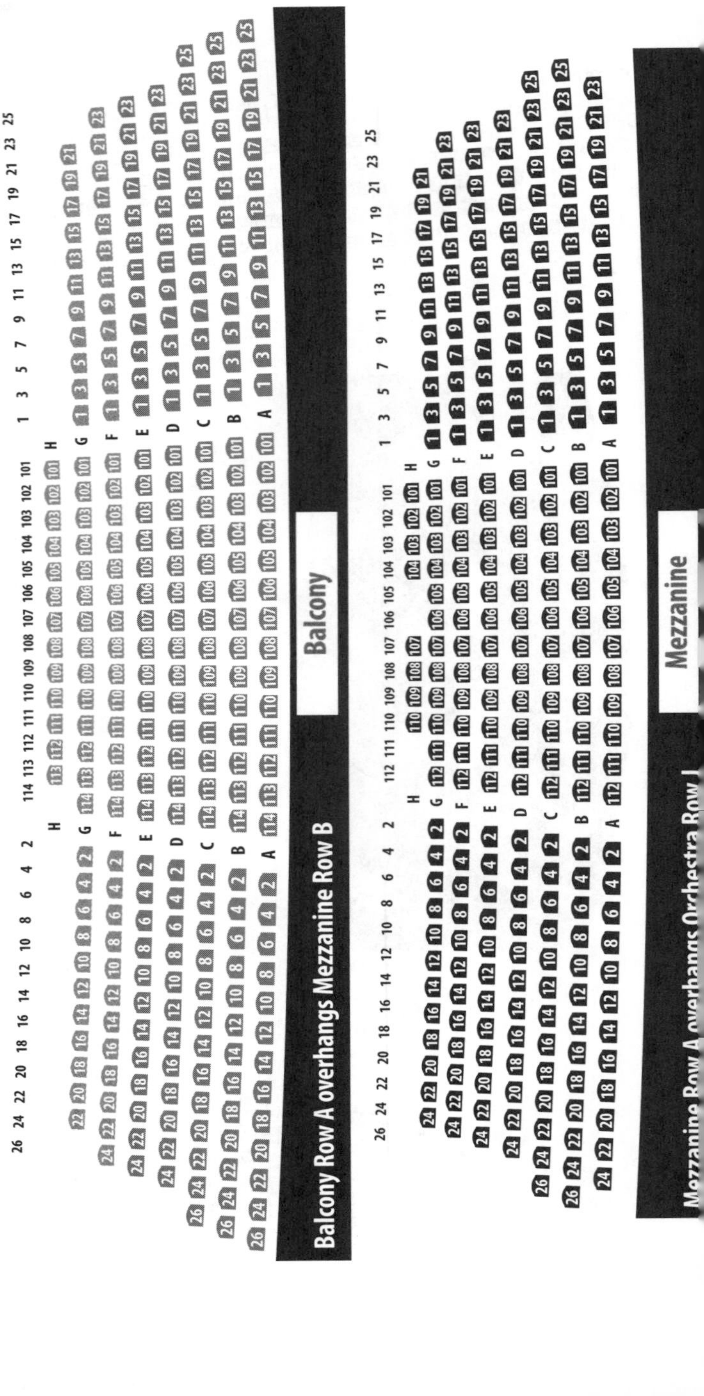

B, D, F, V to Rockefeller Ctr. [47–50th Sts.]   Kinney: 155 West 48th St. [bet. 6th & 7th Aves.]

GMC: 148 West 48th St. [bet. 6th & 7th Aves.]

M6, M7, M10, M27, M50, M104   Midtown Map #12

Orchestra

$$$$
$$$
$$

243 West 47th Street // New York, NY [between Broadway & 8th Avenue]

Telecharge: (212) 239-6200 // Group Sales: (212) 239-6262

[www.shubertorganization.com]

Rear Mezzanine
Front Mezzanine
Mezzanine Row A overhangs Orchestra Row K

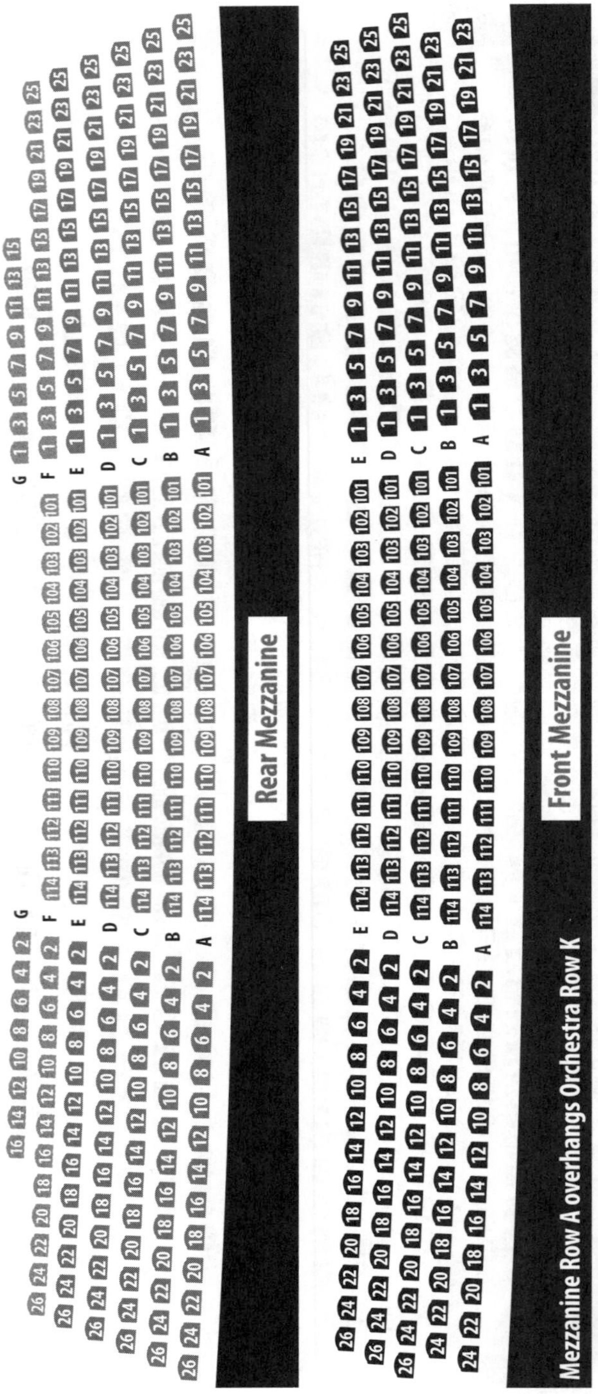

A, C, E to 42nd St. & 8th Ave.

West 47th: 257 West 47th St. [bet. Broadway & 8th Ave.]
Kinney: 253 West 47th St. [bet. Broadway & 8th Ave.]

M6, M7, M10, M27, M50, M104   Midtown Map #11

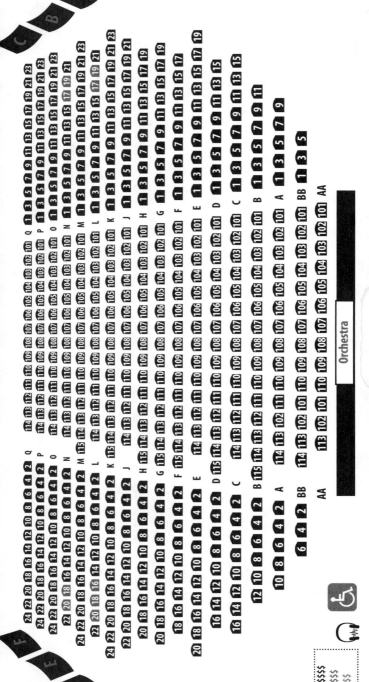

Orchestra

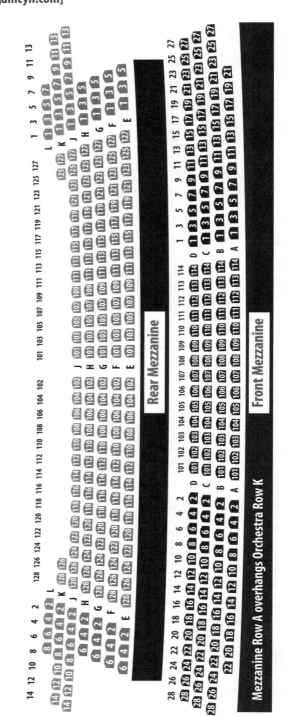

Rear Mezzanine

Front Mezzanine

Mezzanine Row A overhangs Orchestra Row K

Premium Broadway Inner Circle Tickets: (212) 563-2929

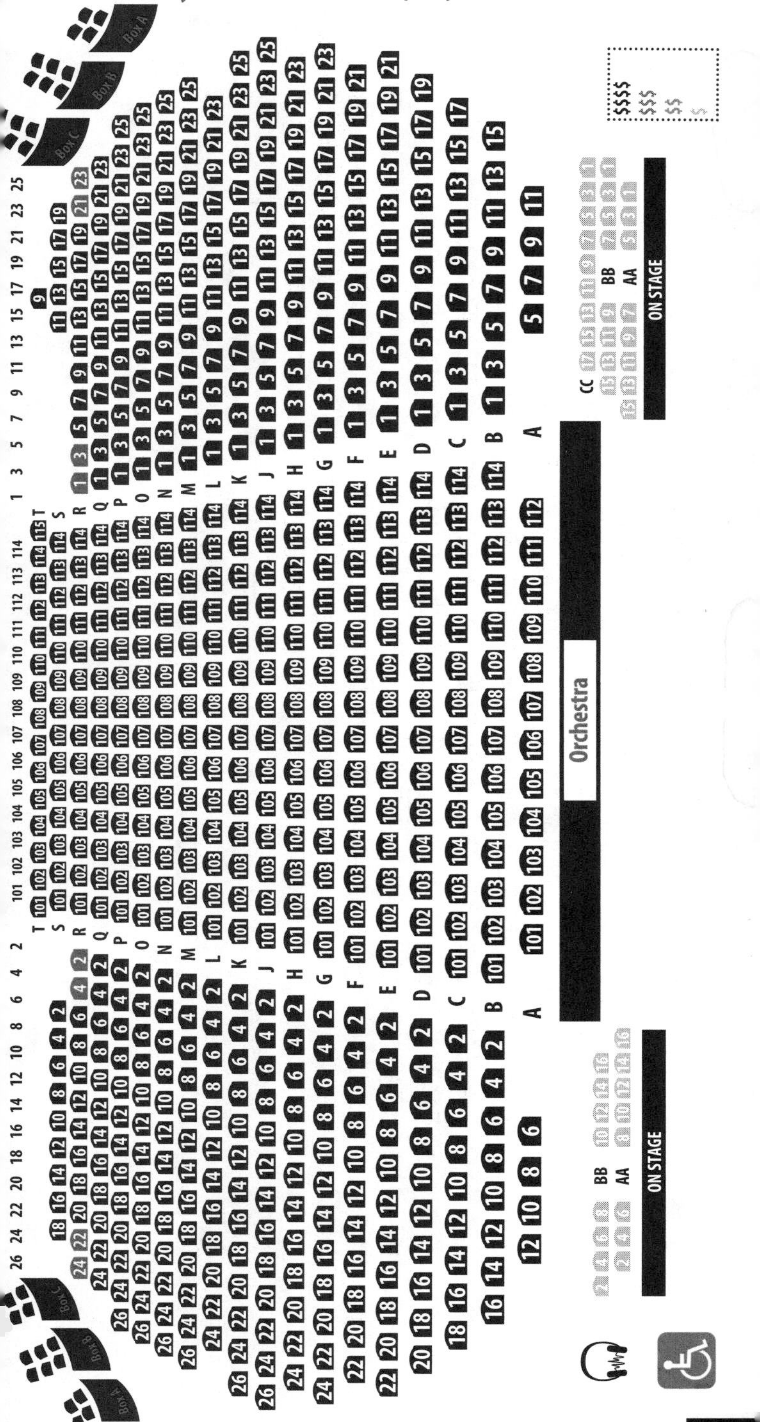

Box A
Box B
Box C

$$$$
$$$
$$
$

ON STAGE

Orchestra

ON STAGE

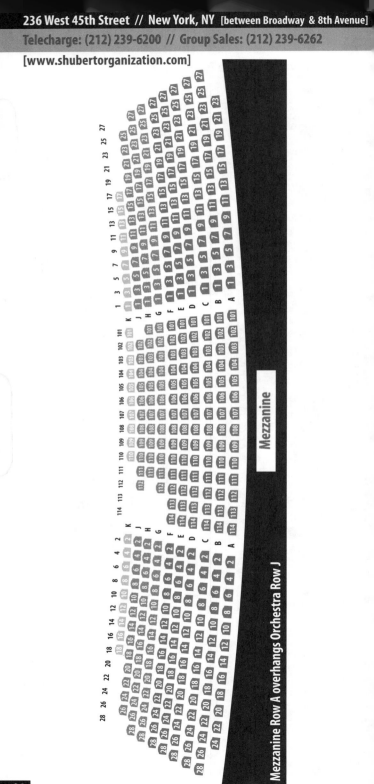

Mezzanine

Mezzanine Row A overhangs Orchestra Row J

1, 2, 3 to 42nd St.   Astor: 1515 Broadway [bet. 43rd & 44th Sts.]

M6, M7, M10, M42, M104   Midtown Map #23

Orchestra

Rear Mezzanine

Front Mezzanine

Front Mezzanine Row A overhangs Orchestra Row N

Orchestra

Mezzanine

Mezzanine Row A overhangs Orchestra Row K

A, C, E, N, Q, R, W to 42nd St. & 8th Ave.
1, 2, 3 to 42nd St. & 7th Ave.

Kinney: 100 West 44th St. [bet. 6th & 7th Aves.]
Astor: 1515 Broadway [bet. 43rd & 44th Sts.]

M6, M7, M10, M42, M104

Midtown Map #31

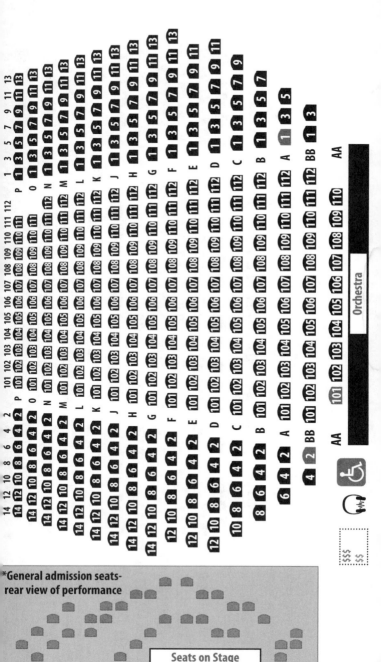

Orchestra

\$\$\$
\$\$

*General admission seats-
rear view of performance

Seats on Stage
Stage Front*

124 West 43rd Street // New York, NY [between Broadway & 6th Aven

Telecharge: (212) 239-6200 // Group Sales: (212) 239-6262

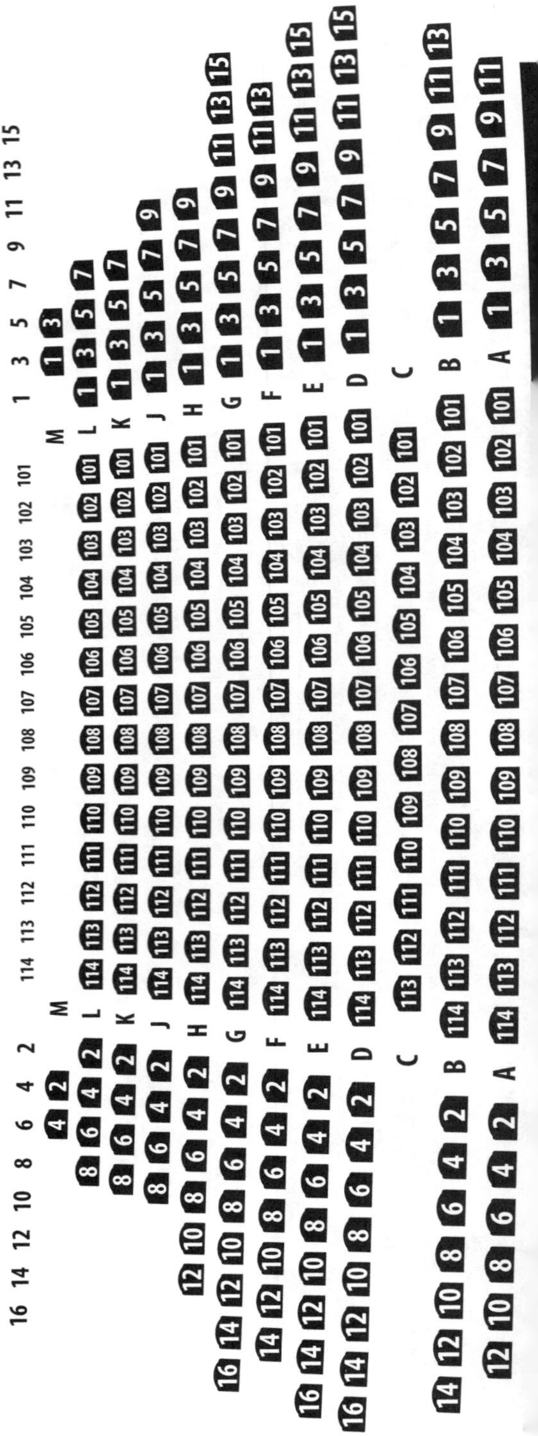

1, 2, 3, 7 to 42nd St. & 7th Ave.
A, C, E to 42nd St. & 8th Ave.

Meyers: 141 West 43rd St. [bet. 6th & 7th Ave.
Astor: 1515 Broadway [bet. 43rd & 44th Sts.]

M6, M7, M10, M27, M50

Midtown Map #40

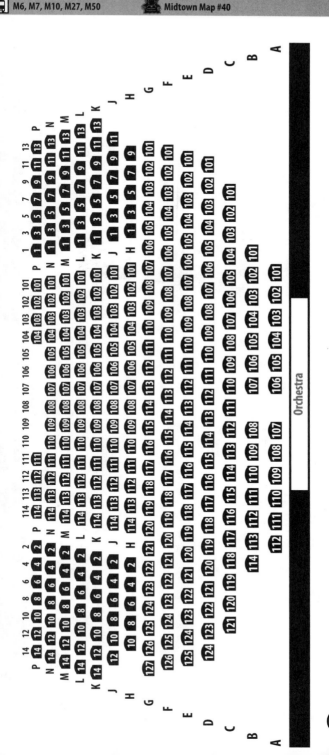

Orchestra

214 West 43rd Street // New York, NY [between 7th & 8th Avenues]

Ticketmaster: (212) 307-4100 // Group Sales: (917) 421-5413

[www.hiltontheatre.com]

Balcony

Balcony Row A overhangs Dress Circle Row B

Dress Circle

Dress Circle Row A overhangs Orchestra Row T

1, 2, 3, S, Q, N, R, W to 42nd St. & 7th Ave.
A, C, E to 42nd St. & 8th Ave.

Kinney: 250 West 41st St. [bet. 6th & 7th Aves.]
Astor: 1515 Broadway [bet. 43rd & 44th Sts.]

M6, M7, M10, M42, M104

Midtown Map #33

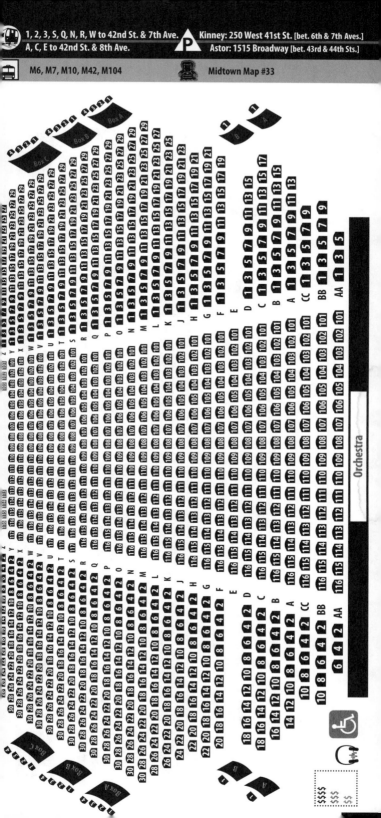

▼ Orchestra ▼

Sec. 1

Sec. 2

Sec. 3

Sec. 4

Sec. 5

Rear Mezzanine

Front Mezzanine

Mezzanine Row A overhangs Orchestra Row H

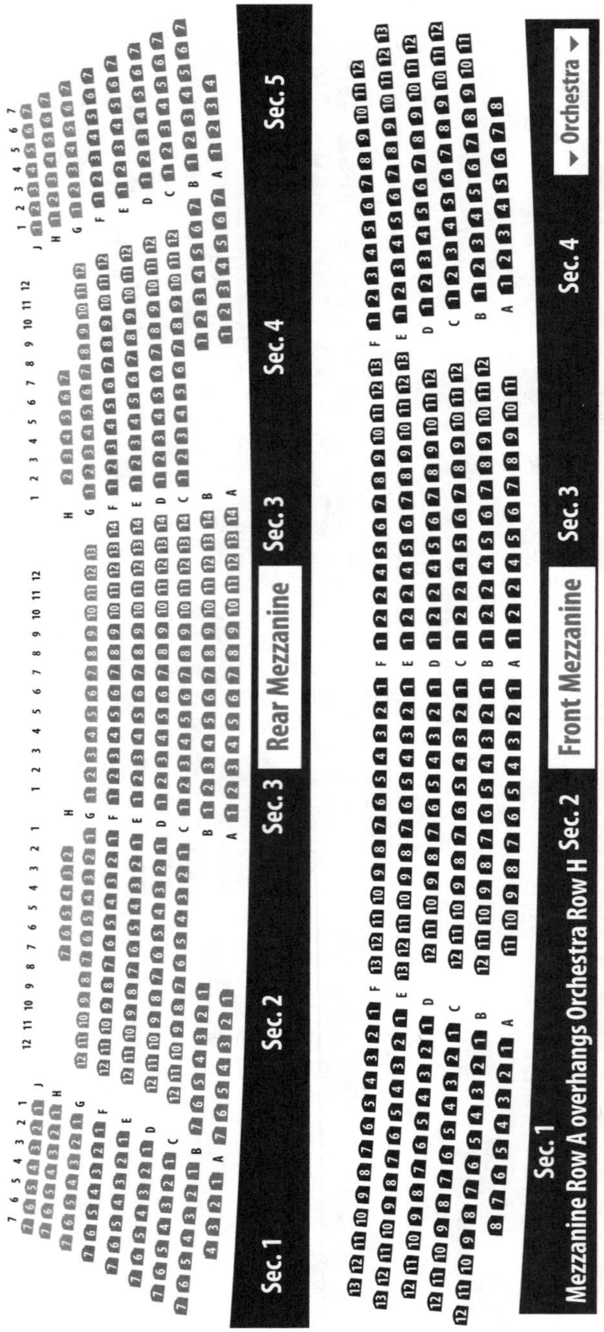

1, 2, 3, 7, N, R, S to 42nd St. & 7th Ave.

Miro: 159 West 45th St. [bet. 6th & 7th Aves.]
Astor: 1515 Broadway [bet. 43rd & 44th Sts.]

M6, M7, M10, M42, M104

Midtown Map #20

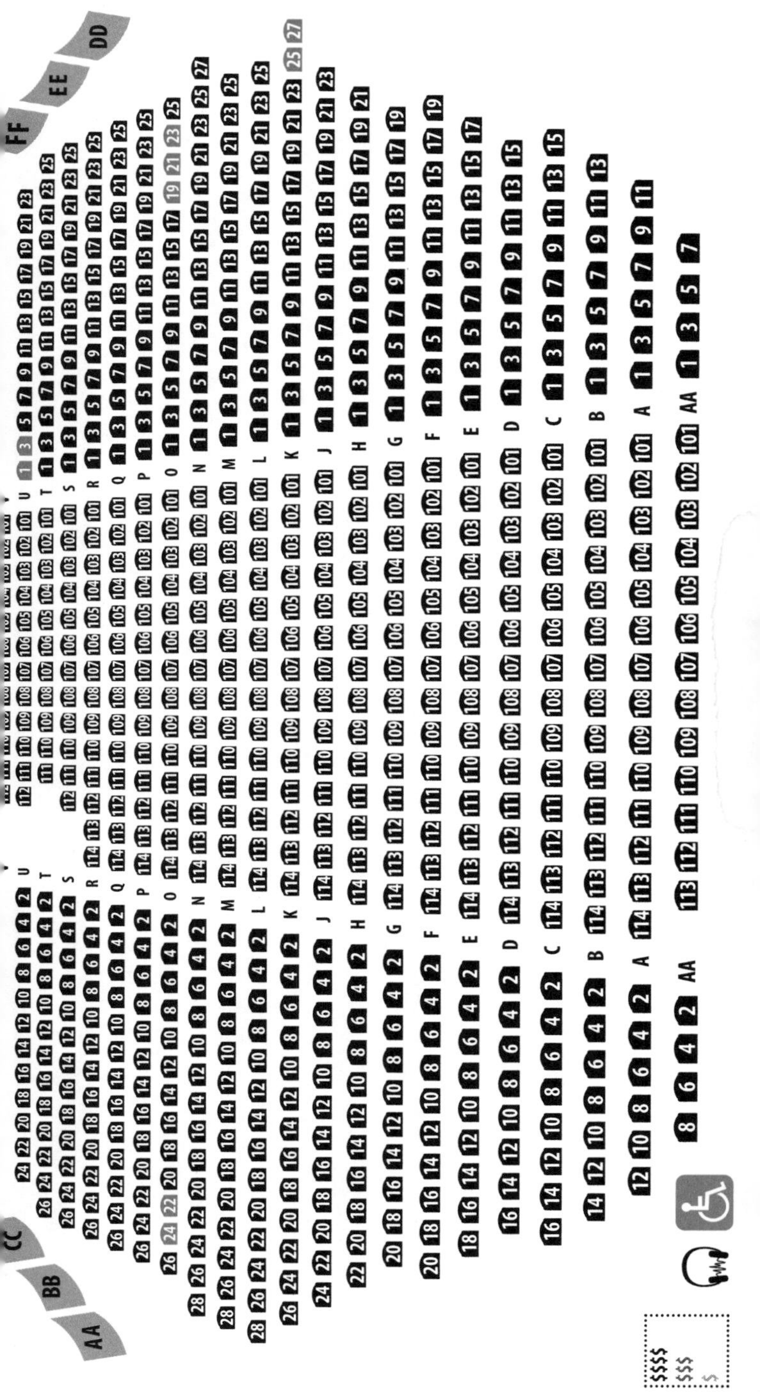

FF EE DD

CC BB AA

$$$$
$$$
$

105

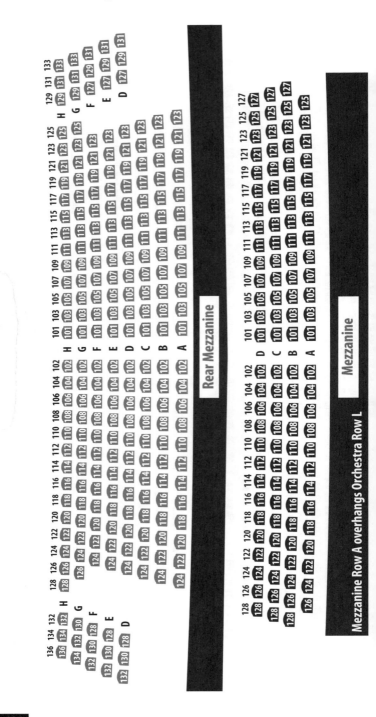

Rear Mezzanine

Mezzanine

Mezzanine Row A overhangs Orchestra Row L

1, 2, 3, 7, N, R, S to 42nd St. & 7th Ave.
A, C, E to 42nd St. & 8th Ave.

Kinney: 100 West 44th St. [bet. 6th & 7th Aves.]
Miro: 139 West 45th St. [bet. 6th & 7th Aves.]

M6, M7, M10, M42, M104

Midtown Map #25

Orchestra

220 West 48th Street // **New York, NY** [between Broadway & 8th Avenue]
Telecharge: (212) 239-6200 // Group Sales: (212) 302-7000

[www.shubertorganization.com]

Balcony

Balcony Row A overhangs Mezzanine Row B

Mezzanine

Mezzanine Row A overhangs Orchestra Row K

B, D, F, V to Rockefeller Ctr. [47–50th Sts.]
1, 9 to 50th St. // N,R to 49th St.

P Kinney: 155 West 48th St. [bet. 6th & 7th Aves.]
GMC: 148 West 48th St. [bet. 6th & 7th Aves.]

M6, M10, M27, M50, M42, M104

Midtown Map #10

Orchestra

$$$$
$$$
$$

205 West 46th Street // New York, NY [between Broadway & 8th Aven

Ticketmaster: (212) 307-4100 // Group Sales: (212) 840-3890

[www.nederlander.org]

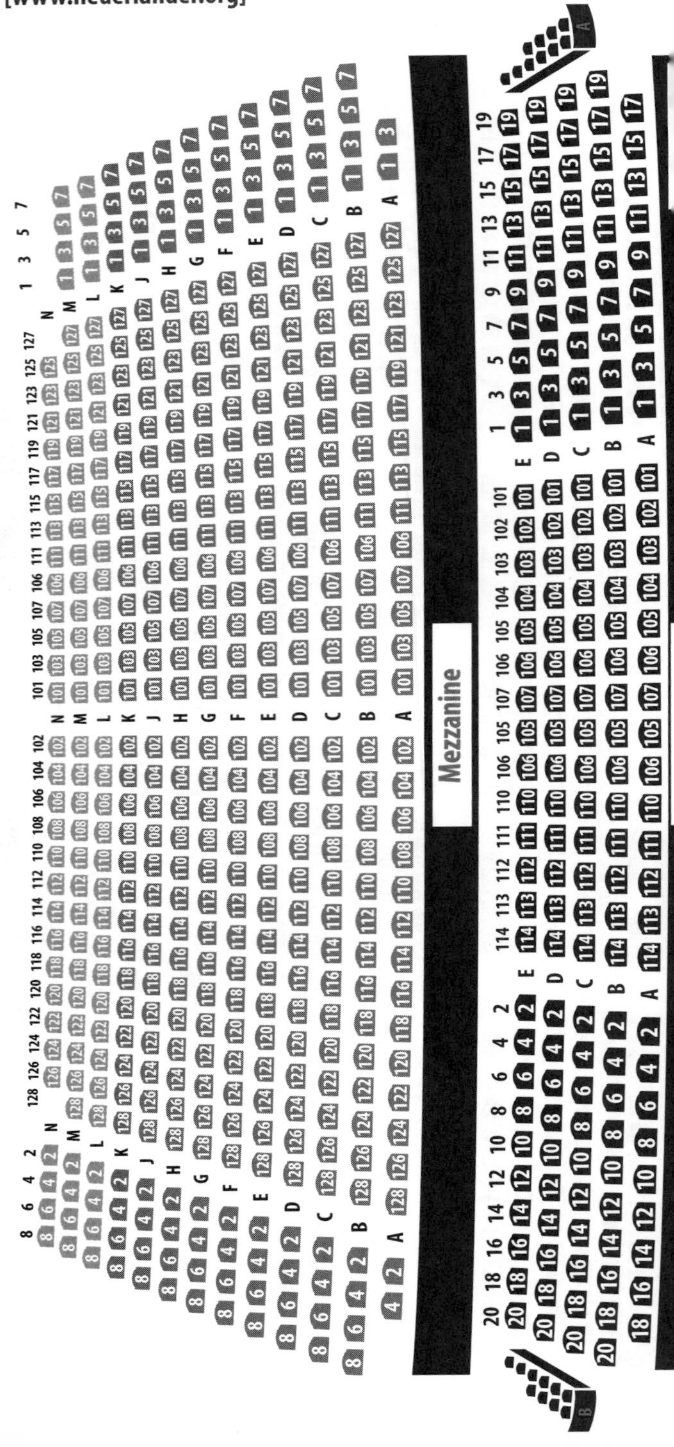

N, R to 42nd St. & 7th Ave.
1, 9, C, E to 50th St.

Trans. 223 W. 46th St. [bet. Broadway & 8th Ave.]
West 47th: 257 W. 47th St. [bet. Broadway & 8th Ave.]

M6, M10, M27, M42, M50, M104   Midtown Map #15

www.luntfontannetheater.com]

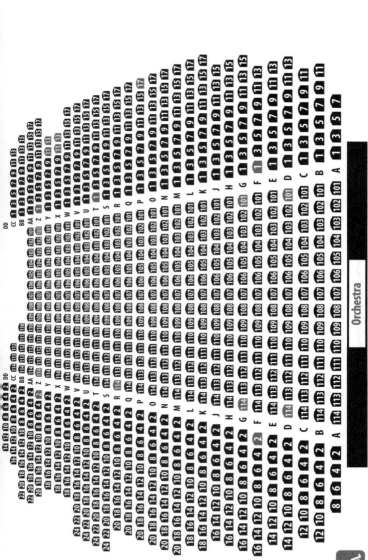

Orchestra

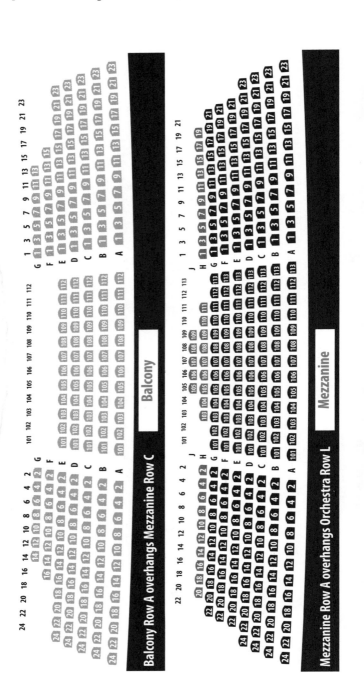

Balcony

Balcony Row A overhangs Mezzanine Row C

Mezzanine

Mezzanine Row A overhangs Orchestra Row L

B, D, F, V to Rockefeller Ctr. [47–50th Sts.]   Miro: 139 West 45th St. [bet. 6th & 7th Aves.]

N, R to 49th St.   Astor: 1515 Broadway [bet. 43rd & 44th Sts.]

M5, M6, M7, M10, M42, M104   Midtown Map #18

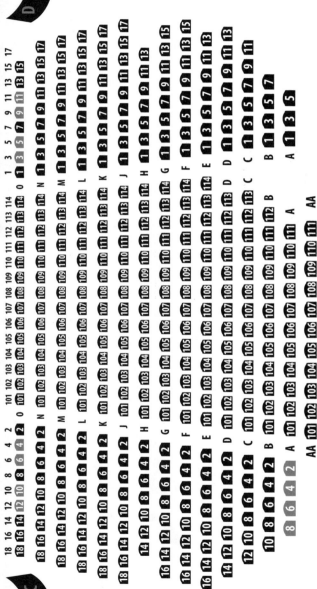

Orchestra

$$$$
$$$
$$
$

Majestic Theatre

245 West 44th Street // **New York, NY** [between Broadway & 8th Avenue]

Telecharge: (212) 239-6200 // Group Sales: (212) 239-6262

[www.shubertorganization.com]

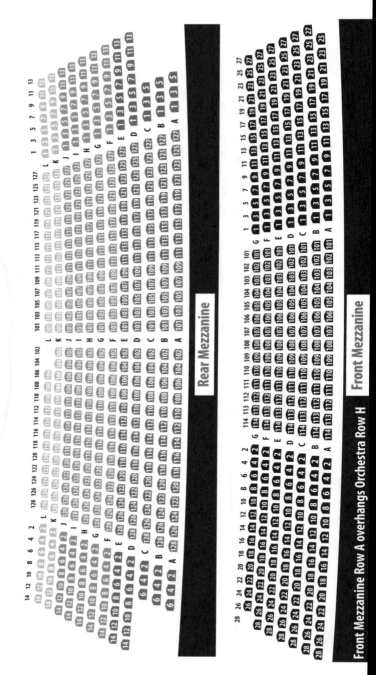

Rear Mezzanine

Front Mezzanine

Front Mezzanine Row A overhangs Orchestra Row H

114

1, 2, 3, 7, 9, N, R, S to 42nd St. & 7th Ave.
A, C, E to 42nd St. & 8th Ave.

Kinney: 100 West 44th St. [bet. 6th & 7th Ave
Astor: 1515 Broadway [bet. 43rd & 44th Sts.]

M6, M7, M10, M42, M104

Midtown Map #27

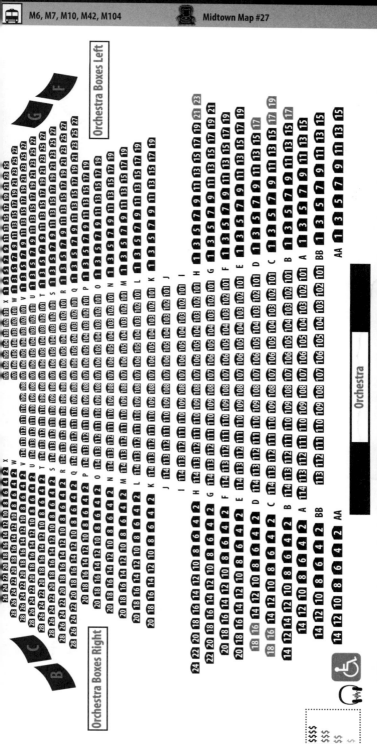

Orchestra Boxes Left

Orchestra Boxes Right

Orchestra

$$$$
$$$
$$
$

1535 Broadway // New York, NY [between 45th & 46th Streets]

Ticketmaster: (212) 307-4100 // Group Sales: (212) 398-8383

[www.nederlander.com]

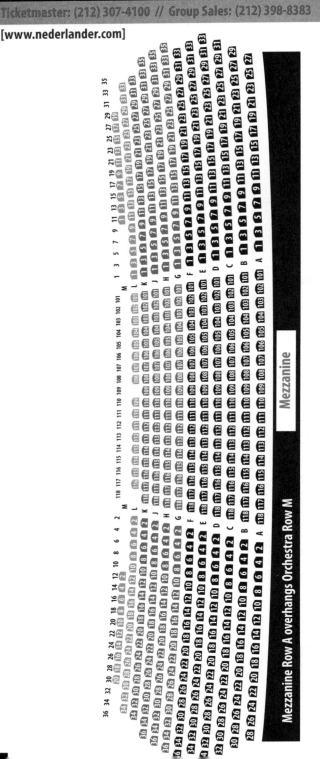

Mezzanine

Mezzanine Row A overhangs Orchestra Row M

to 42nd St. & 7th Ave.   Central: 257 West 47th [bet. Broadway & 8th Ave.]

M6, M7, M10, M27, M42, M50, M104   Midtown Map #17

[www.marquistheatre.com]

Orchestra

$$$$
$$$
$$

200 West 45th Street // New York, NY [between 7th & 8th Avenues]
Ticketmaster: (212) 307-4100 // (800-755-4000)

[www.nederlander.com] [www.minskofftheatre.com]

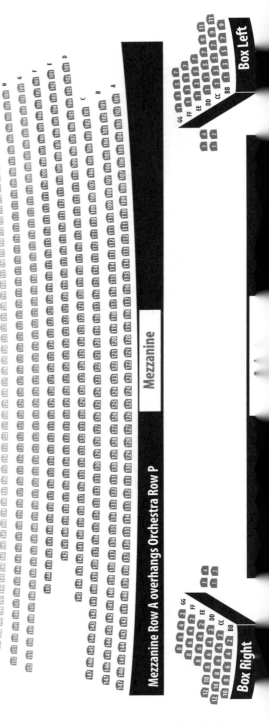

Mezzanine Row A overhangs Orchestra Row P

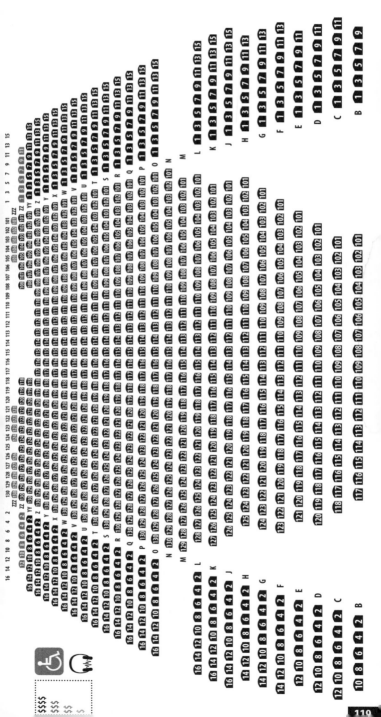

Music Box Theatre

239 West 45th Street // New York, NY [between Broadway & 8th Avenue]

Telecharge: (212) 239-6200 // Group Sales: (212) 239-6262

[www.shubertorganization.com]

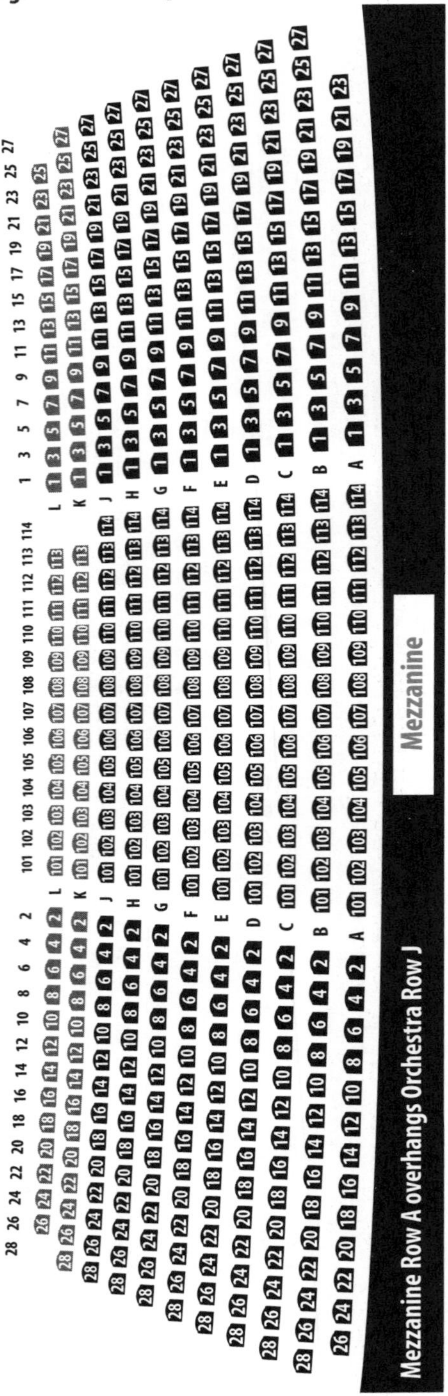

Mezzanine

Mezzanine Row A overhangs Orchestra Row J

1, 2, 3, 7, N, R, S to 42nd St. & 7th Ave.
A, C, E to 42nd St. & 8th Ave.

Kinney: 100 West 44th St. [bet. 6th & 7th Aves.]
Miro: 139 West 45th St. [bet. 6th & 7th Aves.]

M6, M7, M10, M42, M104

Midtown Map #19

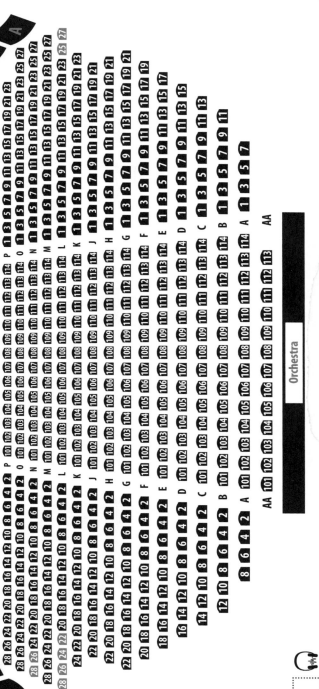

208 West 41st Street // New York, NY [between 7th & 8th Avenues]

Ticketmaster: (212) 307-4100 // Group Sales: (212) 840-3890

[www.nederlander.com] [www.nederlandertheatre.com]

Rear Mezzanine
Front Mezzanine
Mezzanine Row AA overhangs Orchestra Row G

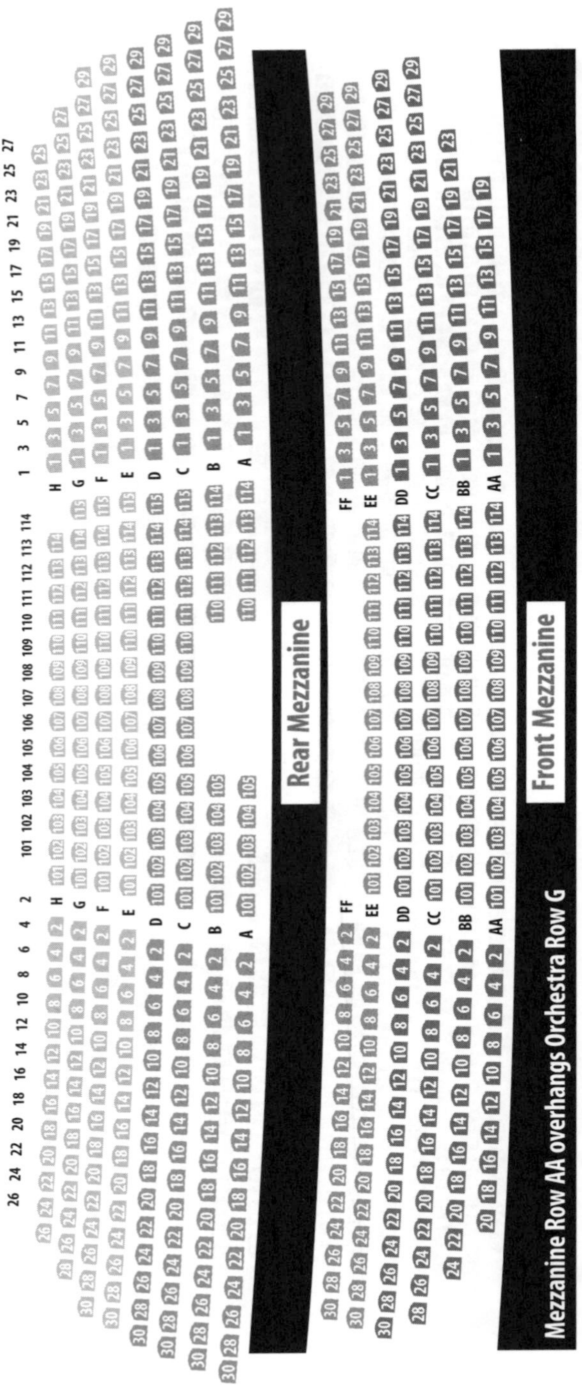

1, 2, 3, 7, N, R, S to 42nd St. & 7th Av.

Kinney: 220 West 41st St. [bet. 7th & 8th Aves.]
Kinney: 236 West 40th St. [bet. 7th & 8th Aves.]

M6, M7, M10, M42, M104

Midtown Map #36

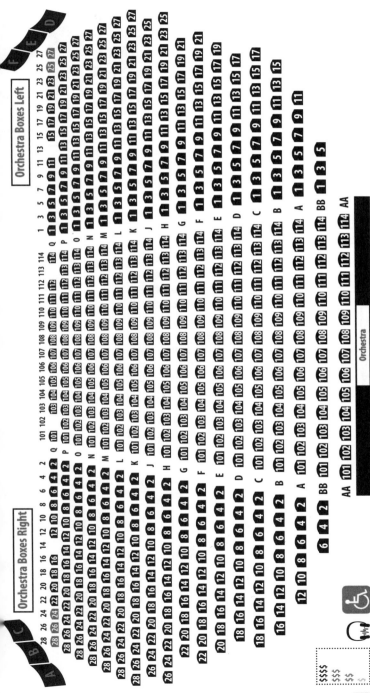

123

Neil Simon Theatre

250 West 52nd Street // New York, NY [between Broadway & 8th Avenue]

Ticketmaster: (212) 307-4100 // Group Sales: (212) 302-7000

[www.nederlander.com] [www.neilsimontheatre.com]

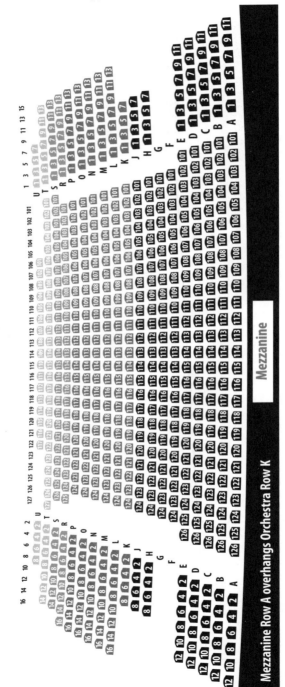

Mezzanine

Mezzanine Row A overhangs Orchestra Row K

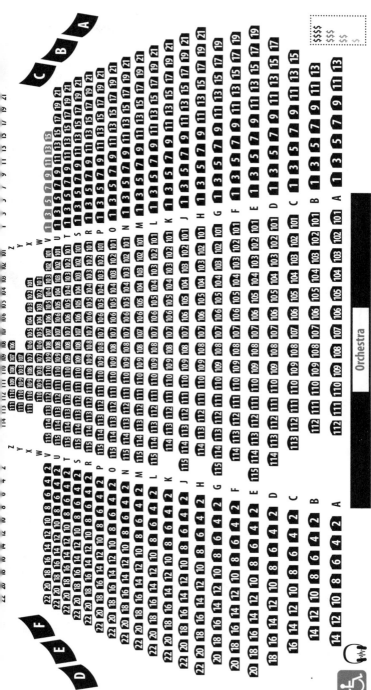

92 Broadway: 1619 Broadway [at 92nd St
Central: 810 7th [at 52nd St.]

M6, M7, M10, M27, M50, M104   Midtown Map #3

Orchestra

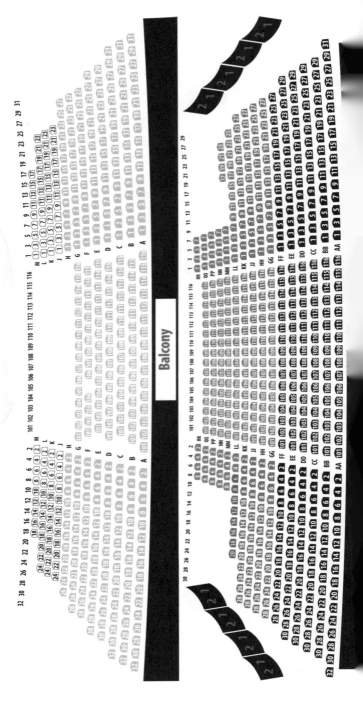

1, 2, 3, 7, N, R, S to 42nd St. & 7th Ave.

Kinney: 264 West 42nd St. [bet. 7th & 8th Ave.]
Cosomo: 360 West 43rd [at 8th Ave.]

M6, M7, M10, M42, M104

Midtown Map #35

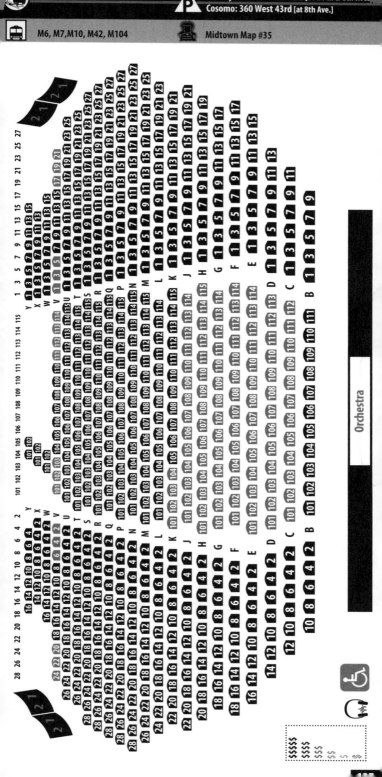

Orchestra

New Victory Theatre

209 West 42nd Street // New York, NY [between Broadway & 8th Avenue]

Box Office: (646) 562-2000 // Group Sales: (646) 222-3000

[www.newvictory.org]

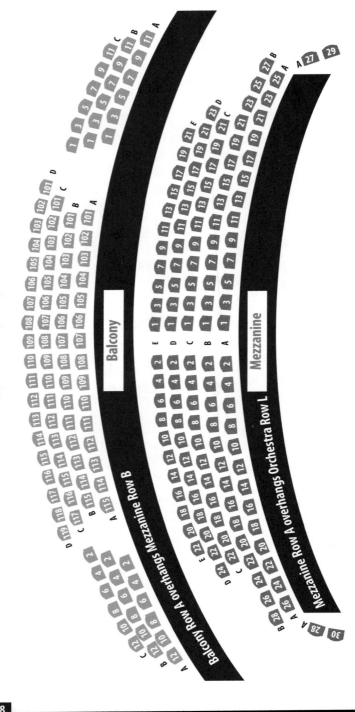

1, 2, 3, 7, N, Q, R, W to 42nd St. & 7th Ave.
A, C, E to 42nd St. & 8th Ave.

Edison: 401 West 42nd St. [at 9th Ave.]
Astor: 1515 Broadway [bet. 43rd & 44th Sts.]

M11, M16, M22, M42, M104

Midtown Map #34

Mezzanine Box L

Orchestra Box Left

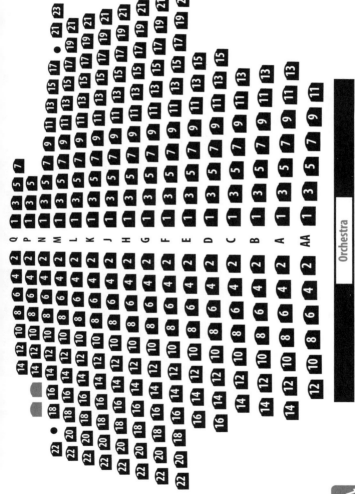

Orchestra

Mezzanine Box R

Orchestra Box Right

$$$$
$$$
$$

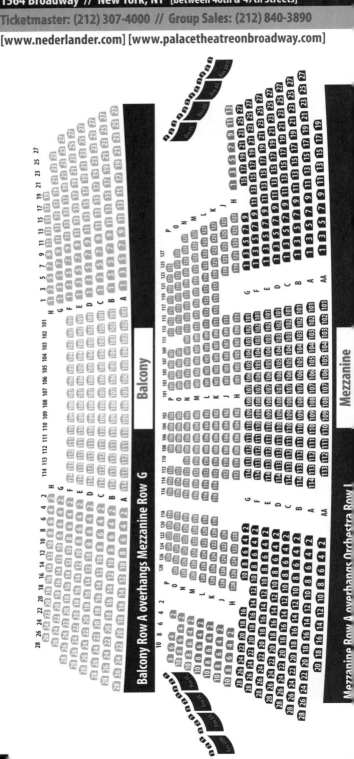

Balcony

Balcony Row A overhangs Mezzanine Row G

Mezzanine

Mezzanine Row A overhangs Orchestra Row I

1, 9, C, E to 50th St.

West 47th: 257 West 47th St. [bet. Broadway & 8th Ave.]
Astor: 1515 Broadway [bet. 43rd & 44th Sts.]

M7, M10, M27, M50, M104   Midtown Map #14

Balcony

Balcony Row A overhangs Mezzanine Row G

Mezzanine

Mezzanine Row A overhangs Orchestra Row I

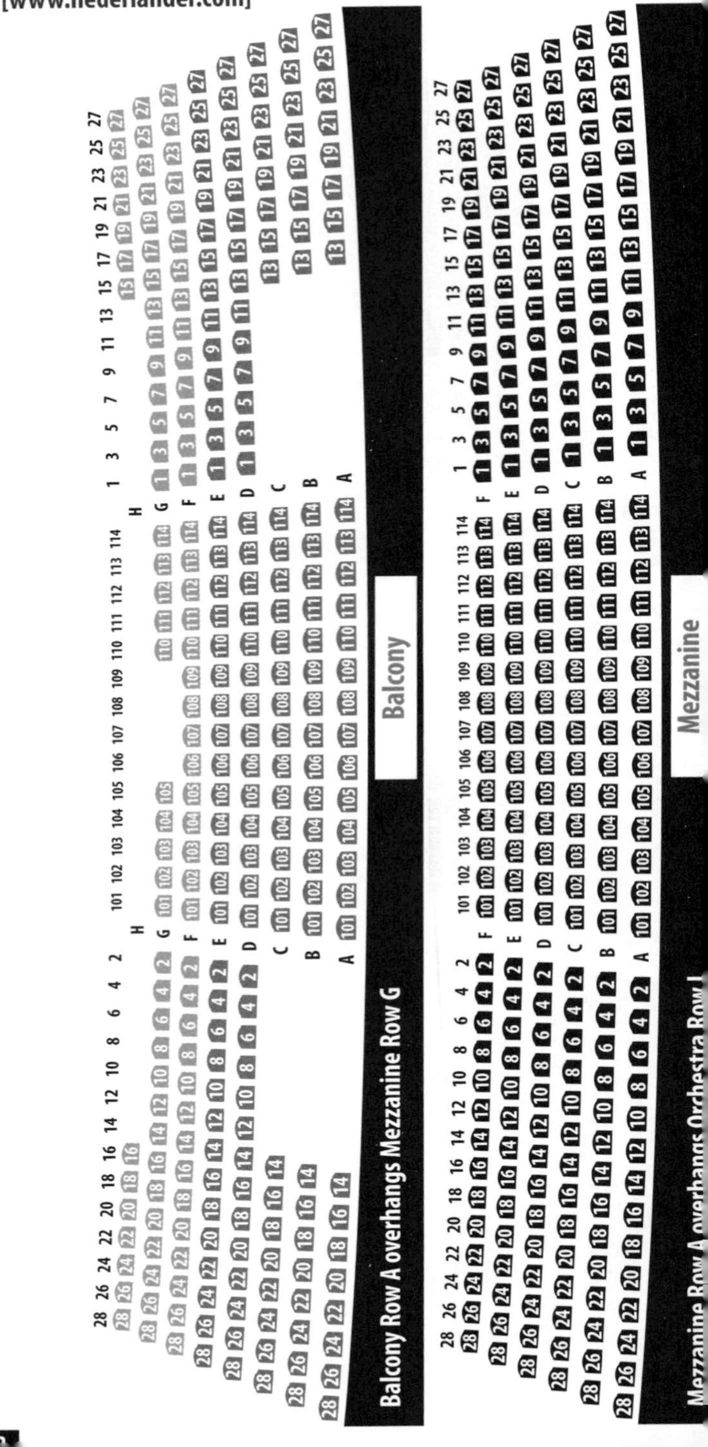

1, 2, 3, 7, N, R, S to 42nd St. & 7th Ave.
1, 9 to 50th St.

P Resource: 164 West 46th St. [bet. 6th & 7th Aves.]
Quik Park: 303 West 46th St. [bet. 8th & 9th Aves.]

M10, M27, M50, M104

Midtown Map #16

www.richardrodgerstheatre.com]

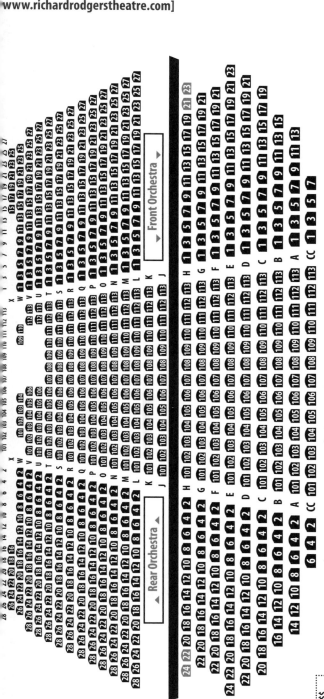

▶ Front Orchestra ▶

◀ Rear Orchestra ◀

$$$$
$$$
$$

Samuel J. Friedman Theatre

261 West 47th Street // **New York, NY** [between Broadway & 8th Avenue]

Telecharge: (212) 239-6200 // Group Sales: (212) 239-6262

[www.mtc-nyc.org]

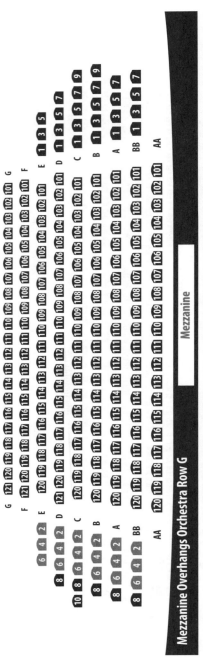

Mezzanine

Mezzanine Overhangs Orchestra Row G

N, R, S, 1, 2, 3, 7, 9 to 42nd & Times Square — Theater: 115 W. 45th St. [bet. 9th & 10th Ave.

A, C, E to Broadway & 8th Ave. — Central: 257 W. 47th St. [bet. Broadway & 8th Ave.]

M6, M7, M10, M42, M104 — Midtown Map #22

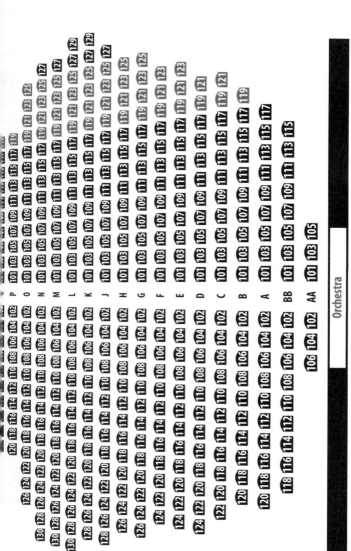

Orchestra

	P	101	103	105	107	109	111	113	115	117	119	121	123	125
	O	101	103	105	107	109	111	113	115	117	119	121	123	125	127
	N	101	103	105	107	109	111	113	115	117	119	121	123	125	127
	M	101	103	105	107	109	111	113	115	117	119	121	123	125	127
	L	101	103	105	107	109	111	113	115	117	119	121	123	125	127
	K	101	103	105	107	109	111	113	115	117	119	121	123	125	127
	J	101	103	105	107	109	111	113	115	117	119	121	123	125	127
	H	101	103	105	107	109	111	113	115	117	119	121	123	125	127
	G	101	103	105	107	109	111	113	115	117	119	121	123	125
	F	101	103	105	107	109	111	113	115	117	119	121	123
	E	101	103	105	107	109	111	113	115	117	119	121	123
	D	101	103	105	107	109	111	113	115	117	119	121
	C	101	103	105	107	109	111	113	115	117	119	121
	B	101	103	105	107	109	111	113	115	117	119
	A	101	103	105	107	109	111	113	115	117	119
	BB	101	103	105	107	109	111	113	115	117
	AA	101	103	105

Balcony

Balcony Row A overhangs Mezzanine Row C

Mezzanine

Mezzanine Row A overhangs Orchestra Row I

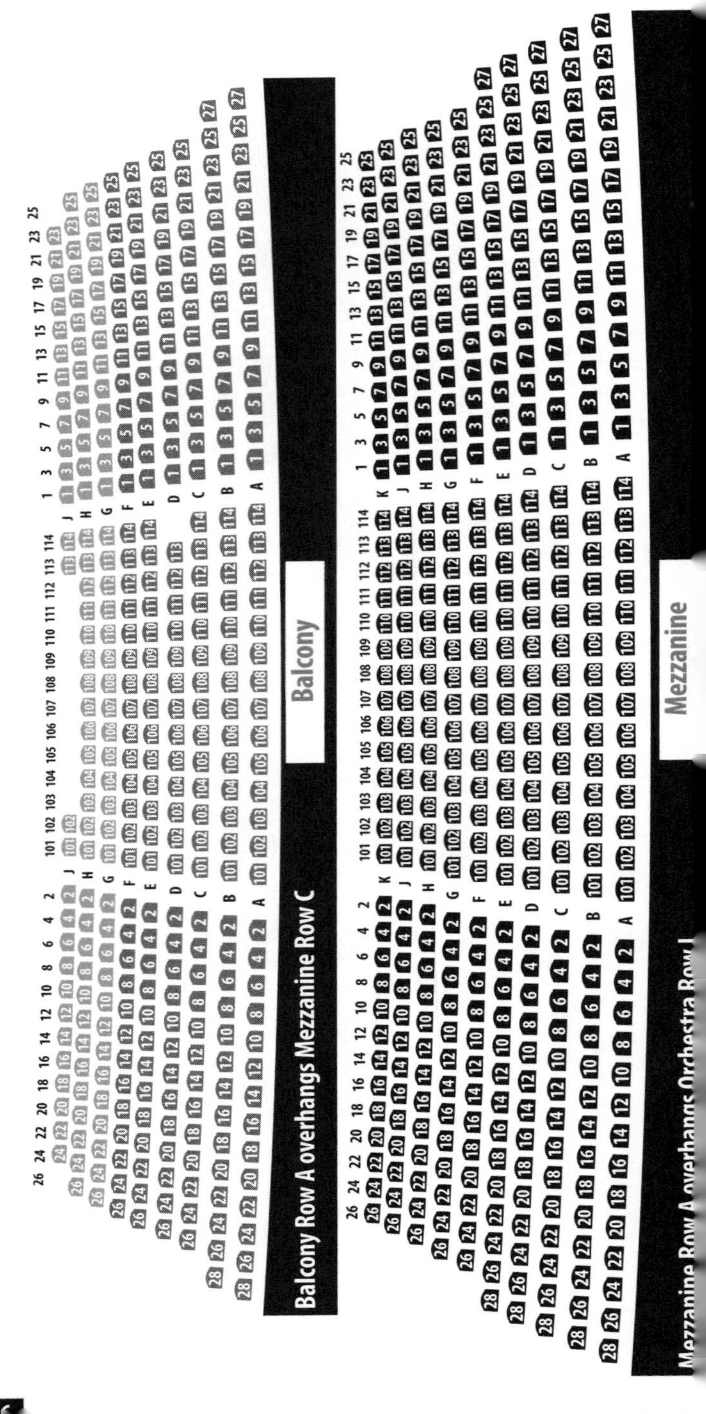

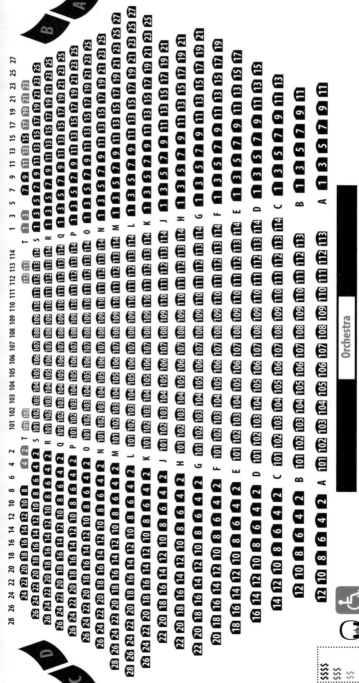

1, 2, 3, 7, N, R, S to 42nd S   7th Ave.   Kinney: 100 West 4th St. [bet. 6th & 7th Aves.]
A, C, E to 42nd St. & 8th Ave.   43rd St: 250 West 43rd St. [bet. 7th & 8th Aves.]

M6, M7, M10, M42, M104   Midtown Map #29

Orchestra

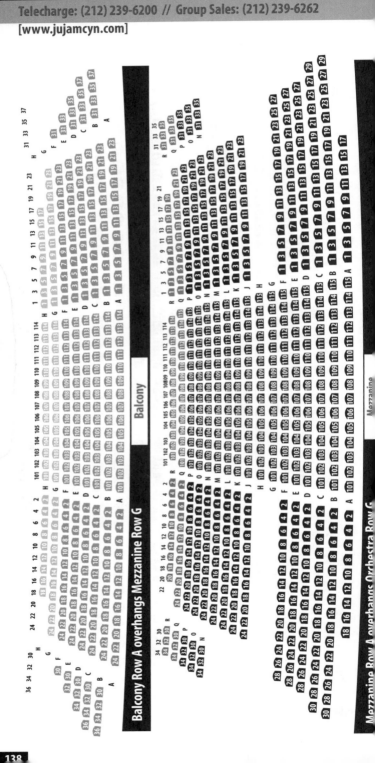

Balcony

Balcony Row A overhangs Mezzanine Row G

Mezzanine Row A overhangs Orchestra Row G

1, 2, 3, 7, N, R, S to 42nd St. & 7th Ave.
A, C, E to 42nd St. & 8th Ave.

Kinney. 100 West 44th St. [bet. 6th & 7th Aves.]
Advance: 249 West 43rd St. [bet. 7th & 8th Aves.]

M6, M7, M10, M42, M104

Midtown Map #32

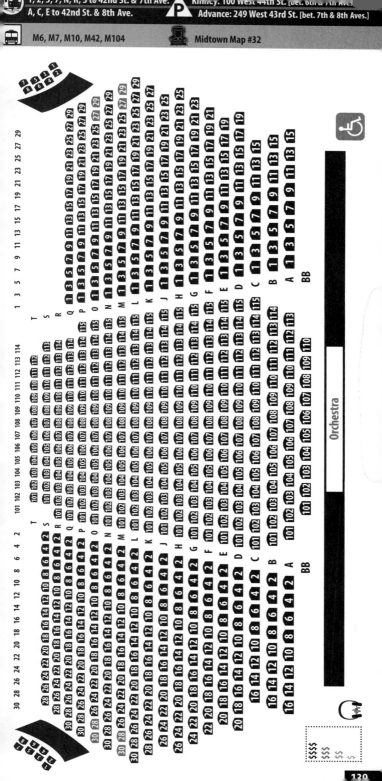

Orchestra

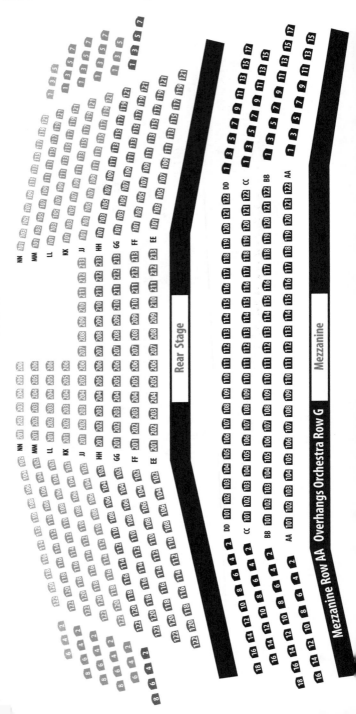

N, R, W to 57th St.

Command: 216 West 54th [bet. Broadway & 7th Ave.]

M6, M7, M10, M27, M50, M104

Midtown Map #44

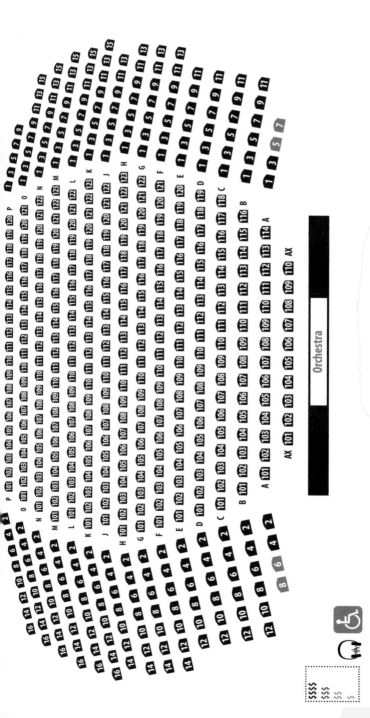

Orchestra

$$$$
$$$
$$
$

Balcony

Balcony Row A overhangs Mezzanine Row P

Mezzanine

Mezzanine Row A overhangs Orchestra Row J

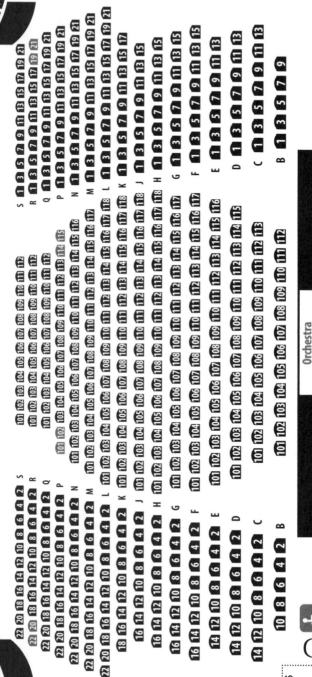

Orchestra

$$$$
$$$
$$

Mezzanine

Mezzanine Row A overhangs Orchestra Row O

1 to 50th St.   GMC: 218 West 50th St. [bet. Broadway & 8th Ave.]

M6, M7, M10, M27, M50, M104   Midtown Map #6

Orchestra

$$$$
$$$
$$

off-broadway theatres

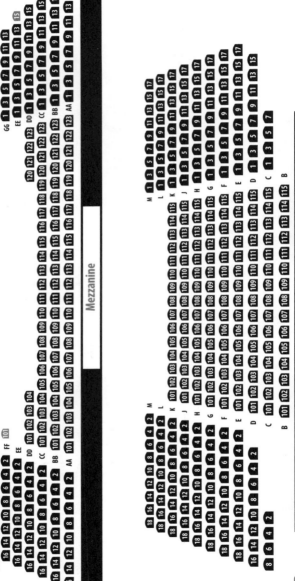

Mezzanine

Stage

Theater A

A, C, E, 1, 9 to 34th St.

509 West 34th St. Garage [bet. 10th & 11th sts.]
Central: 451 10th Ave. [bet. 35th & 36th sts.]

M34, M11, M16

Theater B

Theater C

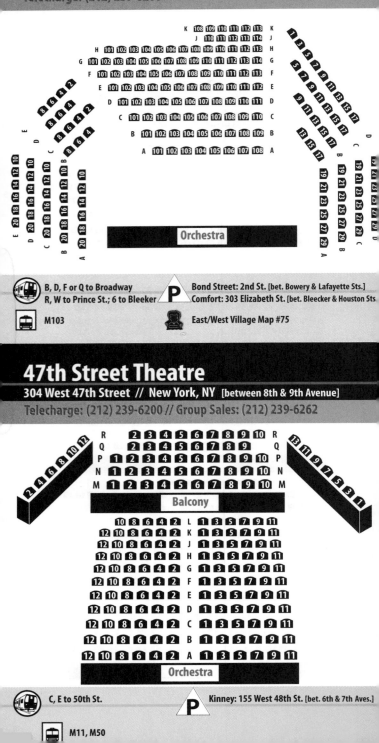

45 Bleecker Street // New York, NY [between Lafayette & Bleecker Sts.]
Telecharge: (212) 239-6200

Orchestra

B, D, F or Q to Broadway
R, W to Prince St.; 6 to Bleeker

M103

Bond Street: 2nd St. [bet. Bowery & Lafayette Sts.]
Comfort: 303 Elizabeth St. [bet. Bleecker & Houston Sts.

East/West Village Map #75

47th Street Theatre
304 West 47th Street // New York, NY [between 8th & 9th Avenue]
Telecharge: (212) 239-6200 // Group Sales: (212) 239-6262

Balcony

Orchestra

C, E to 50th St.

Kinney: 155 West 48th St. [bet. 6th & 7th Aves.]

M11, M50

59 East 59th Street // New York, NY [between Madison & Park Aves.]

Box Office: (212) 573-5959 [www.59e59.org]

Stage

▼ **Theater B** ▼   ▲ **Theater A** ▲

Stage

4, 5, 6, N, R, W to Lexington & 59th St.
N, R, W to 5th Ave.

M1, M2, M3, M4, M101, M102, M103, Q32

P Allied: 58 W. 58th [bet. 5th & 6th Aves.]
Central: 110 East 58th St. [bet. Park & Lex. Aves.]

151

312 W. 36th Street // New York, NY [Between 8th & 9th Avenues]
Box Office: (212) 868-4444 [www.abingtontheatre.org]

A, E, C, 1, 9, 7, R

M104, M42, M16

P 330 West 37th St. [bet. 8th & 9th Sts.]
*Ticket stub discount

Ailey Citigroup Theater at the Joan Weill Center for Dance
405 West 55th Street // New York, NY [at 9th Avenue]
Box Office: (212) 405-9000 [www.alvinailey.org]

1, 9, A, C, B, D to 59th St. & Columbus Circle
N, R, Q, W to 57th St. & 7th Ave.

M57, M11, M30, M31

P 330 West 56th [bet. 8th & 9th Aves.]
Central: 888 8th Ave. [bet. 52nd & 53rd Sts.]

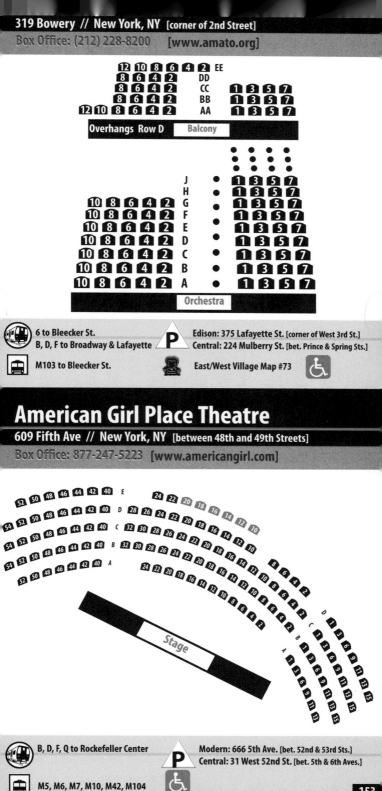

319 Bowery // New York, NY [corner of 2nd Street]

Box Office: (212) 228-8200 [www.amato.org]

Balcony

Overhangs Row D

Orchestra

6 to Bleecker St.
B, D, F to Broadway & Lafayette

M103 to Bleecker St.

Edison: 375 Lafayette St. [corner of West 3rd St.]
Central: 224 Mulberry St. [bet. Prince & Spring Sts.]

East/West Village Map #73

American Girl Place Theatre

609 Fifth Ave // New York, NY [between 48th and 49th Streets]

Box Office: 877-247-5223 [www.americangirl.com]

Stage

B, D, F, Q to Rockefeller Center

M5, M6, M7, M10, M42, M104

Modern: 666 5th Ave. [bet. 52nd & 53rd Sts.]
Central: 31 West 52nd St. [bet. 5th & 6th Aves.]

434 Lafayette Street // New York, NY [between Astor Place & West 4th St.]

Ticketmaster: (212) 307-4100 // Group Sales: (212) 260-8993

[www.blueman.com]

```
                        G  1  3  5  7  9  11 13
    12 10 8 6 4 2       F  1  3  5  7  9  11 13
    12 10 8 6 4 2       E  1  3  5  7  9  11
    12 10 8 6 4 2       D  1  3  5  7  9  11 13
    12 10 8 6 4 2       C  1  3  5  7  9  11 13
    12 10 8 6 4 2       B  1  3  5  7  9  11
    12 10 8 6 4 2       A  1  3  5  7  9  11
```

Mezzanine

Mezzanine overhangs Row HH

```
              106 104 102  SS  101 103 105
          108 106 104 102  RR  101 103 105 107
   114 112 110 108 106 104 102  QQ  101 103 105 107 109 111
   114 112 110 108 106 104 102  PP  101 103 105 107 109 111
   114 112 110 108 106 104 102  OO  101 103 105 107 109 111
   114 112 110 108 106 104 102  NN  101 103 105 107 109 111
   114 112 110 108 106 104 102  MM  101 103 105 107 109 111
   114 112 110 108 106 104 102  LL  101 103 105 107 109 111
   114 112 110 108 106 104 102  KK  101 103 105 107 109 111
   114 112 110 108 106 104 102  JJ  101 103 105 107 109 111
   114 112 110 108 106 104 102  HH  101 103 105 107 109 111
   114 112 110 108 106 104 102  GG  101 103 105 107 109 111
   114 112 110 108 106 104 102  FF  101 103 105 107 109 111
   114 112 110 108 106 104 102  EE
   114 112 110 108 106 104 102  DD  101 103 105 107 109 111
   114 112 110 108 106 104 102  CC  101 103 105 107 109 111
   114 112 110 108 106 104 102  BB  101 103 105 107 109 111
   114 112 110 108 106 104 102  AA  101 103 105 107 109 111
```

Orchestra

Poncho Section: AA to EE 102-114; AA to DD 101-110

$$$$
$$$

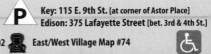

W, R to 8th St. or 6 to Astor Place
B, D, F, Q to Broadway/Lafayette St.

Key: 115 E. 9th St. [at corner of Astor Place]
Edison: 375 Lafayette Street [bet. 3rd & 4th St.]

M2, M3, M5, M13, M101, M102   East/West Village Map #74

154

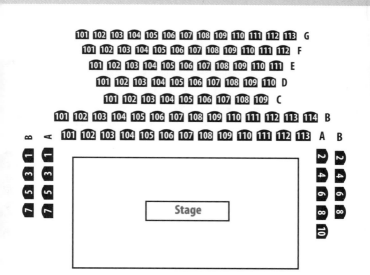

336 West 20th Street // New York, NY [between 8th & 9th Avenues]

Telecharge: (212) 239-6200   [www.atlantictheater.org]

101 102 103 104 105 106 107 108 109 110 111 112 113 114 115 H
101 102 103 104 105 106 107 108 109 110 111 112 113 114 115 116 117 G
101 102 103 104 105 106 107 108 109 110 111 112 113 114 115 116 117 F
101 102 103 104 105 106 107 108 109 110 111 112 113 114 115 116 117 E
101 102 103 104 105 106 107 108 109 110 111 112 113 114 115 116 117 D
101 102 103 104 105 106 107 108 109 110 111 112 113 114 115 116 117 C
101 102 103 104 105 106 107 108 109 110 111 112 113 114 115 116 117 B
101 102 103 104 105 106 107 108 109 110 111 112 113 114 115 116 117 A
101 102 103 104 105 106 107 108 109 110 111 112 113 114 115 116 AA

Stage

Linda Gross

101 102 103 104 105 106 107 108 109 110 111 112 113 G
101 102 103 104 105 106 107 108 109 110 111 112 F
101 102 103 104 105 106 107 108 109 110 111 E
101 102 103 104 105 106 107 108 109 110 D
101 102 103 104 105 106 107 108 109 C
101 102 103 104 105 106 107 108 109 110 111 112 113 114 B
101 102 103 104 105 106 107 108 109 110 111 112 113 A   B

B   A
1 1
3 3
5 5
7 7

2 2
4 4
6 6
8 8
10

Stage

Atlantic Stage 2

C, E to 23rd St.
1, 9 to 18th St.

M11, M20, M23

P 19th St. Garage: 250 West 19th St. [bet. 7th & 8th Aves.]
Kinney: 435 West 23rd St. [bet. 9th & 10th Aves.]

Chelsea Map #68

155

27 Barrow Street // New York, NY [At 7th Avenue, South of Christopher Street]

Box Office: (212) 243-6262 // Group Sales: (212) 243-6565

[www.barrowstreettheatre.com]

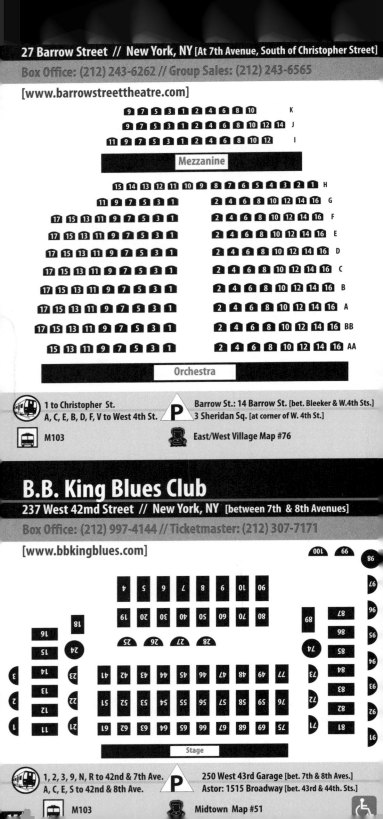

Mezzanine

Orchestra

1 to Christopher St.
A, C, E, B, D, F, V to West 4th St.

M103

Barrow St.: 14 Barrow St. [bet. Bleeker & W.4th Sts.]
3 Sheridan Sq. [at corner of W. 4th St.]

East/West Village Map #76

B.B. King Blues Club
237 West 42md Street // New York, NY [between 7th & 8th Avenues]

Box Office: (212) 997-4144 // Ticketmaster: (212) 307-7171

[www.bbkingblues.com]

Stage

1, 2, 3, 9, N, R to 42nd & 7th Ave.
A, C, E, S to 42nd & 8th Ave.

M103

250 West 43rd Garage [bet. 7th & 8th Aves.]
Astor: 1515 Broadway [bet. 43rd & 44th. Sts.]

Midtown Map #51

127 East 23rd Street // **New York, NY** [between Park Ave. S. & Lexington]
Box Office: (212)307-7171 [www.blendertheater.com]

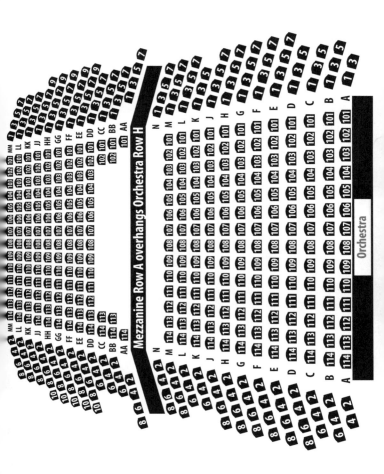

Mezzanine Row A overhangs Orchestra Row H

Orchestra

4, 5, 6, N,R to 23rd St.

East 24: 214 East 24th St. [bet. 2nd & 3rd Aves.]
Lexus: 116 East 24th St. [bet. Park & Lexington Aves.]

M1, M2, M3, M6, M7, M101, M102, M103

Bessie Schonberg Theater (Dance Theater Worksho

219 West 19th Street // New York, NY [between 7th & 8th Avenues]

Box Office: (212) 294-0077 // Group Sales: (212) 924-0077

[www.dtw.org]

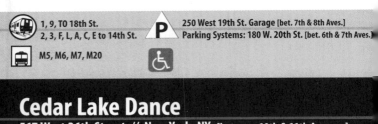

Stage

1, 9, TO 18th St.
2, 3, F, L, A, C, E to 14th St.

M5, M6, M7, M20

250 West 19th St. Garage [bet. 7th & 8th Aves.]
Parking Systems: 180 W. 20th St. [bet. 6th & 7th Aves.]

Cedar Lake Dance

567 West 26th Street // New York, NY [between 10th & 11th Avenues]

Smarttix (212)-868-4444   [www.cedarlakedance.com]

Stage

C, E to 23rd Street

M23

West 26th St.: 513 West 26th [bet. 10th & 11th]
United: 279 10th Ave. [bet. 26th & 27th Sts.]

125 West 22nd Street // New York, NY [between 6th & 7th Avenues]

Box Office: (212) 924-7415

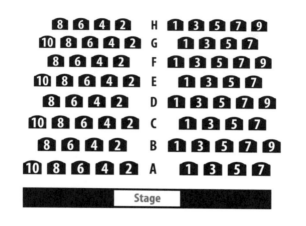

H 8 6 4 2   H   1 3 5 7 9
G 10 8 6 4 2   G   1 3 5 7
F 8 6 4 2   F   1 3 5 7 9
E 10 8 6 4 2   E   1 3 5 7
D 8 6 4 2   D   1 3 5 7 9
C 10 8 6 4 2   C   1 3 5 7
B 8 6 4 2   B   1 3 5 7 9
A 10 8 6 4 2   A   1 3 5 7

Stage

1, 9 to 23rd & 7th Sts.

M23

Kinney: 235 West 22nd St. [bet. 7th & 8th Ave.]
Parking Systems: 120 W. 21st [bet. 7th & 8th Aves.]

Chelsea Map #69

Cherry Lane Theatre
38 Commerce Street // New York, NY [between 7th Avenue & Hudson St.]

Telecharge: (212) 239-6200   [www.cherrylanetheatre.org]

O   1 2 3   O   4 5 6 7 8 9
N   1 2 3 4   N   5 6 7 8 9 10
M   1 2 3 4   M   5 6 7 8 9 10 11 12
L   L   1 2 3 4 5 6 7 8
K   1 2 3 4 5   K   6 7 8 9 10 11 12 13
J   1 2 3 4 5   J   6 7 8 9 10 11 12 13
I   1 2 3 4 5   I   6 7 8 9 10 11 12 13
H   1 2 3 4 5   H   6 7 8 9 10 11 12
G   1 2 3 4 5 6   G   7 8 9 10 11 12 13
F   1 2 3 4 5 6   F   7 8 9 10 11 12 13
E   1 2 3 4 5 6   E   7 8 9 10 11 12
D   1 2 3 4 5 6 7   D   8 9 10 11 12 13
C   1 2 3 4 5 6 7   C   8 9 10 11 12 13
B   1 2 3 4 5 6 7   B   8 9 10 11 12
A   1 2 3 4 5 6 7 8   A   9 10 11 12 13

Stage

1 to Christopher St.
A, B, C, D, E, F, & V to W4th St.

M20

396 Hudson Street [bet. Clarkson & Houston Sts.]
Kinney: 20 Morton Street [bet. Bleecker & 7th Ave.]

East/West Village Map #77

136 East 13th Street // New York, NY [between 3rd & 4th Avenues]

Box Office: (212) 677-4210 ext. 10 // Theatremania: (212) 352-3101

[www.classicstage.org]

F	101 102 103 104 105 106 107 108 109 110 111 112 113 114 115 116 117 118	F
E	101 102 103 104 105 106 107 108 109 110 111 112 113 114 115 116 117	E
D	101 102 103 104 105 106 107 108 109 110 111 112 113 114 115 116 117 118 119 120	D
C	101 102 103 104 105 106 107 108 109 110 111 112 113 114 115 116 117 118 119	C
B	101 102 103 104 105 106 107 108 109 110 111 112 113 114 115 116 117 118 119	B
A	102 103 104 105 106 107 108 109 110 111 112 113 114 115 116 117	A

Stage

4, 5 ,6, L, N, R to 14th St.

P
Manhattan: 190 E. 12th St. [corner of 3rd Ave.]
13th St. Garage: 98 E. 13th St. [corner of 4th Ave.]

M1, M3, M9, M14, M18, M101, M102

Union Square Map #110

Players Theatre
115 MacDougal Street // New York, NY [between W 3rd & Bleeker Sts.]

Box Office: (212) 475-1449 [www.theplayerstheatre.com]

Stage

A, B, C, D, E, F, Q to West 4th St.

P
8MC: 122 West 3rd St. [bet. 6th & MacDougal Sts.]
Minetta Garage: 122 W. 3rd St. [bet. 6th & MacDougal St♦

M5, M6, M10

East/West Village Map #83

55 Mercer Street // **New York, NY** [between Broome & Grand St.]

Box Office: (212) 925-1900 [www.cultureproject.org]

M	9	8	7	6	5	4	3	2		M
L	10	9	8	7	6	5	4	3	2	1	L
K	10	9	8	7	6	5	4	3	2	1	K
J	10	9	8	7	6	5	4	3	2	1	J
H	10	9	8	7	6	5	4	3	2	1	H
G	10	9	8	7	6	5	4	3	2	1	G
F	10	9	8	7	6	5	4	3	2	1	F
E	10	9	8	7	6	5	4	3	2	1	E
D	10	9	8	7	6	5	4	3	2	1	D
C	10	9	8	7	6	5	4	3	2	1	C
B	10	9	8	7	6	5	4	3	2	1	B
A	10	9	8	7	6	5	4	3	2	1	A

Stage

C, E, 6 to Spring St.
N, R to Prince St.

M1

Champion: 411 Broadway [bet. Lispenard & Canal Sts.]
One: 81 Mercer St. [bet. Broome & Spring Sts.]

DiCapo Opera Theatre (St. Jean Baptiste Church)
184 East 76th Street // **New York, NY** [between Lexington & 3rd Avenues]

Box Office: (212) 288-9438 [www.dicapo.com]

L	17	16	15	14	13	12	11	10	9	8	7	6	5	4	3	2	1	L
K	17	16	15	14	13	12	11	10	9	8	7	6	5	4	3	2	1	K
J	17	16	15	14	13	12	11	10	9	8	7	6	5	4	3	2	1	J
I	17	16	15	14	13	12	11	10	9	8	7	6	5	4	3	2	1	I
H	17	16	15	14	13	12	11	10	9	8	7	6	5	4	3	2	1	H
G	17	16	15	14	13	12	11	10	9	8	7	6	5	4	3	2	1	G
F	17	16	15	14	13	12	11	10	9	8	7	6	5	4	3	2	1	F
E	17	16	15	14	13	12	11	10	9	8	7	6	5	4	3	2	1	E
D	17	16	15	14	13	12	11	10	9	8	7	6	5	4	3	2	1	D
C	17	16	15	14	13	12	11	10	9	8	7	6	5	4	3	2	1	C
B	17	16	15	14	13	12	11	10	9	8	7	6	5	4	3	2	1	B
A	17	16	15	14	13	12	11	10	9	8	7	6	5	4	3	2	1	A

Stage

4, 5, 6 to 77th Street

M101, M102, M103

GMC: 332 East 76th St. [bet. 2nd & 1st Aves.]
Rapid: 155 East 76th St. [bet. 3rd & Lexington Aves.]

101 East 15th Street // New York, NY [between 14th & 15th Sts.]
Telecharge: (212) 239-6200 [www.dr2theatre.com]

Stage

4, 5, 6, L, N, R to 14th St.

M1, M2, M3, M6, M7, M9, M14, M101, M102, M103

Parking 16: 101 E. 16th St. [bet. Irving & Union
101 E 16th Assoc. [bet. Irving & Union Sq.]

Union Square Map #111

Gramercy Arts Theatre & Repertorio Españo
138 East 27th Street // New York, NY [between Lexington & 3rd Avenues]
Box Office: (212) 889-2850 [www.repertorio.org]

Balcony

Orchestra

6 to 28th St. & Park Ave. South
N, R to 28th St. & Broadway

M23, M101, M102

Excellent: 155 29th St. [bet. Lexington & 3rd Aves.
Park East: 240 East 27th [bet. 26th & 27th Sts.]

The Irish Repertory Theatre

132 West 22nd Street // New York, NY [between 6th & 7th Avenues]

Box Office: (212) 727-2737 [www.irishrepertorytheatre.com]

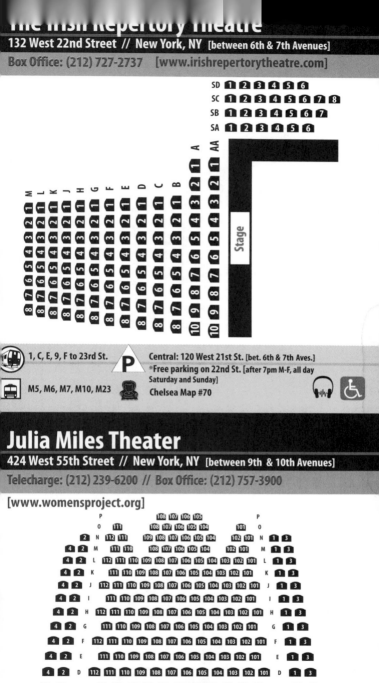

1, C, E, 9, F to 23rd St.

M5, M6, M7, M10, M23

Central: 120 West 21st St. [bet. 6th & 7th Aves.]
*Free parking on 22nd St. [after 7pm M-F, all day Saturday and Sunday]
Chelsea Map #70

Julia Miles Theater

424 West 55th Street // New York, NY [between 9th & 10th Avenues]

Telecharge: (212) 239-6200 // Box Office: (212) 757-3900

[www.womensproject.org]

Orchestra

1, 9, A, B, C, D to 59th St.

M6, M7, M27, M50, M57

Imperial: 300 West 55th St. [bet. 8th & 9th Aves.]
GMC: 622 West 57th St. [bet. 11th & 12th Aves.]

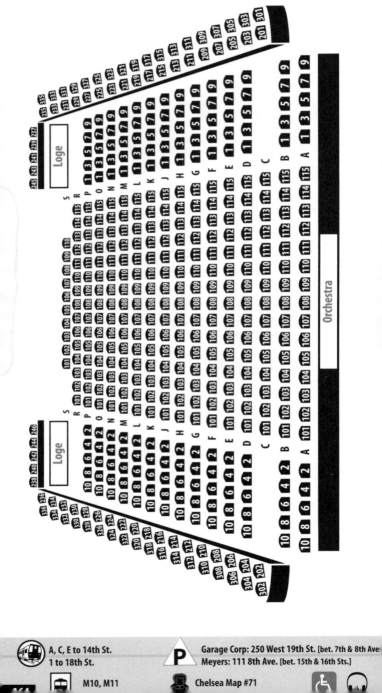

A, C, E to 14th St.
1 to 18th St.

M10, M11

Garage Corp: 250 West 19th St. [bet. 7th & 8th Ave]
Meyers: 111 8th Ave. [bet. 15th & 16th Sts.]

Chelsea Map #71

695 Park Avenue // New York, NY [68th St. between Park & Lexington Aves.]

Box Office: (212) 772-4448 [www.kayeplayhouse.hunter.cuny.edu]

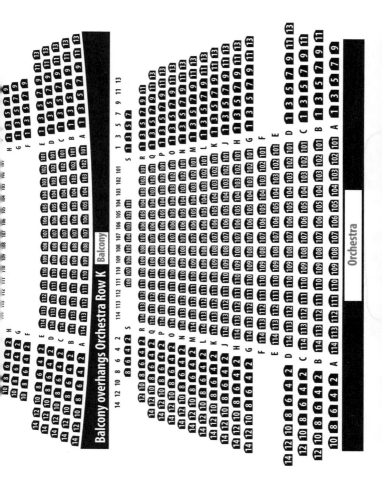

Balcony overhangs Orchestra Row K

Balcony

Orchestra

6 to 68th St.
B, F to 63rd St.

M66, M98, M101, M102, M103

P Almar: 95 East 69th St. [bet. 68th & 69th Sts.]
   Almar: 700 Park Ave. [corner of 69th St.]

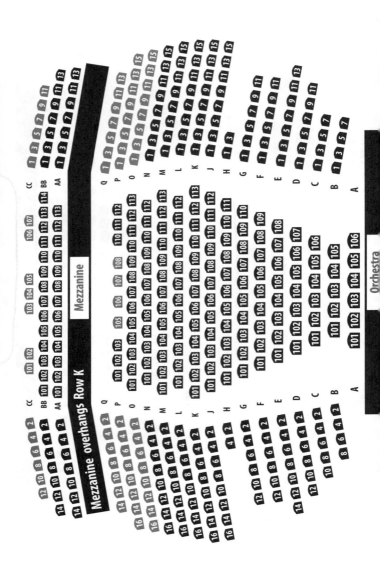

Laura Pels (Roundabout Theatre Company)

231 West 39th Street // New York, NY [between 6th & 7th Avenues.]

Box Office: (212) 719-1300 // Group Sales: (212) 719-9393

[www.roundabouttheatre.org]

Mezzanine

Mezzanine overhangs Row K

Orchestra

N, R, 1, 2, 3 to Times Square

M5, M6, M7, M20

P 39 West: 310 W. 39th [bet. 8th & 9th Aves.]
Astor: 1515 Broadway [bet. 43rd & 44th Sts.]

Midtown Map #53

422 West 42nd Street // **New York, NY** [between 9th Ave. & Dwyer St.]

Box Office: (212) 239-6200 // **Group Sales: (212) 239-6262**

[www.shubertorganization.com]

Stage

1, 2, 3, 7, N, Q, R, W to 42nd St.

P Edison: 427 W. 42nd St. [corner of Dyer & 42nd Sts.]
Edison: 401 W. 42nd St. [corner of 9th Ave.]

M10, M11, M20, M42

Westside Map #65

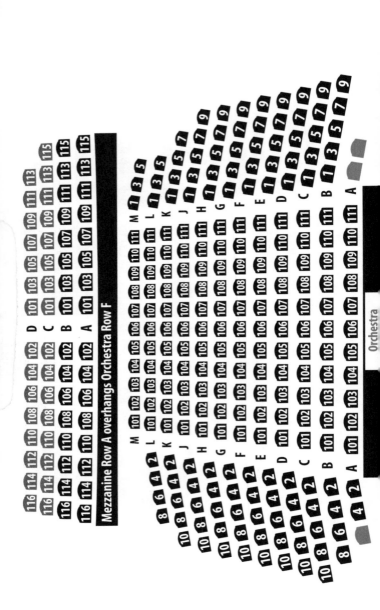

Mezzanine Row A overhangs Orchestra Row F

Orchestra

$$$$
$$$

A, C, E, B, D, F, V to W. 4th St.

P Apple West 11th: 222 W. 11th [*discount with tix]
3 Sherdian Sq. [bet. Bleecker & W. 4th Sts.]

M8, M10

East/West Village Map #78

The McGinn/Cazale Theatre (Second Stage Theatre)
2162 Broadway 4th Floor // New York, NY [between 76th & 77th Sts.]
Box Office: (212) 246-4422 [www.2st.com]

1, 2, 3 to 72nd St.

M5, M7, M11, M72, M104

P Carousel: 201 W. 75th St. [bet. Broadway & Amsterdam Ave.]
Central: 214 W. 80th St. [bet. Broadway & Amsterdam Ave.]

Second Stage Theatre (Midtown)
307 West 43rd Street // New York, NY [corner of 8th Avenue]
Box Office: (212) 246-4422 // Group Sales: (212) 787-8302 x203

[www.2st.com]

1, 2, 3, 7, N, R, S to 42nd St.
A, C, E to 42nd St.

M42, M104

P Central: 322 West 44th St. [bet. 8th & 9th Aves.]
Astor: 1515 Broadway [bet. 43rd & 44th Sts.]

Westside Map #55

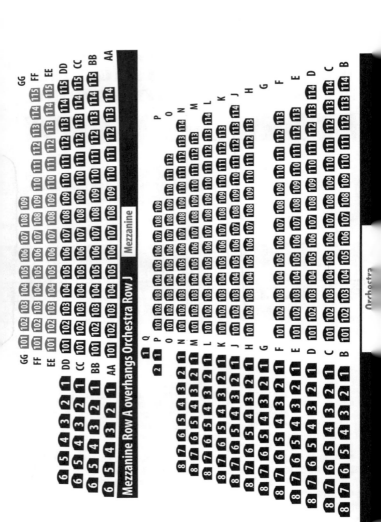

18 Minetta Lane // **New York, NY** [between 6th Avenue & MacDougal Stree

Ticketmaster: (212) 307-4100 // Box Office: (212) 420-8000

Mezzanine

Mezzanine Row A overhangs Orchestra Row J

Orchestra

A, B, C, D, E, F, Q to W. 4th St.

Minetta: 122 W. 3rd St. [bet. 6th & MacDougal St.]
3 Sherdian Sq. [bet. Bleecker & W. 4th Sts.]

M3, M5, M10

East/West Village Map #79

340 West 50th Street // New York, NY [between 8th & 9th Avenues]

Telecharge: (212) 239-6200 // Group Sales: (212) 239-6262

[www.newworldstages.com]

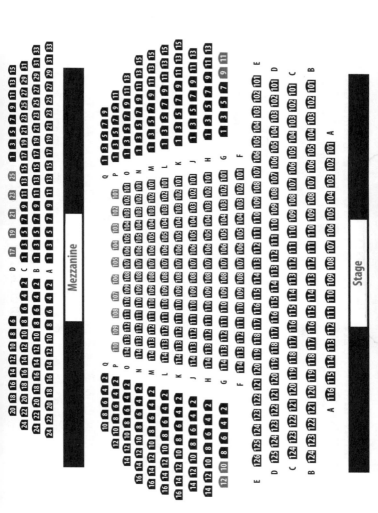

Mezzanine

Stage

1 at 50th St.
C, E at 50th St.

P Central: 888 8th Ave. [bet. 52nd & 53rd. Sts.]
Central: 810 7th Ave. [corner of 52nd St.]

Midtown Map #50

Mezzanine

▼ Orchestra ▼

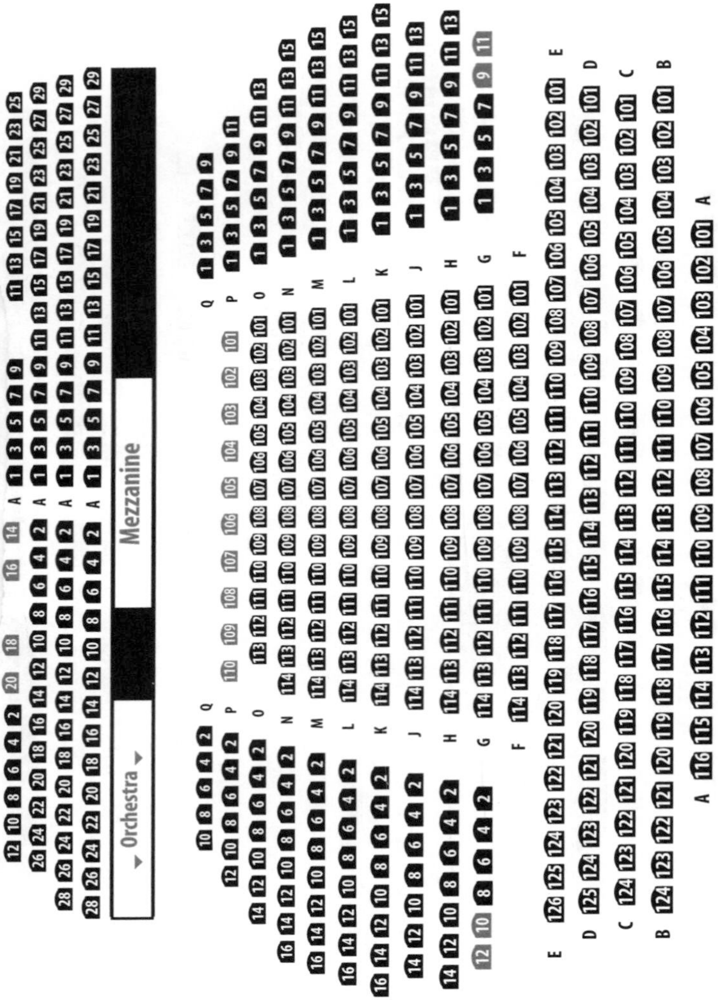

Stage Three

C, E at 50th St.   P   Central: 810 7th Ave. [corner of 52nd St.]

M1   Midtown Map #50

Stage

Stage Two

Stage

Stage Four

340 West 50th Street // New York, NY [between 8th & 9th Avenues]

Telecharge: (212) 239-6200 // Group Sales: (212) 239-6262

[www.newworldstages.com]

Mezzanine

Stage

1 at 50th St.
C, E at 50th St.

M1

Central: 888 8th Ave. [bet. 52nd & 53rd. Sts.]
Central: 810 7th Ave. [corner of 52nd St.]

Midtown Map #50

Mint Theater Company

311 West 43rd Street, 5th Floor // New York, NY [between 8th & 9th Avenue

Box Office: (212) 315-0231   [www.minttheater.org]

Stage

1, 2, 3, 7, A, C, E, N, R to 42nd. St.

M10, M42, M104

Astor: 1515 Broadway [bet. 43rd & 44th Sts.]
Kinney: 289 W. 52nd St. [bet. 7th & 8th Aves.]

Westside Map #62

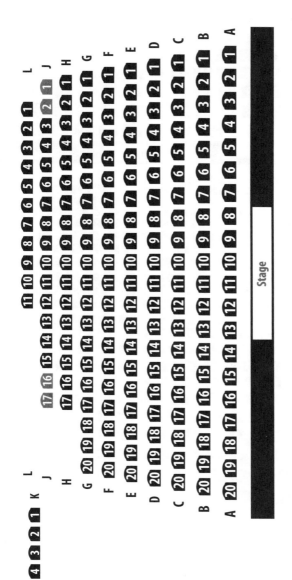

6 to Astor Place
N, R to 8th St.

M8, M15, M21, M101, M102, M103

P Master: 64 Cooper Sq. [bet. Astor Pl. & E. 4th St.]
Wooster: 303 E. 6th St. [bet. 1st & 2nd Aves.]

East/West Village Map #80

175

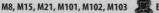

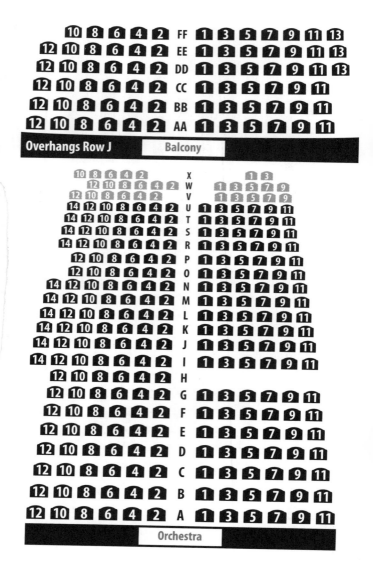

126 Second Avenue // **New York, NY** [between 7th Ave. & St. Marks Place]

Box Office: (212) 477-2477 // Group Sales: (212) 302-7000

[www.stomponline.com]

Overhangs Row J — Balcony

Orchestra

$$$$
$$

N, R to 8th St.
6 to Astor Place

M13, M15, M102, M103

P Canny: 220 East 9th St. [bet. 2nd & 3rd Aves.]
Central: 310 E. 11th St. [bet. 1st & 2nd. Aves.]

East/West Village Map #81

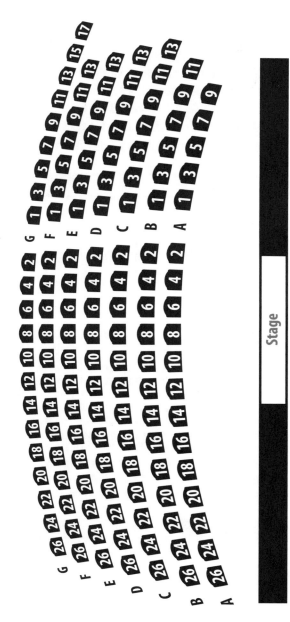

F to 2nd Ave.
4, 5, 6 to Astor Place

M1, M15

P Central: 310 E. 11th St. [bet. 1st & 2nd. Aves.]
   Key: 115 E. 9th St. [bet. 3rd & 4th Aves.]

East/West Village Map #82

177

F ① ② ③ ④ ⑤ ⑥ ⑦ ⑧ ⑨ ⑩ ⑪ ⑫ ⑬ ⑭ ⑮ ⑯ F
E ① ② ③ ④ ⑤ ⑥ ⑦ ⑧ ⑨ ⑩ ⑪ ⑫ ⑬ ⑭ ⑮ ⑯ E
D ① ② ③ ④ ⑤ ⑥ ⑦ ⑧ ⑨ ⑩ ⑪ ⑫ ⑬ ⑭ ⑮ ⑯ D
C ① ② ③ ④ ⑤ ⑥ ⑦ ⑧ ⑨ ⑩ ⑪ ⑫ ⑬ ⑭ ⑮ ⑯ C
B ① ② ③ ④ ⑤ ⑥ ⑦ ⑧ ⑨ ⑩ ⑪ ⑫ ⑬ ⑭ ⑮ ⑯ B
A ① ② ③ ④ ⑤ ⑥ ⑦ ⑧ ⑨ ⑩ ⑪ ⑫ ⑬ ⑭ ⑮ ⑯ A

Stage

Peter Jay Sharp

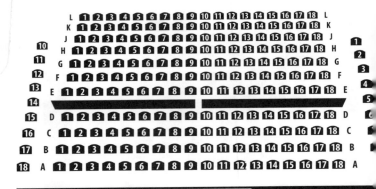

L ① ② ③ ④ ⑤ ⑥ ⑦ ⑧ ⑨ ⑩ ⑪ ⑫ ⑬ ⑭ ⑮ ⑯ ⑰ ⑱ L
K ① ② ③ ④ ⑤ ⑥ ⑦ ⑧ ⑨ ⑩ ⑪ ⑫ ⑬ ⑭ ⑮ ⑯ ⑰ ⑱ K
J ① ② ③ ④ ⑤ ⑥ ⑦ ⑧ ⑨ ⑩ ⑪ ⑫ ⑬ ⑭ ⑮ ⑯ ⑰ ⑱ J
⑩ H ① ② ③ ④ ⑤ ⑥ ⑦ ⑧ ⑨ ⑩ ⑪ ⑫ ⑬ ⑭ ⑮ ⑯ ⑰ ⑱ H ①
⑪ G ① ② ③ ④ ⑤ ⑥ ⑦ ⑧ ⑨ ⑩ ⑪ ⑫ ⑬ ⑭ ⑮ ⑯ ⑰ ⑱ G ②
⑫ F ① ② ③ ④ ⑤ ⑥ ⑦ ⑧ ⑨ ⑩ ⑪ ⑫ ⑬ ⑭ ⑮ ⑯ ⑰ ⑱ F ③
⑬ E ① ② ③ ④ ⑤ ⑥ ⑦ ⑧ ⑨ ⑩ ⑪ ⑫ ⑬ ⑭ ⑮ ⑯ ⑰ ⑱ E ④
⑭ ⑤
⑮ D ① ② ③ ④ ⑤ ⑥ ⑦ ⑧ ⑨ ⑩ ⑪ ⑫ ⑬ ⑭ ⑮ ⑯ ⑰ ⑱ D ⑥
⑯ C ① ② ③ ④ ⑤ ⑥ ⑦ ⑧ ⑨ ⑩ ⑪ ⑫ ⑬ ⑭ ⑮ ⑯ ⑰ ⑱ C
⑰ B ① ② ③ ④ ⑤ ⑥ ⑦ ⑧ ⑨ ⑩ ⑪ ⑫ ⑬ ⑭ ⑮ ⑯ ⑰ ⑱ B
⑱ A ① ② ③ ④ ⑤ ⑥ ⑦ ⑧ ⑨ ⑩ ⑪ ⑫ ⑬ ⑭ ⑮ ⑯ ⑰ ⑱ A

Stage

Main Stage

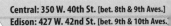

1, 2, 3, N, R, Q to 42nd St. & 7th Ave.

P Central: 350 W. 40th St. [bet. 8th & 9th Aves.]
Edison: 427 W. 42nd St. [bet. 9th & 10th Aves.]

M42, M104

Westside Map #67

425 Lafayette Street // **New York, NY** [between Astor Place & 4th Street]

Box Office: (212) 967-7555 // Group Sales: (212) 539-8621

[www.publictheater.org]

*All Public Theater Facilities are Handicap Accessible

6 to Astor Place
B, D, F, Q to Broadway & Lafayette St.

M2, M3, M5, M6, M8, M15, M101

410 Lafayette Garage [bet. W. 4th St. & Astor Pl.]
Edison: 375 Lafayette St. [bet. W. 3rd & Bond St.]

East/West Village Map #84

M	301 302 303 304 305 306						309 310 311 312 313 314						M
L	301 302 303 304 305						309 310 311 312 313 314						L
K	301 302 303 304 305 306 307						309 310 311 312 313 314 315						K
J	301 302 303 304 305 306 307						309 310 311 312 313 314 315						J
H	301 302 303 304 305 306 307						309 310 311 312 313 314 315						H
G	301 302 303 304 305 306						309 310 311 312 313 314						G
F	301 302 303 304 305 306 307						309 310 311 312 313 314 315						F
E	301 302 303 304 305 306 307						309 310 311 312 313 314 315						E
D	301 302 303 304 305 306 307						309 310 311 312 313 314 315						D
C	301 302 303 304 305 306						309 310 311 312 313 314						C
B	301 302 303 304 305 306 307						309 310 311 312 313 314 315						B
A	301 302 303 304 305 306 307						309 310 311 312 313 314 315						A

Stage

Luesther Hall

O	1 2 3 4 5 6						8 9 10 11 12 13						
N	1 2 3 4 5 6 7						9 10 11 12 13 14 15						
M	1 2 3 4 5 6						8 9 10 11 12 13						
L	1 2 3 4 5 6 7 8 9 10 11 12 13 14 15												
K	1 2 3 4 5 6 7 8 9 10 11 12 13 14 15												
J	1 2 3 4 5 6 7 8 9 10 11 12 13 14 15												
H	1 2 3 4 5 6 7 8 9 10 11 12 13 14 15												
G	1 2 3 4 5 6 7 8 9 10 11 12 13												
F	1 2 3 4 5 6 7 8 9 10 11 12 13 14 15												
E	1 2 3 4 5 6 7 8 9 10 11 12 13 14 15												
D	1 2 3 4 5 6 7 8 9 10 11 12 13 14 15												
C	1 2 3 4 5 6 7 8 9 10 11 12 13												
B	1 2 3 4 5 6 7 8 9 10 11 12 13 14 15												
A	1 2 3 4 5 6 7 8 9 10 11 12 13 14 15												

Stage

Martinson

B, D, F, Q to Broadway & Lafayette St.

Edison: 375 Lafayette St. [bet. W. 3rd & Bond St.]

M2, M3, M5, M6, M8, M15, M101   East/West Village Map #84

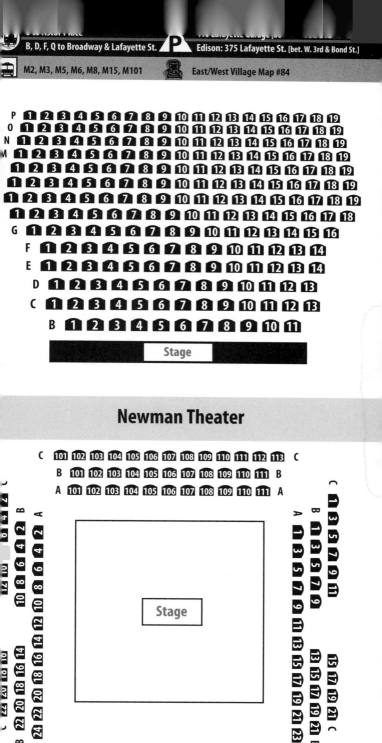

Stage

Newman Theater

Stage

Shiva

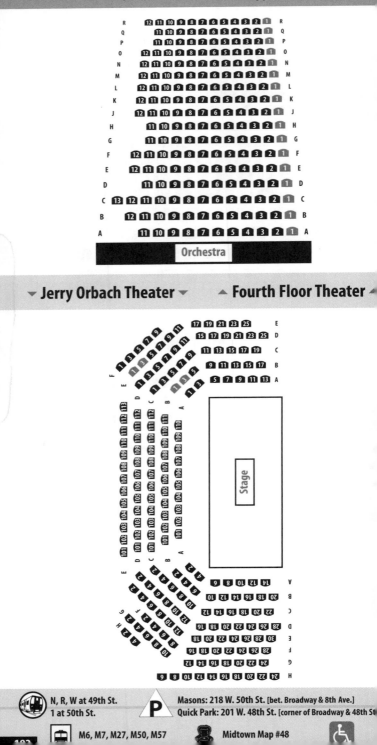

Orchestra

▼ Jerry Orbach Theater ▼   ▲ Fourth Floor Theater ▲

Stage

N, R, W at 49th St.
1 at 50th St.

Masons: 218 W. 50th St. [bet. Broadway & 8th Ave.]
Quick Park: 201 W. 48th St. [corner of Broadway & 48th St]

M6, M7, M27, M50, M57

Midtown Map #48

Plan 1

```
8 6 4 2   O  101 102 103 104 105 106 107 108 109 110 111 112 113 114  OO   1 3 5 7
8 6 4 2   N  101 102 103 104 105 106 107 108 109 110 111 112 113 114  NN   1 3 5 7
8 6 4 2   M  101 102 103 104 105 106 107 108 109 110 111 112 113 114 MM   1 3 5 7
8 6 4 2   L  101 102 103 104 105 106 107 108 109 110 111 112 113 114  LL   1 3 5 7
8 6 4 2   K  101 102 103 104 105 106 107 108 109 110 111 112 113 114  KK   1 3 5 7
8 6 4 2   J  101 102 103 104 105 106 107 108 109 110 111 112 113 114  JJ   1 3 5 7
8 6 4 2   H  101 102 103 104 105 106 107 108 109 110 111 112 113 114  HH   1 3 5 7
8 6 4 2   G  101 102 103 104 105 106 107 108 109 110 111 112 113 114  GG   1 3 5 7
8 6 4 2   F  101 102 103 104 105 106 107 108 109 110 111 112 113 114  FF   1 3 5 7
8 6 4 2   E  101 102 103 104 105 106 107 108 109 110 111 112 113 114  EE   1 3 5 7
8 6 4 2   D  101 102 103 104 105 106 107 108 109 110 111 112 113 114  DD   1 3 5 7
8 6 4 2   C  101 102 103 104 105 106 107 108 109 110 111 112 113 114  CC   1 3 5 7
8 6 4 2   B  101 102 103 104 105 106 107 108 109 110 111 112 113 114  BB   1 3 5 7
8 6 4 2   A  101 102 103 104 105 106 107 108 109 110 111 112 113 114  AA   1 3 5 7
```

Plan 2

```
8 6 4 2   PP  101 102 103 104 105 106 107 108 109 110 111 112 113 114  PP   1 3 5 7
8 6 4 2   OO  101 102 103 104 105 106 107 108 109 110 111 112 113 114  OO   1 3 5 7
8 6 4 2   NN  101 102 103 104 105 106 107 108 109 110 111 112 113 114  NN   1 3 5 7 9 11
8 6 4 2   MM  101 102 103 104 105 106 107 108 109 110 111 112 113 114  MM   1 3 5 7 9 11
8 6 4 2   LL  101 102 103 104 105 106 107 108 109 110 111 112 113 114  LL   1 3 5 7 9 11
8 6 4 2   KK  101 102 103 104 105 106 107 108 109 110 111 112 113 114  KK   1 3 5 7 9 11
8 6 4 2   JJ  101 102 103 104 105 106 107 108 109 110 111 112 113 114  JJ   1 3 5 7 9 11
8 6 4 2   HH  101 102 103 104 105 106 107 108 109 110 111 112 113 114  HH   1 3 5 7 9 11
8 6 4 2   GG  101 102 103 104 105 106 107 108 109 110 111 112 113 114  GG   1 3 5 7 9 11
8 6 4 2   FF  101 102 103 104 105 106 107 108 109 110 111 112 113 114  FF   1 3 5 7 9 11
8 6 4 2   EE  101 102 103 104 105 106 107 108 109 110 111 112 113 114  EE   1 3 5 7 9 11
8 6 4 2   DD  101 102 103 104 105 106 107 108 109 110 111 112 113 114  DD   1 3 5 7 9 11
6 4 2   CC  101 102 103 104 105 106 107 108 109 110 111 112 113 114  CC   1 3 5 7 9 11
6 4 2   BB  101 102 103 104 105 106 107 108 109 110 111 112 113 114  BB   1 3 5 7
          AA  101 102 103 104 105 106 107 108 109 110 111 112 113 114  AA
```

Stage

Plan 1: Theater Presentations
Plan 1+2: Seated Concert Presentations

A, C at High St.; 2, 3 at Clark St.;
F at York St.

B25

Park Kwik: 21 Front st. & Dock St.
Dumbo: 50 Main St. [bet. Howard Alley & Front St.

15 Vandam Street // New York, NY [between 6th & 7th Avenues]
Telecharge: (212) 239-6200 // Group Sales: (212) 691-1555

[www. sohoplayhouse.com]

| P |
| O |
| N |
| M |
| L |
| K |
| J |
| I |
| H |
| G |
| F |
| E |
| D |
| C |
| B |
| A |
| BB |
| AA |

Stage

A, C,E to Spring St.
1, 9 to Houston St.

M6, M20

P Metrowest: 214 West Houston [bet. 6th & Varick St.]
Central: 14 Charlton [bet. 6th & Varick St.]

St. Luke's Theatre
308 West 46th Street // New York, NY [between 8th & 9th Avenues]
Telecharge: (212) 239-6200 // Group Sales: (212) 889-4300

[www. stlukesnyc.org]

F	13 12 11 10 9 8 7 6 5 4 3 2 1	F
E	13 12 11 10 9 8 7 6 5 4 3 2 1	E
D	13 12 11 10 9 8 7 6 5 4 3 2 1	D
C	12 11 10 9 8 7 6 5 4 3 2 1	C
B	15 14 13 12 11 10 9 8 7 6 5 4 3	B
A	18 17 16 15 14 13 12 11 10 9 8 7 6 5 4 3 2 1	A

Stage

1, 2, 3, 7, N, R, S to 42nd St. & 7th Ave.
A, C, E to 42nd St. & 8th Ave.

M6, M7, M10, M11, M42, M104

P Quik Park: 303 W. 46th St. [bet. 8th & 9th Av
Astor: 1515 Broadway [bet. 43rd & 44th Sts.

Westside Map #58

229 West 42nd Street // New York, NY [between 7th & 8th Avenues]

Ticketcentral: (212) 279-4200 // Box Office: (646) 223-3010

[www. dukeon42.org]

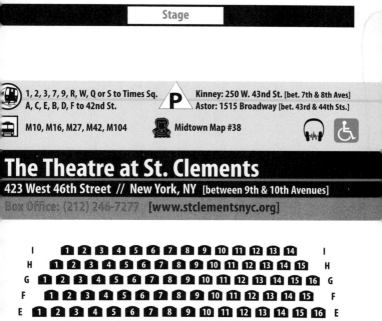

Stage

1, 2, 3, 7, 9, R, W, Q or S to Times Sq.
A, C, E, B, D, F to 42nd St.

M10, M16, M27, M42, M104

Kinney: 250 W. 43nd St. [bet. 7th & 8th Aves]
Astor: 1515 Broadway [bet. 43rd & 44th Sts.]

Midtown Map #38

The Theatre at St. Clements

423 West 46th Street // New York, NY [between 9th & 10th Avenues]

Box Office: (212) 246-7277 [www.stclementsnyc.org]

Stage

A, C, E to 50th St. & 8th Ave.
1, 2, 3, 7, N to 42nd St. & 7th Ave.

M10, M11, M42, M104

GMC: 257 W. 47th St. [bet. Broadway & 8th Ave.]
Kinney: 253 W. 47th St. [bet. Broadway & 8th Ave.]

Westside Map #57

Orchestra

A, C, E, 1, 2, 3, 7, S to 42nd St. & Times Square

M6, M7, M10, M16, M20, M27, M42, M104

P — Astor: 1515 Broadway [bet. 43rd & 44th Sts.]
Central: 251 W. 40th [bet. 7th & 8th Aves.]

555 West 42nd Street // New York, NY [between 10th & 11th Avenues]

Box Office: (212) 244-7529 [www.signaturetheatre.org]

	H	121 120 119 118 117 116 115 114 113 112 111 110 109 108 107 106 105 104 103 102	H
	G	121 120 119 118 117 116 115 114 113 112 111 110 109 108 107 106 105 104 103 102	G
	F	121 120 119 118 117 116 115 114 113 112 111 110 109 108 107 106 105 104 103 102	F
	E	121 120 119 118 117 116 115 114 113 112 111 110 109 108 107 106 105 104 103 102	E
	D	121 120 119 118 117 116 115 114 113 112 111 110 109 108 107 106 105 104 103 102	D
	C	121 120 119 118 117 116 115 114 113 112 111 110 109 108 107 106 105 104 103 102	C
	B	121 120 119 118 117 116 115 114 113 112 111 110 109 108 107 106 105 104 103 102	B
	A	121 120 119 118 117 116 115 114 113 112 111 110 109 108 107 106 105 104 103 102	A

Stage

A, C, E to 42nd St. & 8th Ave.
1, 2, 3, 7, N, R, W, Q, S to 42nd St. & 7th Ave.

M42, M11

P Begg's: 500 W. 43rd St. [corner of 10th Ave.]
Edison: 427 W. 42nd St. [bet. 9th & 10th Aves.]

Westside Map #56

Theatre Row (Lion Theatre)

410 West 42nd Street // New York, NY [between 9th & 10th Avenues]

TicketCentral: (212) 279-4200 // Box Office: (212) 594-2826

[www.theatrerow.org]

Stage

A, C, E to 42nd St. & 8th Ave.
1, 2, 3, 7, 9, N, R, Q, W, S at 42nd. & 7th.

M11, M42

P Edison: 427 W. 42nd [bet. 9th & 10th Aves.]
Edison: 401 W. 42nd [bet. 9th & 10th Aves.]

Westside Map #59

410 West 42nd Street // New York, NY [between 9th & 10th Avenues]

TicketCentral: (212) 279-4200 // Box Office: (212) 594-2826

[www.theatrerow.org]

I 1 2 3 4 5 6 7 8 9 10 11 12 13 14 15 16 17 18 19 20 21 I
H 1 2 3 4 5 6 7 8 9 10 11 12 13 14 15 16 17 18 19 20 21 22 H
G 1 2 3 4 5 6 7 8 9 10 11 12 13 14 15 16 17 18 19 20 21 22 G
F 1 2 3 4 5 6 7 8 9 10 11 12 13 14 15 16 17 18 19 20 21 22 F
E 1 2 3 4 5 6 7 8 9 10 11 12 13 14 15 16 17 18 19 20 21 22 E
D 1 2 3 4 5 6 7 8 9 10 11 12 13 14 15 16 17 18 19 20 21 22 D
C 1 2 3 4 5 6 7 8 9 10 11 12 13 14 15 16 17 18 19 20 21 22 C
B 1 2 3 4 5 6 7 8 9 10 11 12 13 14 15 16 17 18 19 20 21 22 23 B
A 1 2 3 4 5 6 7 8 9 10 11 12 13 14 15 16 17 18 19 20 21 22 23 A

Stage

*All Theater Row Facilities are Handicap Accessible

Acorn

1 2 3 4 5 6 7 8 9 10 11 12 13 14 15 G
1 2 3 4 5 6 7 8 9 10 11 12 13 14 15 F
1 2 3 4 5 6 7 8 9 10 11 12 13 14 15 E
1 2 3 4 5 6 7 8 9 10 11 12 13 14 15 D
1 2 3 4 5 6 7 8 9 10 11 12 13 14 15 C
1 2 3 4 5 6 7 8 9 10 11 12 13 14 15 B
1 2 3 4 5 6 7 8 9 10 11 12 13 14 15 A

Stage

Beckett

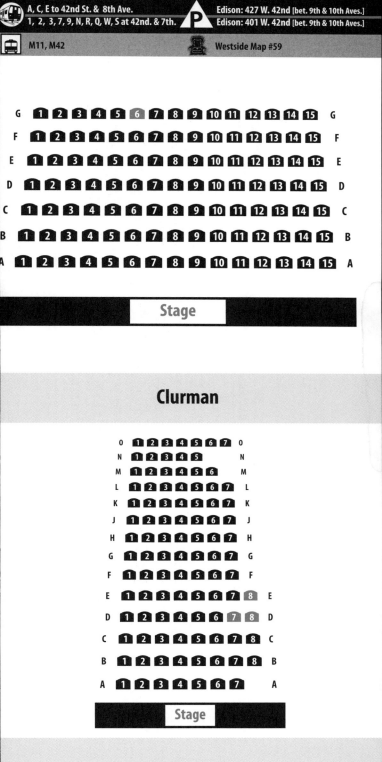

A, C, E to 42nd St. & 8th Ave.

1, 2, 3, 7, 9, N, R, Q, W, S at 42nd. & 7th.

Edison: 427 W. 42nd [bet. 9th & 10th Aves.]

Edison: 401 W. 42nd [bet. 9th & 10th Aves.]

M11, M42

Westside Map #59

Stage

Clurman

Stage

Kirk

Union Square Theatre

100 East 17th Street // New York, NY [between Park Avenue & Irving Place]

Ticketmaster: (212) 307-4100 // **Group Sales: (212) 889-4300**

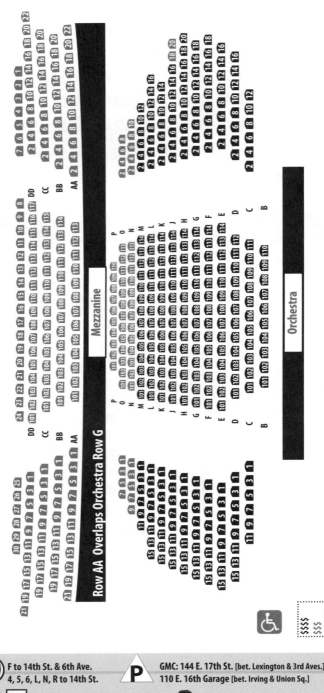

Mezzanine

Row AA Overlaps Orchestra Row G

Orchestra

F to 14th St. & 6th Ave.
4, 5, 6, L, N, R to 14th St.

GMC: 144 E. 17th St. [bet. Lexington & 3rd Aves.]
110 E. 16th Garage [bet. Irving & Union Sq.]

M1, M2, M3, M7, M14, M101, M102

Union Square Map #112

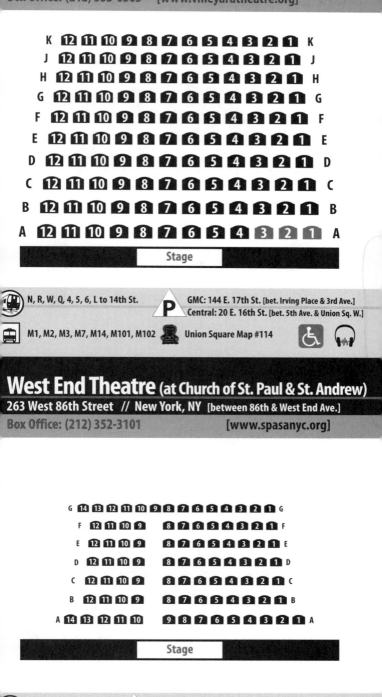

108 East 15th Street // New York, NY [between 4th Ave. & Irving Place]

Box Office: (212) 353-0303 [www.vineyardtheatre.org]

Stage

N, R, W, Q, 4, 5, 6, L to 14th St.

GMC: 144 E. 17th St. [bet. Irving Place & 3rd Ave.]
Central: 20 E. 16th St. [bet. 5th Ave. & Union Sq. W.]

M1, M2, M3, M7, M14, M101, M102   Union Square Map #114

West End Theatre (at Church of St. Paul & St. Andrew)

263 West 86th Street // New York, NY [between 86th & West End Ave.]

Box Office: (212) 352-3101 [www.spasanyc.org]

Stage

1 to 86th St.

Central: 150 W. 83rd St. [bet. Amsterdam & Columbus Aves.]
Active: 280 W.87th St. [bet. West End & Broadway]

M104, M86, M7, M11

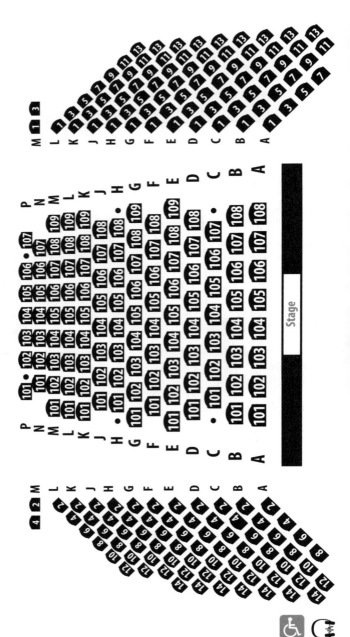

Downstairs

A, C, E, 1, 9, 2, 3, R, N to
Times Square & 42nd St.

Edison: 401 W. 42nd St. [bet. 9th & 10th Aves.]
Central: 322 W. 44th [bet. 8th & 9th Aves.]

M10, M11, M16, M42, M104   Westside Map #60

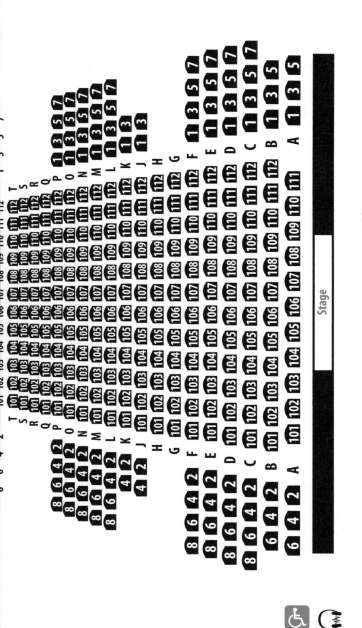

Upstairs

World Underground Theatre

1501 Broadway // New York, NY [between 43rd Street & Broadway]

Box Office: (212) 398-3439 // Group Sales: (212) 971-7205

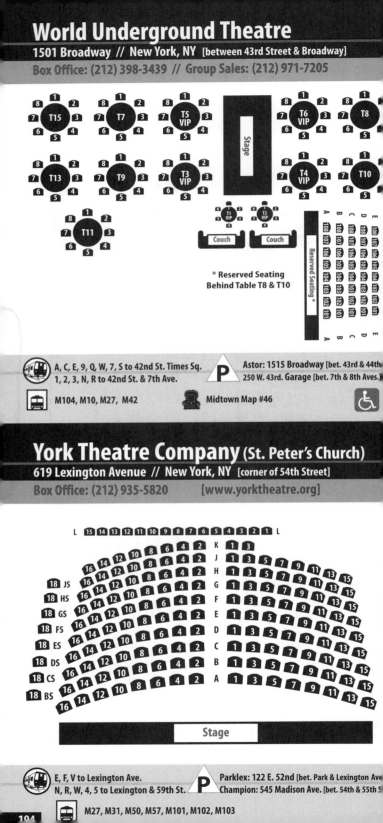

Stage

T15, T7, T5 VIP, T6 VIP, T8

T13, T9, T3 VIP, T4 VIP, T10

T11, T1 VIP, T2 VIP

Couch Couch

* Reserved Seating
Behind Table T8 & T10

Reserved Seating *

A, C, E, 9, Q, W, 7, S to 42nd St. Times Sq.
1, 2, 3, N, R to 42nd St. & 7th Ave.

P Astor: 1515 Broadway [bet. 43rd & 44th]
250 W. 43rd. Garage [bet. 7th & 8th Aves.]

M104, M10, M27, M42

Midtown Map #46

York Theatre Company (St. Peter's Church)

619 Lexington Avenue // New York, NY [corner of 54th Street]

Box Office: (212) 935-5820 [www.yorktheatre.org]

Stage

E, F, V to Lexington Ave.
N, R, W, 4, 5 to Lexington & 59th St.

P Parklex: 122 E. 52nd [bet. Park & Lexington Ave]
Champion: 545 Madison Ave. [bet. 54th & 55th St]

M27, M31, M50, M57, M101, M102, M103

194

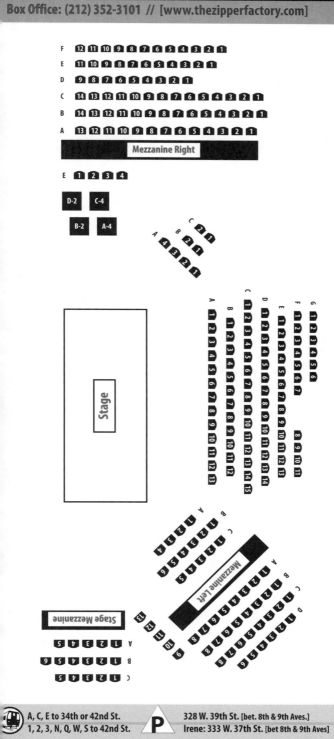

Mezzanine Right

Stage

Mezzanine Left

Stage Mezzanine

A, C, E to 34th or 42nd St.
1, 2, 3, N, Q, W, S to 42nd St.

328 W. 39th St. [bet. 8th & 9th Aves.]
Irene: 333 W. 37th St. [bet 8th & 9th Aves]

M10, M11, M16, M20, M27, M42, M104

195

Seascap

APOLLO

APOLLO

Harlem...
Come see the greatness
YOUR world famous Apollo Theater
has to offer.

concert halls

New York City Opera

1395 Lexington Ave. // New York, NY [between 91st & 92nd Street]
Y-Charge: (212) 415-5500 // Group Sales: (212) 415-5447
[www.92y.org]

Orchestra ▶

Balcony

Balcony Row A overhangs Orchestra Row S

4, 5, 6 to 86th St.

M1, M2, M3, M86, M96, M101, M102, M103

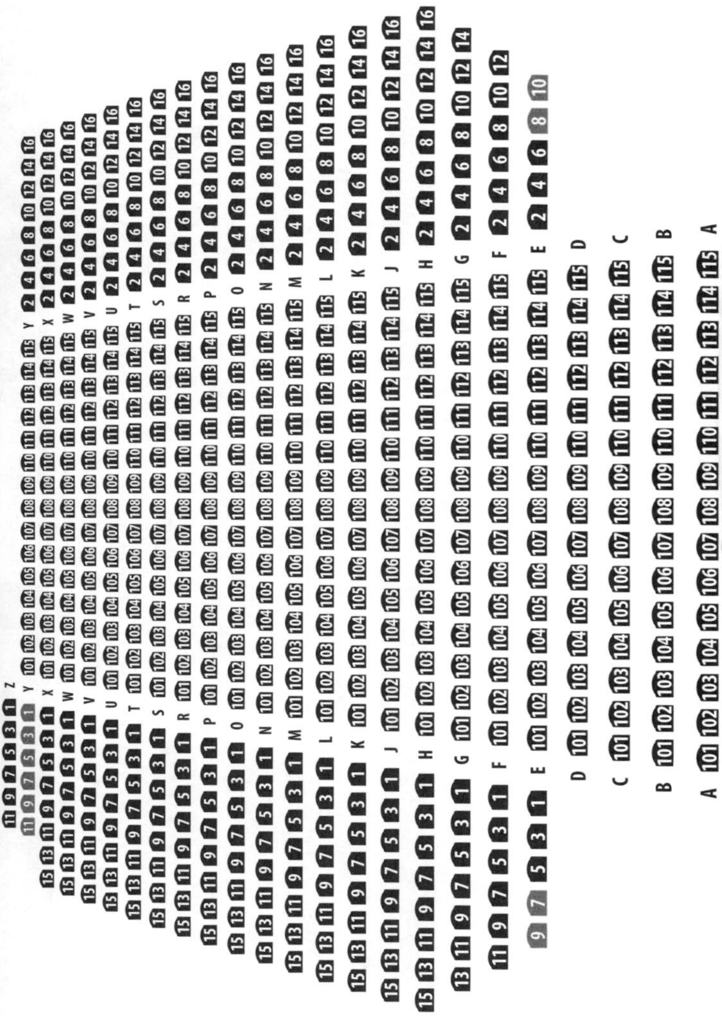

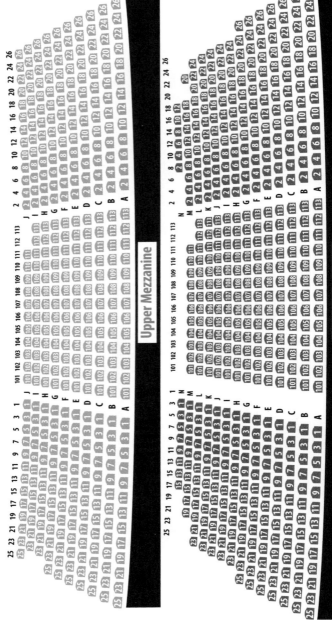

Upper Mezzanine

Lower Mezzanine

Mezzanine Row A overhangs Orchestra Row H

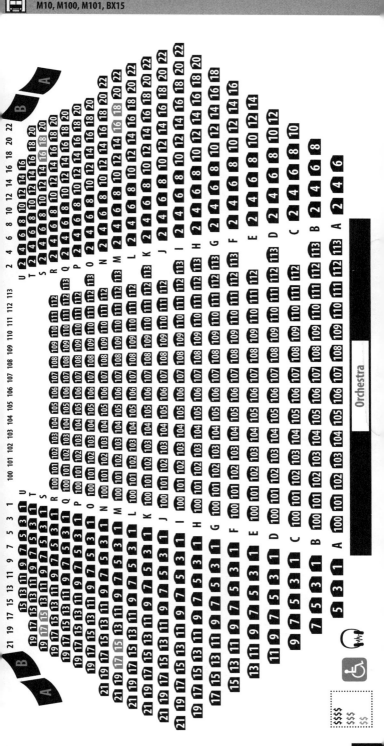

A, B, C, D, 2, 3 to 125th St.
Metro North to 125th St.

Garage: 120 W. 126th St. [bet. 7th & Lenox Ave.]
126th St.: 215 W. 125th St. [bet. 7th & Douglass Aves.]

M10, M100, M101, BX15

Orchestra

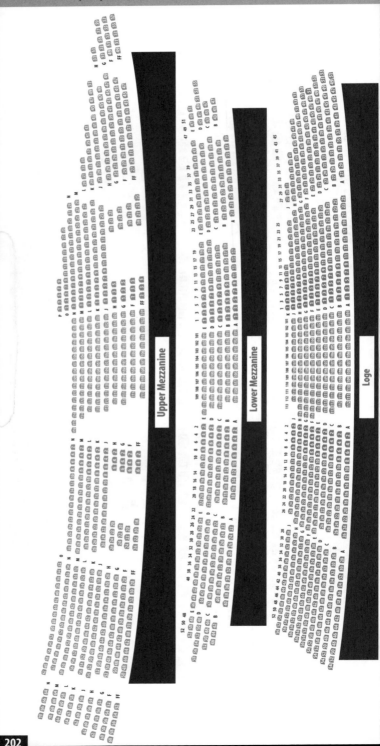

Upper Mezzanine

Lower Mezzanine

Loge

1, 2, 3 to 72nd St.
9, B, C to 72nd St.

Kinney. 201 West 75th St. [bet. Broadway & Amsterdam Aves.]
TCP Ansmia: 2169 Broadway [btwn. 73rd & 74th Sts.]

M79

Orchestra

$$$$
$$$
$$

Brooklyn Academy of Music (Harvey Theater)

30 Lafayette Avenue // Brooklyn, NY

Box Office: (718) 636-4100 // Group Sales: (718) 623-7885

[www.bam.org]

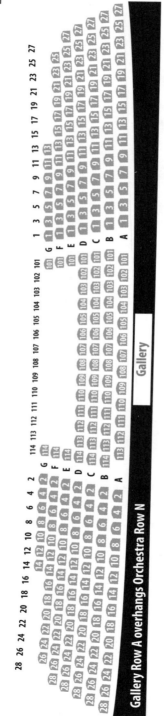

Gallery

Gallery Row A overhangs Orchestra Row N

2, 3, 4, 5, B, C, G, N, P, Q, R to Atlantic Ave.
C to Lafayette St. or G to Fulton St.

P Lot 1: Ashland bet. Fulton & Lafayette Ave.
Lot 2: Ashland Pl. & Lafayette Ave.

B25, B26, B45, B52, B63, B67. Call BAM Bus at (718) 636-4100

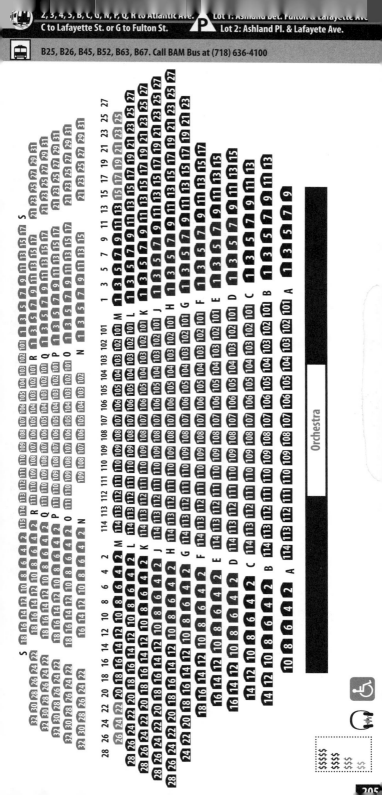

Orchestra

Brooklyn Academy of Music (Opera House)

30 Lafayette Avenue // Brooklyn, NY

Ticketmaster: (212) 636-4100 // Group Sales: (718) 623-7885

[www.bam.org]

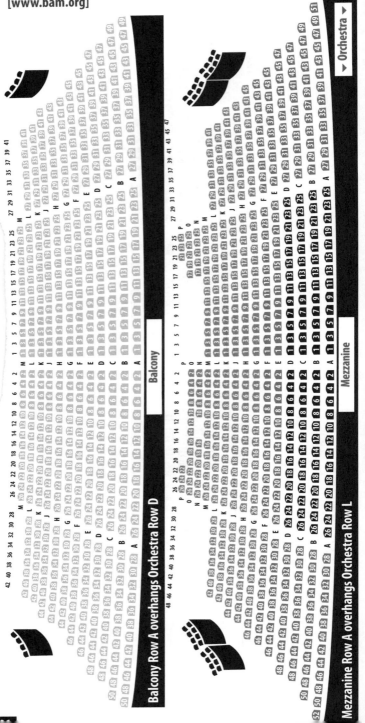

▶ Orchestra ▶

Balcony

Balcony Row A overhangs Orchestra Row D

Mezzanine

Mezzanine Row A overhangs Orchestra Row L

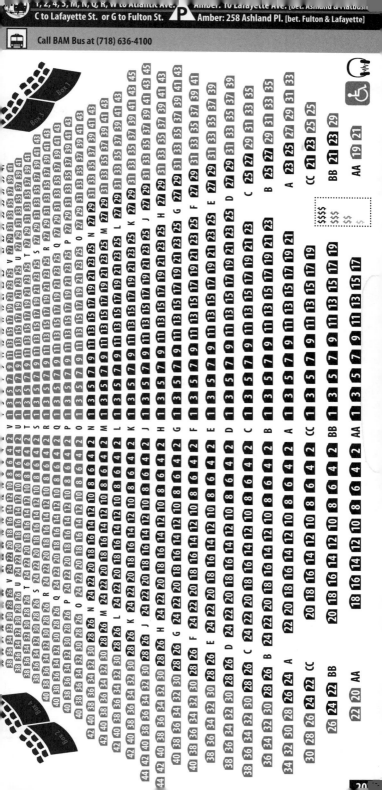

1, 2, 4, 5, M, N, Q, R, W to Atlantic Ave. / C to Lafayette St. or G to Fulton St.

Amber: 10 Lafayette Ave. [bet. Ashland & Flatbush]

Amber: 258 Ashland Pl. [bet. Fulton & Lafayette]

Call BAM Bus at (718) 636-4100

881 Seventh Avenue // New York, NY [at 57th Street]

Box Office: (212) 247-7800 // Group Sales: (212) 903-9705

[www.carnegiehall.org]

A, B, C, D, 1, 2 to 59th St. [Columbus Circle]
N, R, Q, W to 57th St.

P 58th & 7th. 100 W. 58th [bet. 6th & 7th Ave.]
Central: 888 7th Ave. [corner of 56th & 7th Ave.]

M5, M6, M7, M10, M30, M31, M57, M104   Midtown Map #42

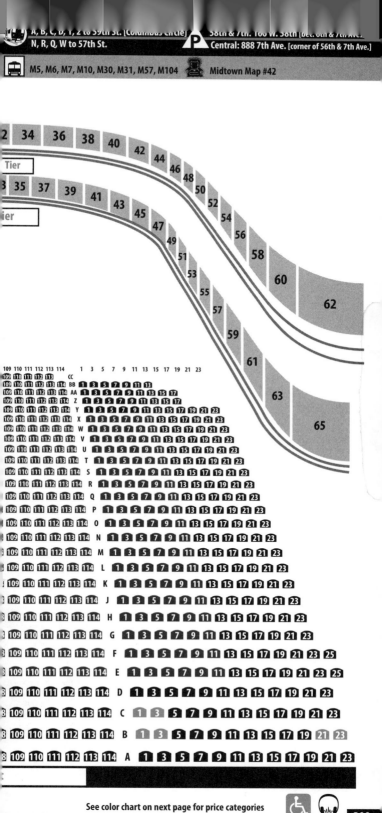

See color chart on next page for price categories

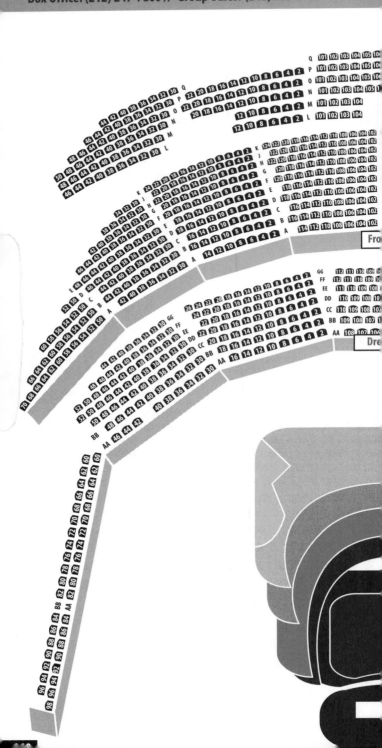

[www.carnegiehall.org]

Center Balcony

Balcony

Dress Circle

Second Tier Center

First Tier

Parquet

Prime Parquet

$$$$$$
$$$$$
$$$$
$$$
$$
$

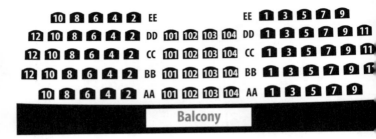

Balcony seating

10	8	6	4	2	EE					EE	1	3	5	7	9	
12	10	8	6	4	2	DD	101	102	103	104	DD	1	3	5	7	9	11
12	10	8	6	4	2	CC	101	102	103	104	CC	1	3	5	7	9	11
12	10	8	6	4	2	BB	101	102	103	104	BB	1	3	5	7	9	1
10	8	6	4	2	AA	101	102	103	104	AA	1	3	5	7	9	

Balcony

Orchestra seating

	101	102	103	104	105	106	107	108	109	110	111	112	113	114	
O	101	102	103	104	105	106	107	108	109	110	111	112	113	114	O
N	101	102	103	104	105	106	107	108	109	110	111	112	113	114	N
M	101	102	103	104	105	106	107	108	109	110	111	112	113	114	M
L	101	102	103	104	105	106	107	108	109	110	111	112	113	114	L
K	101	102	103	104	105	106	107	108	109	110	111	112	113	114	K
J	101	102	103	104	105	106	107	108	109	110	111	112	113	114	J
H	101	102	103	104	105	106	107	108	109	110	111	112	113	114	H
G	101	102	103	104	105	106	107	108	109	110	111	112	113	114	G
F	101	102	103	104	105	106	107	108	109	110	111	112	113	114	F
E	101	102	103	104	105	106	107	108	109	110	111	112	113	114	E
D	101	102	103	104	105	106	107	108	109	110	111	112	113	114	D
C	101	102	103	104	105	106	107	108	109	110	111	112	113	114	C
B	101	102	103	104	105	106	107	108	109	110	111	112	113	114	B
A	101	102	103	104	105	106	107	108	109	110	111	112	113	114	A

Orchestra

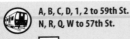

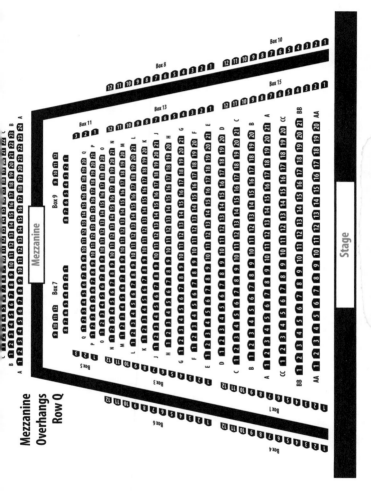

A, B, C, D, 1, 2 to 59th St.
N, R, Q, W to 57th St.

58th & 7th: 166 W. 58th [bet. 6th & 7th Aves.]
Central: 888 7th Ave. [corner of 56th & 7th Ave.]

M5, M6, M7, M10, M30, M31, M57, M104

Midtown Map #42

213

First Balcony / Grand Tier

Grand Tier Row A overhangs Orchestra Row H

Upper Levels shown on next page

B, D, E to 53rd St.   Kinney: 109 W. 56th St. [bet. 6th & 7th Aves.]

M5, M6, M7, M30, M31, M57, M104   Midtown Map #41

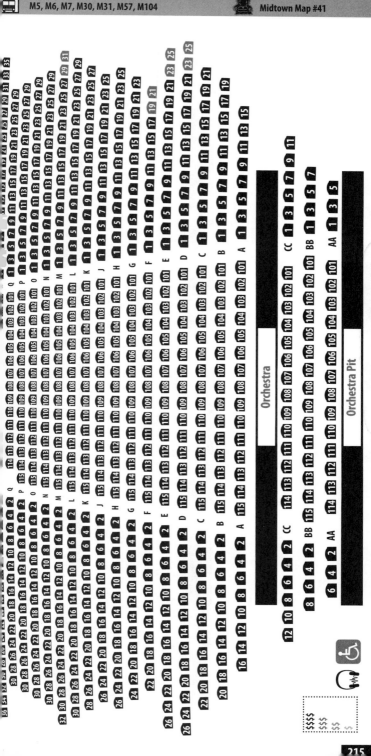

Rear Gallery

Front Gallery Row A overhangs First Balcony Row E Second Balcony / Front Gallery

216

Rear Mezzanine

First Balcony Middle / Mezzanine

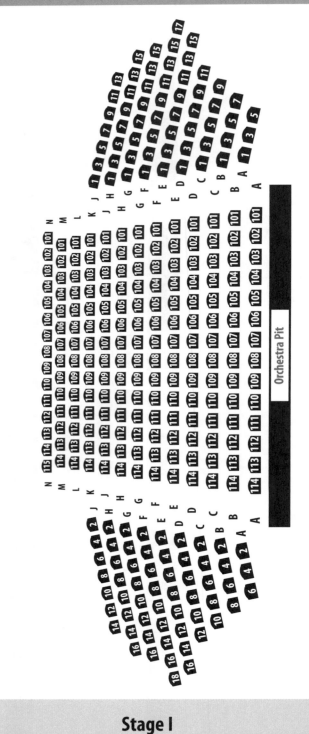

Stage I

B, D, E to 53rd St.

Burlington: 131 W. 50 ...[bet. 6th & 7th Av...
Kinney: 175 W. 56th St. [bet. 6th & 7th Aves.]

M5, M6, M7, M30, M31, M57, M104

Midtown Map #47

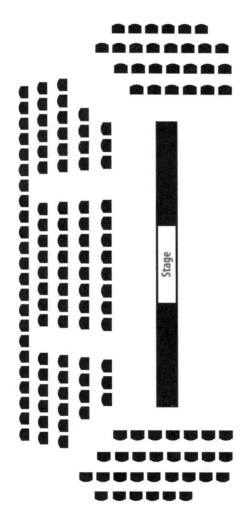

Stage II

* General admission: no seat numbers or rows

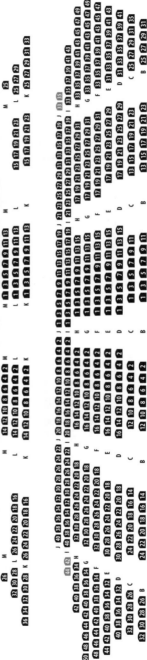

Balcony

Orchestra

Overhangs Row K

1 to 66th & Broadway
A, B, C, D to Columbus Circle

P Continental: 10 W. 66th St. (bet. Cent. Park W. & Broadway)
AMPCO: 61 W. 62nd St. (bet. Broadway & Columbus Ave.)

M5, M7, M10, M11, M20, M66, M105

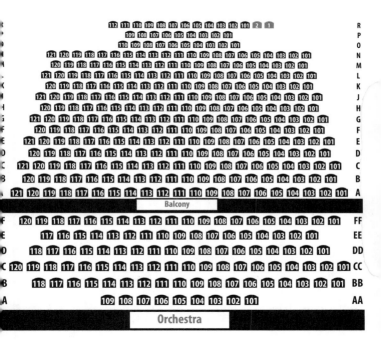

55 East 59th Street // New York, NY [between Park and Madison Avenues]
Box Office: (212) 355-6160 [www.fiaf.org]

```
                    R  112 111 110 109 108 107 106 105 104 103 102 101  2  1   R
                    P      109 108 107 106 105 104 103 102 101              P
                    O      110 109 108 107 106 105 104 103 102 101          O
     N 121 120 119 118 117 116 115 114 113 112 111 110 109 108 107 106 105 104 103 102 101  N
     M 120 119 118 117 116 115 114 113 112 111 110 109 108 107 106 105 104 103 102 101  M
     L 121 120 119 118 117 116 115 114 113 112 111 110 109 108 107 106 105 104 103 102 101  L
     K 120 119 118 117 116 115 114 113 112 111 110 109 108 107 106 105 104 103 102 101  K
     J 121 120 119 118 117 116 115 114 113 112 111 110 109 108 107 106 105 104 103 102 101  J
     H 120 119 118 117 116 115 114 113 112 111 110 109 108 107 106 105 104 103 102 101  H
     G 121 120 119 118 117 116 115 114 113 112 111 110 109 108 107 106 105 104 103 102 101  G
     F 120 119 118 117 116 115 114 113 112 111 110 109 108 107 106 105 104 103 102 101  F
     E 121 120 119 118 117 116 115 114 113 112 111 110 109 108 107 106 105 104 103 102 101  E
     D 120 119 118 117 116 115 114 113 112 111 110 109 108 107 106 105 104 103 102 101  D
     C 121 120 119 118 117 116 115 114 113 112 111 110 109 108 107 106 105 104 103 102 101  C
     B 120 119 118 117 116 115 114 113 112 111 110 109 108 107 106 105 104 103 102 101  B
     A 121 120 119 118 117 116 115 114 113 112 111 110 109 108 107 106 105 104 103 102 101  A
```

Balcony

```
    FF 120 119 118 117 116 115 114 113 112 111 110 109 108 107 106 105 104 103 102 101  FF
    EE     117 116 115 114 113 112 111 110 109 108 107 106 105 104 103 102 101          EE
    DD     118 117 116 115 114 113 112 111 110 109 108 107 106 105 104 103 102 101      DD
    CC 120 119 118 117 116 115 114 113 112 111 110 109 108 107 106 105 104 103 102 101  CC
    BB     118 117 116 115 114 113 112 111 110 109 108 107 106 105 104 103 102 101      BB
    AA             109 108 107 106 105 104 103 102 101                                  AA
```

Orchestra

4, 5, 6, F, N, R, W to 59th St.
N, R to 59th St.

P   59th and 5th: 26 E 59th St. [bet. Madison & Park Aves.]
GMC: 200 Central Park South [at 58th St.]

M1 M2 M3, M4 M31 M57

Grace Rainey Rodgers (Metropolitan Museum of Art)

100 Fifth Avenue // New York, NY [Corner of 82nd St. & 5th Ave.]

Box Office: (212) 570-3949 // Group Sales: (212) 570-3792

[www.metmuseum.org]

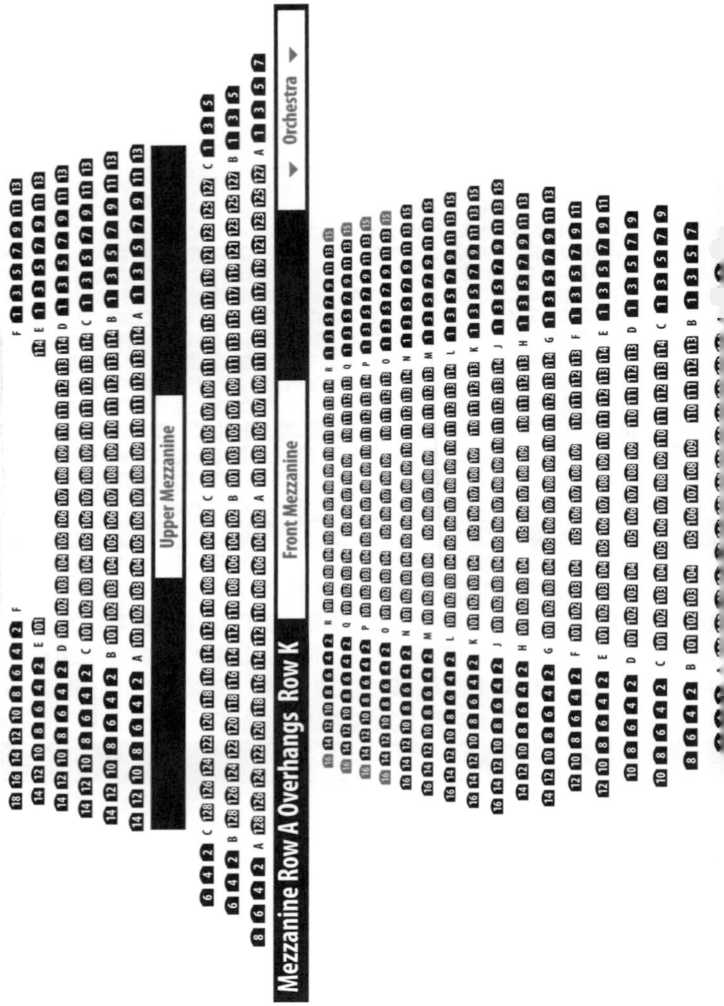

Upper Mezzanine
Front Mezzanine
Orchestra
Mezzanine Row A Overhangs Row K

1, 6 to 86th

Garage onsite: 5th Ave. & 80th St.

M1, M2, M3, M4, M86

25 Madison Avenue // New York, NY [Between 58th & 59th Sts.]

Box Office: (212) 685-0008 x560 // Group Sales: (212) 685-0008 x561

www.morganlibrary.org]

		11	10	9	8	7	6	5	4	3	2	1		O

O

N 15 14 13 12 11 10 9 8 7 6 5 4 3 2 1 N

M 15 14 13 12 11 10 9 8 7 6 5 4 3 2 1 M

L 15 14 13 12 11 10 9 8 7 6 5 4 3 2 1 L

K 15 14 13 12 11 10 9 8 7 6 5 4 3 2 1 K

J 15 14 13 12 11 10 9 8 7 6 5 4 3 2 1 J

I 15 14 13 12 11 10 9 8 7 6 5 4 3 2 1 I

H 15 14 13 12 11 10 9 8 7 6 5 4 3 2 1 H

G 15 14 13 12 11 10 9 8 7 6 5 4 3 2 1 G

F 15 14 13 12 11 10 9 8 7 6 5 4 3 2 1 F

E 15 14 13 12 11 10 9 8 7 6 5 4 3 2 1 E

D 15 14 13 12 11 10 9 8 7 6 5 4 3 2 1 D

C 15 14 13 12 11 10 9 8 7 6 5 4 3 2 1 C

B 15 14 13 12 11 10 9 8 7 6 5 4 3 2 1 B

A 15 14 13 12 11 10 9 8 7 6 5 4 3 2 1 A

FF 15 14 13 12 11 10 9 8 7 6 5 4 3 2 1 FF

EE 15 14 13 12 11 10 9 8 7 6 5 4 3 2 1 EE

DD 13 12 11 10 9 8 7 6 5 4 3 2 1 DD

Stage

 6 to 33rd; 4, 5, 6, 7 to Grand Central
B, D, F, Q to 42nd Street

P MHM: 61 W. 35th St. [bet. 5th & 6th Aves.]
Central: 222 Lexington Ave. [33rd & 34th St.]

M2. M3. M4. Q32 to 36th St. PATH to 33rd St.

223

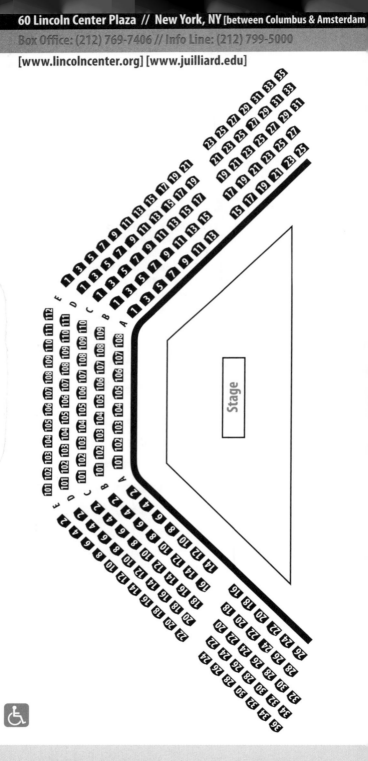

60 Lincoln Center Plaza // New York, NY [between Columbus & Amsterdam]

Box Office: (212) 769-7406 // Info Line: (212) 799-5000

[www.lincolncenter.org] [www.juilliard.edu]

Stage

Stephanie P. McClelland Drama Theater

1, 2 to 60th Street // 1, 2, 3 to 72nd St.
A, B, C, D to 59th St.

Lincoln Center Park & Lock. West 65th St.
[bet. Amsterdam & Broadway] Reserve: (212) 721-6500

M5, M7, M11, M66, M104

Lincoln Center Map #92

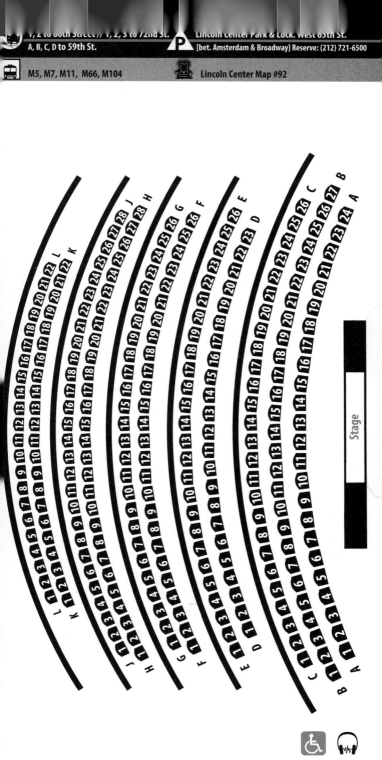

Paul Recital Hall

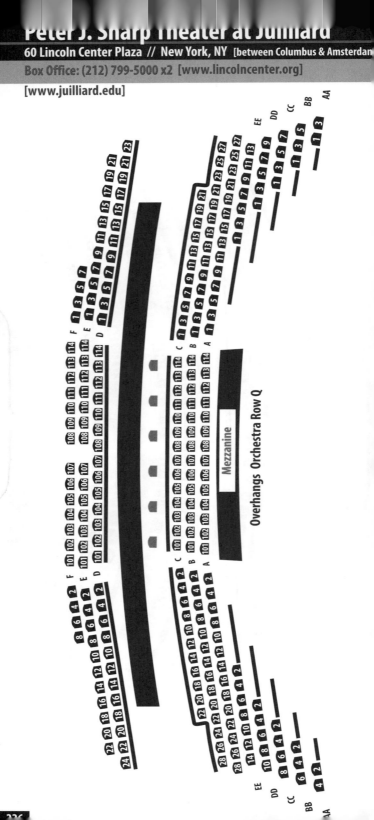

1, 2 to 66th Street // 1, 2, 3 to 72nd St.

A, B, C, D to 59th St.

Lincoln Center Park & Lock. West 65th St.
[bet. Amsterdam & Broadway] Reserve: (212) 721-6500

M5, M7, M11, M66, M104

Lincoln Center Map #92

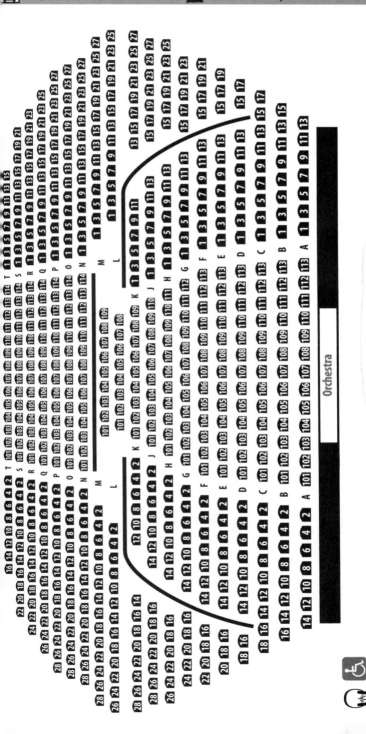

Orchestra

Lehman Center for the Performing Arts
250 Bedford Park Blvd. West // Bronx, NY [between Columbus & Amsterd

Box Office: (718) 960-8833   [www.lehmancenter.org]

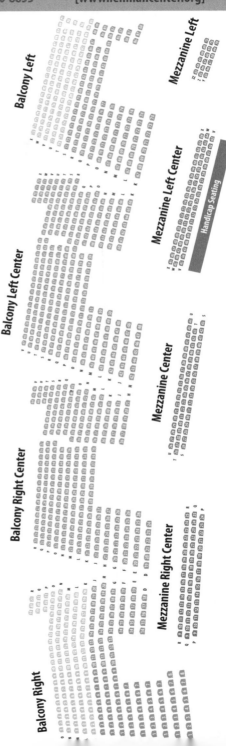

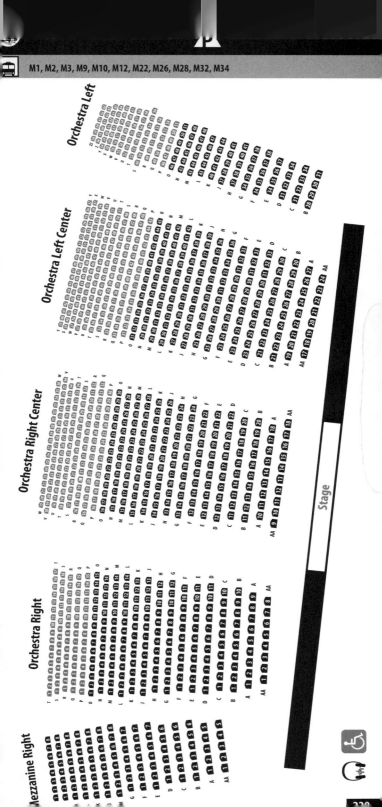

Orchestra Left

Orchestra Left Center

Orchestra Right Center

Orchestra Right

Mezzanine Right

Stage

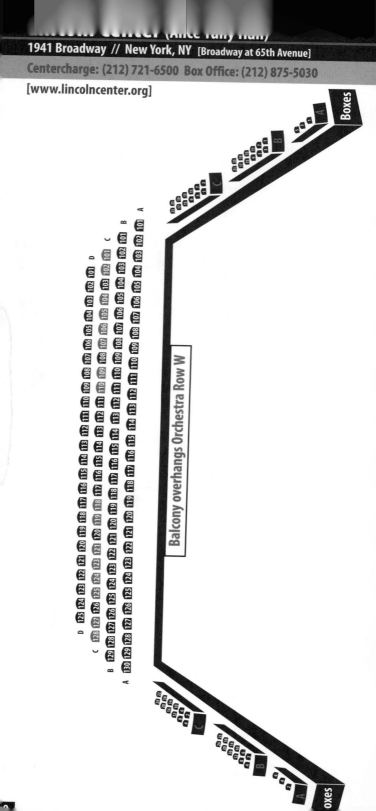

Lincoln Center (Alice Tully Hall)

1941 Broadway // New York, NY [Broadway at 65th Avenue]

Centercharge: (212) 721-6500 Box Office: (212) 875-5030

[www.lincolncenter.org]

Boxes

Balcony overhangs Orchestra Row W

A, B, C, D to 59th St.

Lincoln Center Park & Lock: West 6!
[bet. Amsterdam & Broadway] Reserve: (212) 721-6500

M5, M7, M10, M11, M66, M104   Lincoln Center Map #91

Orchestra

A, B, C, D to 59th St.   [bet. Amsterdam & Broadway] Reserve: (212) 721-6500

M5, M7, M10, M11, M66, M104   Lincoln Center Map #90

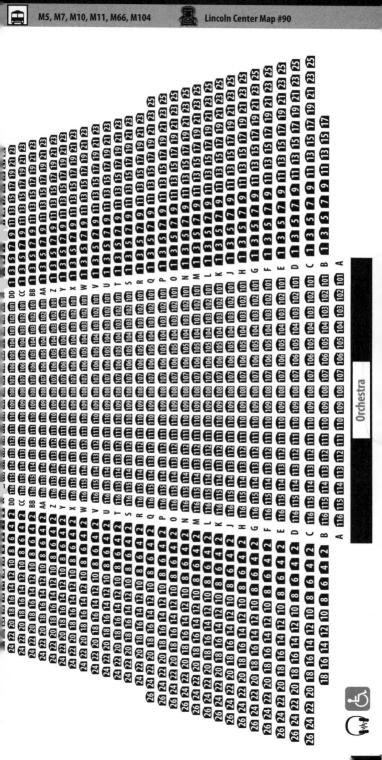

Orchestra

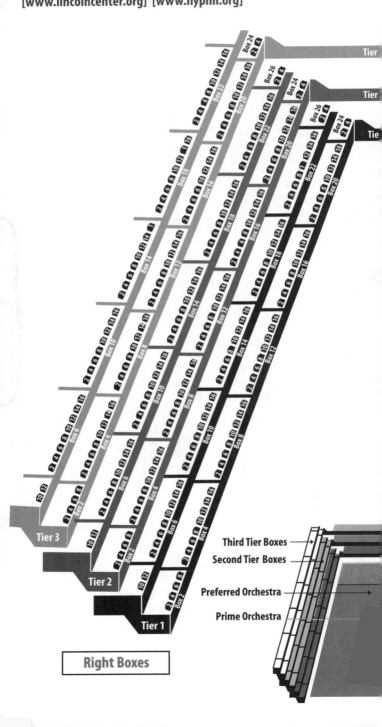

Third Tier Boxes
Second Tier Boxes
Preferred Orchestra
Prime Orchestra

Right Boxes

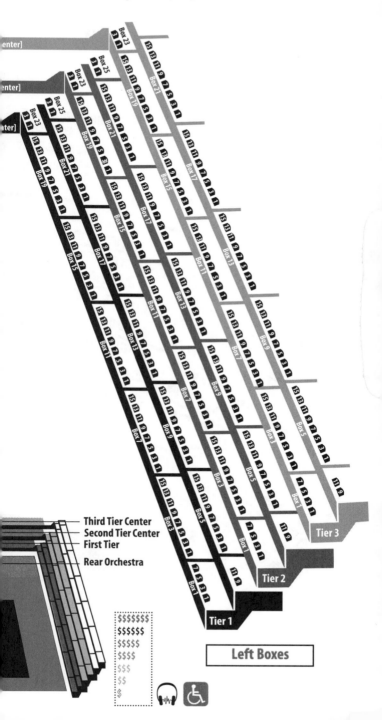

NY Philharmonic Info: (212) 875-5709

NY Philharmonic Tickets: (212) 875-5656

NY Philharmonic Group Sales: (212) 875-5672

Third Tier Center
Second Tier Center
First Tier
Rear Orchestra

$$$$$$$
$$$$$$
$$$$$
$$$$
$$$
$$
$

Tier 1

Tier 2

Tier 3

Left Boxes

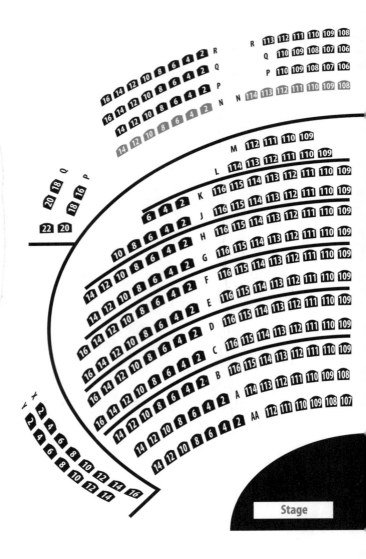

[www.lincolncenter.org] [www.jalc.org] [www.jazzatlincolncenter.org]

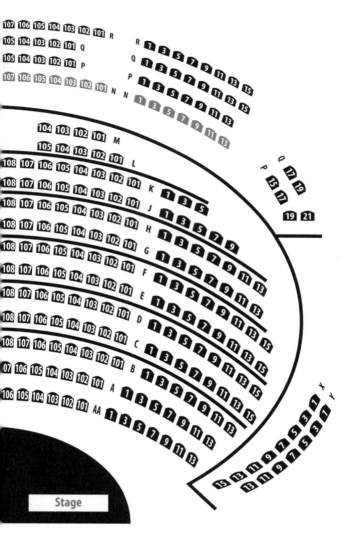

Lincoln Center (Mitzi E. Newhouse Theater)

150 West 65th Street // New York, NY [between Broadway & Amsterdam]

Telecharge: (212) 239-6200 // Group Sales: (212) 889-4300

[www.lincolncenter.org]

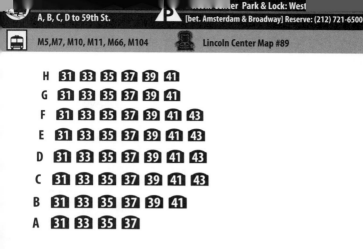

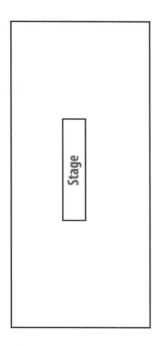

A, B, C, D to 59th St.

Park & Lock: West
[bet. Amsterdam & Broadway] Reserve: (212) 721-6500

M5, M7, M10, M11, M66, M104

Lincoln Center Map #89

H 31 33 35 37 39 41
G 31 33 35 37 39 41
F 31 33 35 37 39 41 43
E 31 33 35 37 39 41 43
D 31 33 35 37 39 41 43
C 31 33 35 37 39 41 43
B 31 33 35 37 39 41
A 31 33 35 37

Stage

A 30 32 34 36
B 30 32 34 36 38 40
C 30 32 34 36 38 40 42
D 30 32 34 36 38 40 42
E 30 32 34 36 38 40 42
F 30 32 34 36 38 40 42
G 30 32 34 36 38 40
H 30 32 34 36 38 40

239

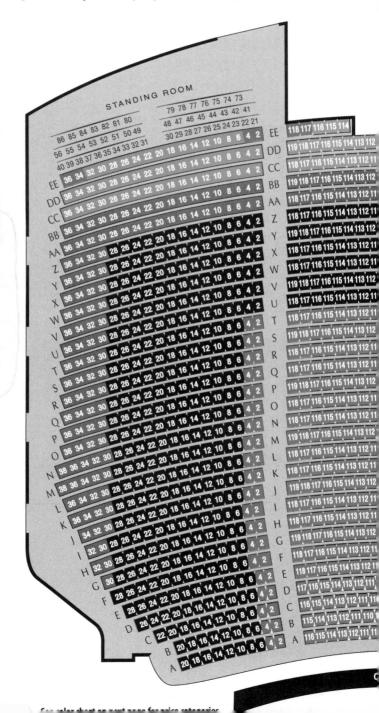

See color chart on next page for price categories

A, B, C, D to 59th St.　　[bet. Amsterdam & Broadway] Reserve: (212) 721-6500

M5, M7, M10, M11, M66, M104　　Lincoln Center Map #87

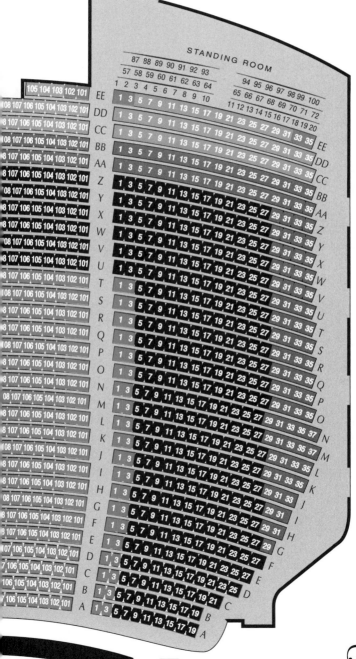

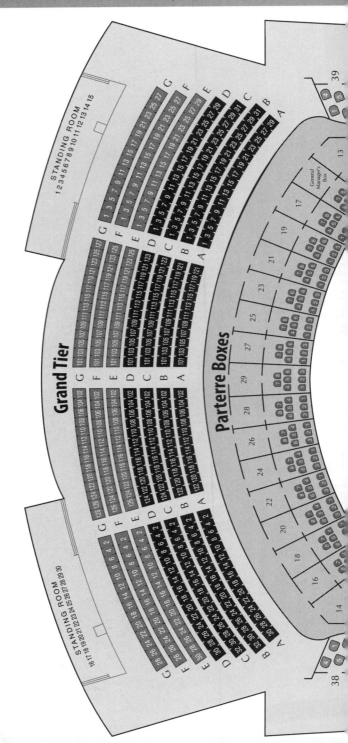

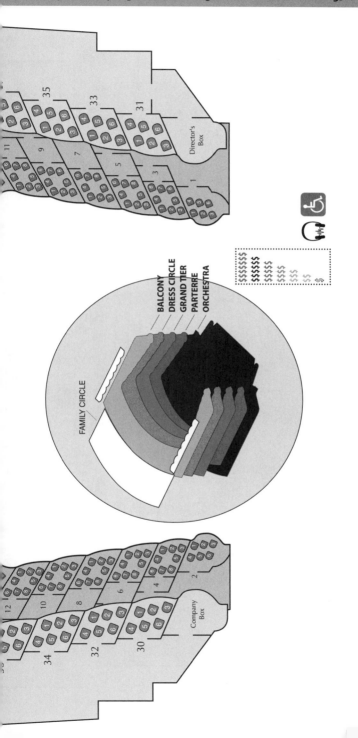

FAMILY CIRCLE

BALCONY
DRESS CIRCLE
GRAND TIER
PARTERRE
ORCHESTRA

$$$$$$$
$$$$$$
$$$$$
$$$$
$$$
$$
$

Director's Box

Company Box

35 33 31
34 32 30

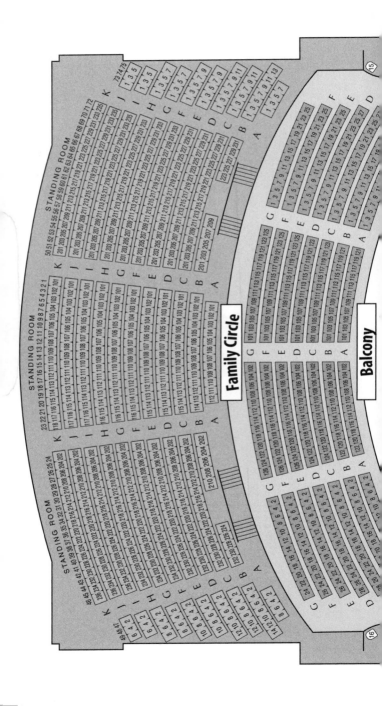

Lincoln Center (Metropolitan Opera House

30 Lincoln Center Plaza // New York, NY [Columbus between 62nd & 65th S

Box Office: (212) 362-6000 // Group Sales: (212) 501-3410

Family Circle

Balcony

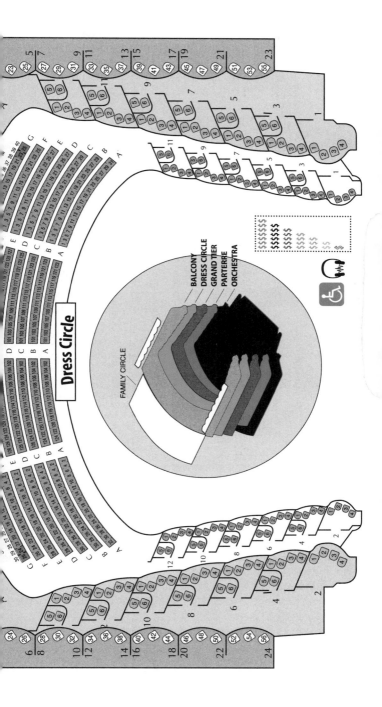

Dress Circle

FAMILY CIRCLE

BALCONY
DRESS CIRCLE
GRAND TIER
PARTERRE
ORCHESTRA

Lincoln Center (New York State Theater)

20 Lincoln Center Plaza // New York, NY [Columbus between 62nd & 65th S

Box Office: (212) 870-5570 // Centercharge: (212) 721-6500

[www.nycballet.org] [www.nycopera.com] [lincolncenter.org]

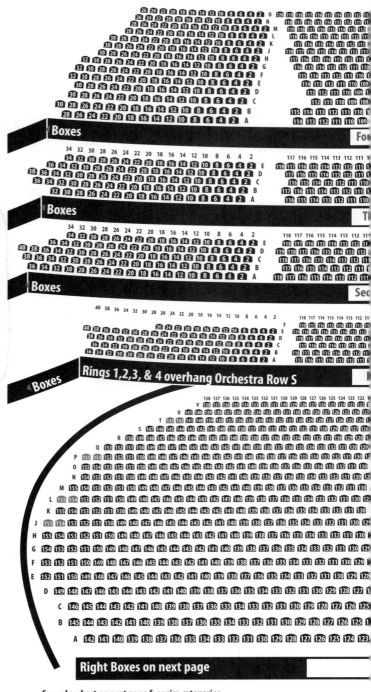

Boxes

Boxes

Boxes

Boxes — Rings 1, 2, 3, & 4 overhang Orchestra Row S

Boxes

Right Boxes on next page

See color chart on next page for price categories

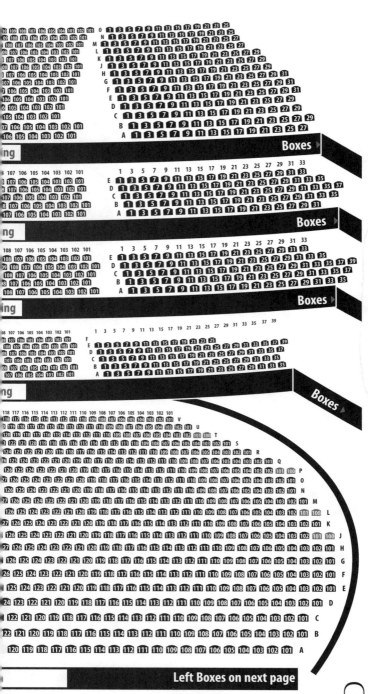

Boxes ▶

Boxes ▶

Boxes ▶

Boxes ▶

Left Boxes on next page

Handicap seats: T100, T101, T142, T143; P100, P101, P154, P155;
J100, J101, J154, J155; I100, I101, I154, I155

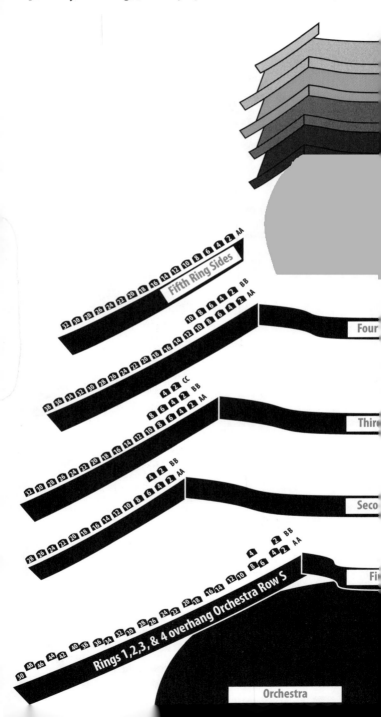

Lincoln Center (New York State Theater)

20 Lincoln Center Plaza // New York, NY [Columbus between 62nd & 65th St

Box Office: (212) 870-5570

[www.nycballet.org] [www.nycopera.com] [lincolncenter.org]

Fifth Ring Sides

Four

Thir

Seco

Fi

Rings 1,2,3, & 4 overhang Orchestra Row S

Orchestra

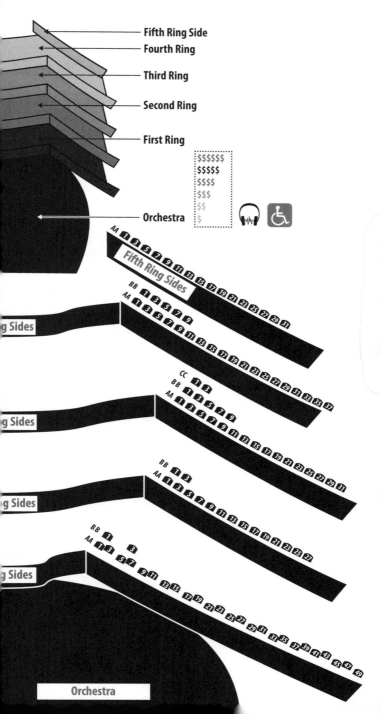

Fifth Ring Side
Fourth Ring
Third Ring
Second Ring
First Ring

$$$$$$
$$$$$
$$$$
$$$
$$
$

Orchestra

Fifth Ring Sides

Sides

Sides

Sides

Sides

Orchestra

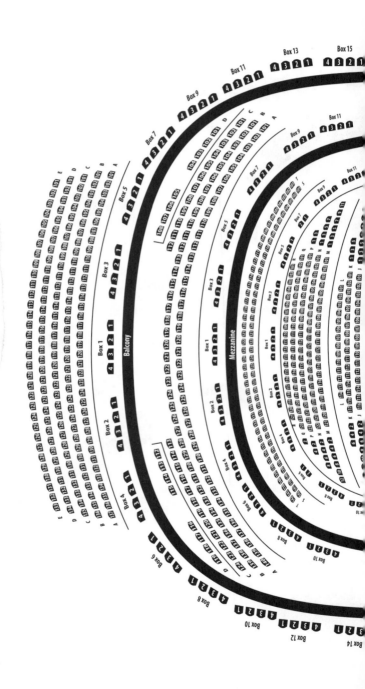

A, B, C, D to 59th St.   [bet. Amsterdam & Broadway] Reserve: (212) 721-6500

M5, M7, M10, M11, M66, M104   Lincoln Center Map #94

www.lincolncenter.org] [www.jalc.org] [www.jazzatlincolncenter.org]

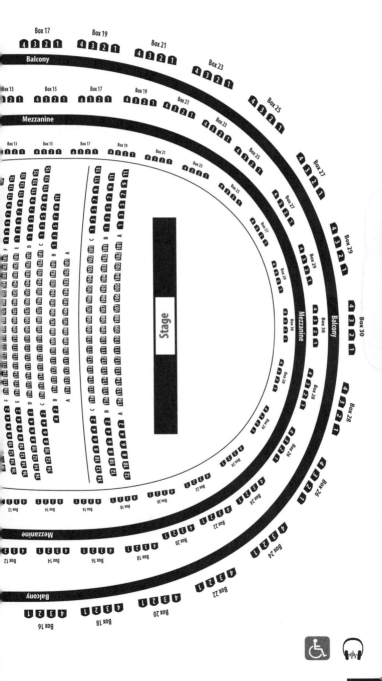

Lincoln Center (Vivian Beaumont Theater)

150 West 65th Street // **New York, NY** [between Broadway & Amsterdam]

Telecharge: (212) 239-6200 // Group Sales: (212) 889-4300

Box Office: (212) 362-7600

A, B, C, D to 59th St.

P [bet. Amsterdam & Broadway] Reserve: (212) 721-6500

M5, M7, M10, M11, M66, M104   Lincoln Center Map #89

[www.lincolncenter.org]   [lct.org]

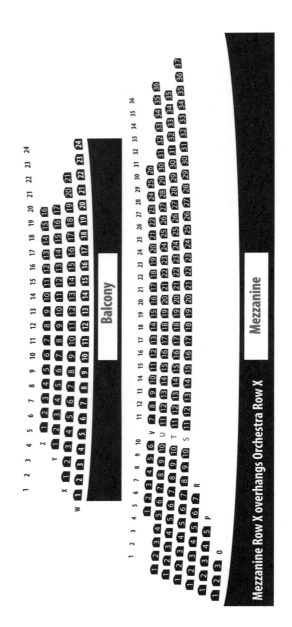

Balcony

Mezzanine

Mezzanine Row X overhangs Orchestra Row X

Orchestra

...hattan S...

120 Claremont Avenue // New York, NY [between Broadway & 122nd Stree...

Box Office: (917) 493-4428 // Info Line: (917) 493-4528

[www.msmnyc.edu]

NN

MM

LL KK JJ HH GG FF

EE DD CC BB AA

Balcony

Overhangs Orchestra Row K

John C. Borden Auditorium

P to 140th St. [Columbia Univ.]   GMC.   2nd & ... [bet. Amsterdam & Broadway]

Claremont: 621 W. 120th St. [corner of Claremont Ave.]

M4, M104

Orchestra

♿ 🦻

Merkin Concert Hall (Abraham Goodman Hou...

129 West 67th Street // New York, NY [between Broadway & Amsterdam Av...

Box Office: (212) 501-3330 [www.kaufman-center.org]

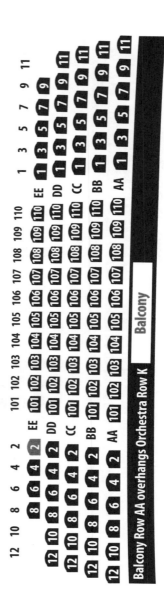

Balcony

Balcony Row AA overhangs Orchestra Row K

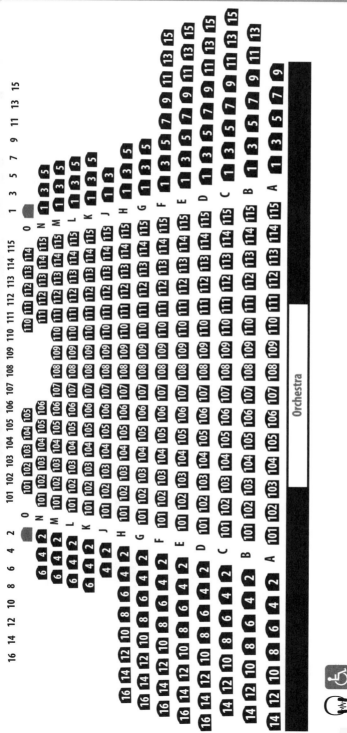

Orchestra

Balcony

Balcony Row AA overhangs Orchestra Row K

1 train to 116th St.

Claremont: 621 W. 120th St. [bet. Claremont Ave. & Broadwa...

GGMC: 512 W. 112th St. [bet. Amsterdam & Broadway]

M4, M60, or M104 to 116th St.

Orchestra

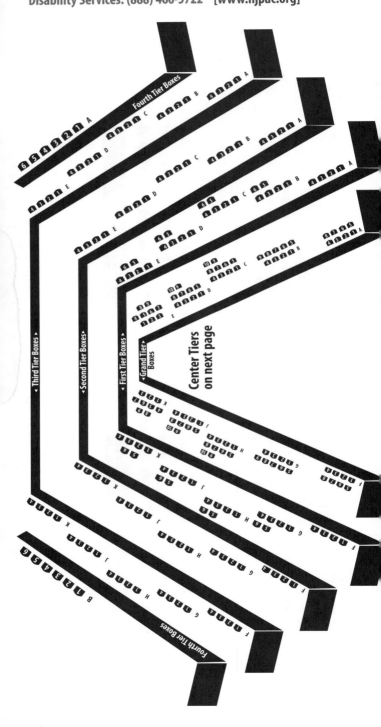

Fourth Tier Boxes

Third Tier Boxes ▸

Second Tier Boxes ▸

First Tier Boxes ▸

Grand Tier Boxes ▸

Center Tiers
on next page

Fourth Tier Boxes

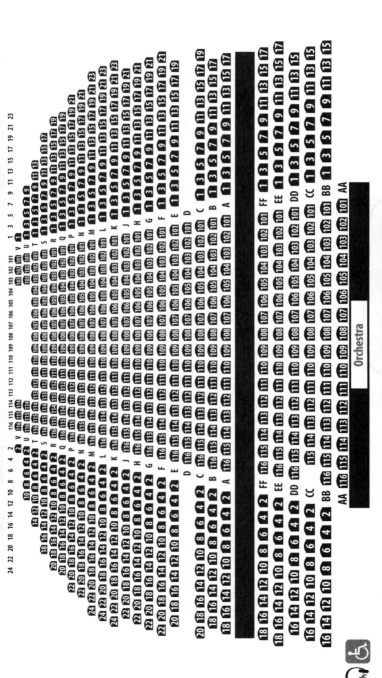

Orchestra

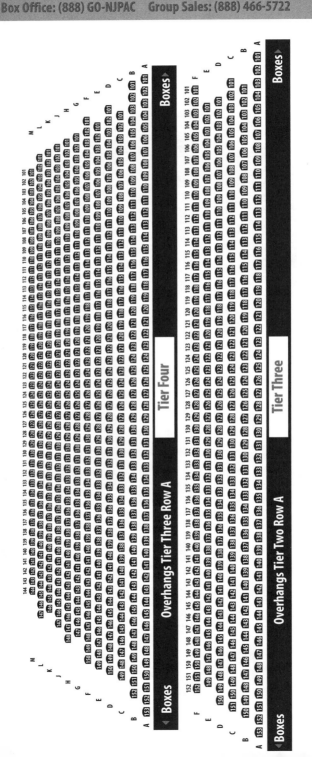

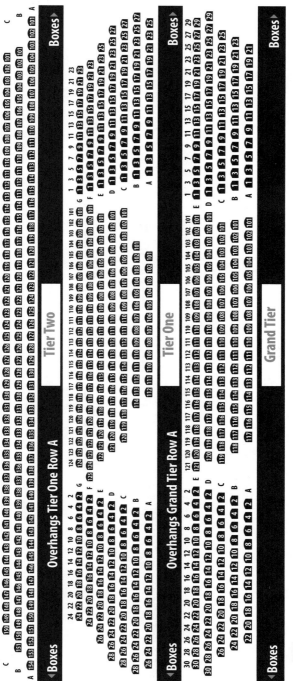

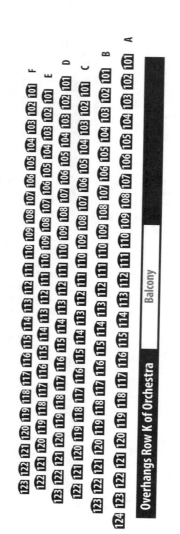

Overhangs Row K of Orchestra

Balcony

1515 Broadway // **New York, NY** [44th & Broadway]

Box Office: (212) 930-1950 x1940 // Concert Hotline: (212) 930-1959

Ticketmaster (212) 307-7171

to 42nd & Times Square | Astor: 1515 Broadway [bet. 43rd & 44th Sts.]

M5, M6, M7, M27, M50 | Midtown Map #49

[www.nokiatheatrenyc.com]

Mezzanine

Rows S, R, Q, P, O, N, M, L, K, J, H, G, F, E, D, C, B, A

Promenade

Rows YY, XX, WW, VV, UU, TT, SS, RR, QQ, PP, OO, NN

Rows MM, LL, KK

Rows JJ, HH, GG, FF, EE, DD, CC, BB, AA

Rows DDD, CCC, BBB, AAA

Stage

[www.artscenter.com]

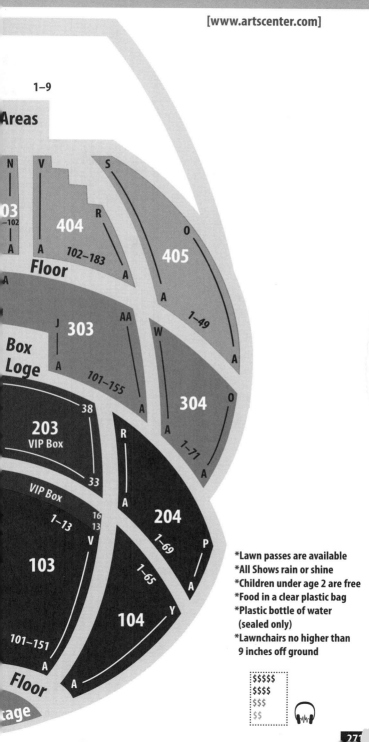

1–9

Areas

N

V

S

03
–102

404

R

405

A

A

102–183

O

Floor

A

A

A

AA

J

303

W

1–49

**Box
Loge**

A

101–155

A

304

38

O

203
VIP Box

R

A

1–71

33

A

VIP Box

16
13

204

1–13

P

V

1–69

A

103

1–65

Y

101–151

104

A

A

Floor

stage

*Lawn passes are available
*All Shows rain or shine
*Children under age 2 are free
*Food in a clear plastic bag
*Plastic bottle of water
 (sealed only)
*Lawnchairs no higher than
 9 inches off ground

$$$$$
$$$$
$$$
$$

271

1260 Avenue of Americas // New York, NY [at 50th Street]
Ticketmaster: (212) 307-7171 // Group Sales: (212) 456-6080

[www.radiocity.com]

D, B, F to 50th St. [Rockefeller Center]   GMC: 218 W. 50th St. [bet. Broadway & 8th Av

Kinney: 155 W. 48th St. [bet. 6th & 7th Sts.]

M5, M6, M7, M27, M50   Midtown Map #43

Orchestra

$$$$
$$$
$$
$

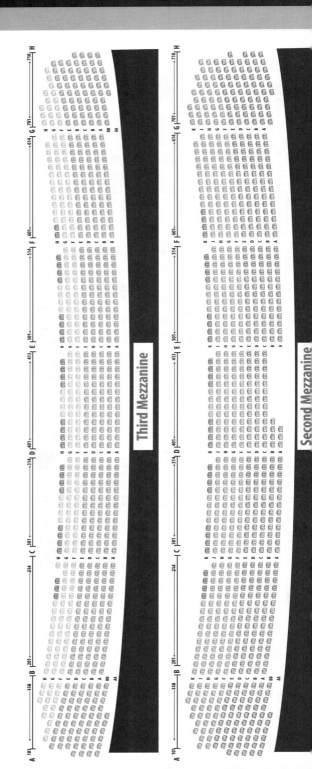

Third Mezzanine

Second Mezzanine

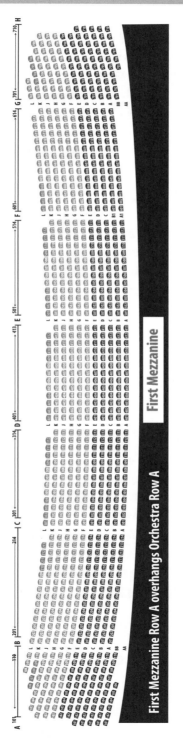

First Mezzanine Row A overhangs Orchestra Row A

First Mezzanine

$$$$
$$$
$$
$

275

Skirball Center for the Performing Arts (NYU

566 LaGuardia Place // New York, NY [Washington Square South]

Box Office: (212) 992-8484 // Ticket Central: (212) 279-4200

[www.skirballcenter.nyu.edu]

Row E — 3 1 ... E 115 114 113 112 111 110 109 1
Row D — 15 13 11 9 7 5 3 1 D 115 114 113 112 111 110 109 1
Row C — 13 11 9 7 5 3 1 C 115 114 113 112 111 110 109 1
Row B — 13 11 9 7 5 3 1 B 115 114 113 112 111 110 109 1
Row A — 11 9 7 5 3 1 A 115 114 113 112 111 110 109 1

BB — 21 19 17 15 13 11 9 7 5 3 1
AA — 23 21 19 17 15 13 11 9 7 5 3 1

Row U — 112 111 110 109 108 107
Row T — 15 13 11 9 7 5 3 1 T 115 114 113 112 111 110 109 1
Row S — 15 13 11 9 7 5 3 1 S 115 114 113 112 111 110 109 1
Row R — 13 11 9 7 5 3 1 R 115 114 113 112 111 110 109 1
Row Q — 13 11 9 7 5 3 1 Q 115 114 113 112 111 110 109 1

RR — 13 11 9 7 5 3 1
QQ — 19 17 15 13 11 9 7 5 3 1

Row P — 7 5 3 1 P 114 113 112 111 110 109 1
Row O — 11 9 7 5 3 1 O 114 113 112 111 110 109 1
Row N — 11 9 7 5 3 1 N 114 113 112 111 110 109 1
Row M — 11 9 7 5 3 1 M 115 114 113 112 111 110 109 1
Row L — 11 9 7 5 3 1 L 115 114 113 112 111 110 109 1
Row K — 11 9 7 5 3 1 K 115 114 113 112 111 110 109 1
Row J — 11 9 7 5 3 1 J 115 114 113 112 111 110 109 1
Row I — 11 9 7 5 3 1 I 115 114 113 112 111 110 109 1
Row H — 13 11 9 7 5 3 1 H 115 114 113 112 111 110 109 1
Row G — 13 11 9 7 5 3 1 G 115 114 113 112 111 110 109 1
Row F — 13 11 9 7 5 3 1 F 115 114 113 112 111 110 109 1
Row E — 13 11 9 7 5 3 1 E 115 114 113 112 111 110 109 1
Row D — 13 11 9 7 5 3 1 D 115 114 113 112 111 110 109 1
Row C — 15 13 11 9 7 5 3 1 C 115 114 113 112 111 110 109 1
Row B — 15 13 11 9 7 5 3 1 B 115 114 113 112 111 110 109 1
Row A — A 115 114 113 112 111 110 109 1

PBR — 1 3 5 7 9

OBR — 17 15 13 11 / 15 13 11 / 9 7 5 / 3 1

Row CC — 9 7 5 3 1 CC 114 113 112 111 110 109 1
Row BB — 5 3 1 BB 114 113 112 111 110 109 1
Row AA — 3 1 AA 114 113 112 111 110 109 1

A, B, C, D, E, F, V to W. 4th St.
1 to Christopher St. 6 to Astor Pl.

P Minetta. 122 West 3rd St. [bet.
Thomson St.: 221 Thompson St. [bet. Bleeker & 3rd St.]

East/West Village Map Map #102

107 106 105 104 103 102 101 E 2 4 6 8 10 12
107 106 105 104 103 102 101 D 2 4 6 8 10 12 14 16
107 106 105 104 103 102 101 C 2 4 6 8 10 12 14
107 106 105 104 103 102 101 B 2 4 6 8 10 12 14
107 106 105 104 103 102 101 A 2 4 6 8 10 12

Balcony

06 105 104 103 102 101 100 U
107 106 105 104 103 102 101 T 2 4
107 106 105 104 103 102 101 S 2 4 6 8 10 12 14 16
107 106 105 104 103 102 101 R 2 4 6 8 10 12 14
107 106 105 104 103 102 101 Q 2 4 6 8 10 12 14

BB
2 4 6 8 10 12 14 16 18 20 22 24 26
AA
2 4 6 8 10 12 14 16 18 20 22

Parterre

107 106 105 104 103 102 101 p 2 4 6 8
107 106 105 104 103 102 101 o 2 4 6 8 10 12
107 106 105 104 103 102 101 N 2 4 6 8 10 12
107 106 105 104 103 102 101 M 2 4 6 8 10 12
107 106 105 104 103 102 101 L 2 4 6 8 10 12
107 106 105 104 103 102 101 K 2 4 6 8 10 12
107 106 105 104 103 102 101 J 2 4 6 8 10 12
107 106 105 104 103 102 101 I 2 4 6 8 10 12
107 106 105 104 103 102 101 H 2 4 6 8 10 12 14
107 106 105 104 103 102 101 G 2 4 6 8 10 12 14
107 106 105 104 103 102 101 F 2 4 6 8 10 12 14
107 106 105 104 103 102 101 E 2 4 6 8 10 12 14
107 106 105 104 103 102 101 D 2 4 6 8 10 12 14
107 106 105 104 103 102 101 C 2 4 6 8 10 12 14 16
107 106 105 104 103 102 101 B 2 4 6 8 10 12 14 16
107 106 105 104 103 102 101 A

RR
2 4 6 8 10 12 14 16 18 20
QQ

PBL
10 8 6 4 2

OBL
18 20 22 24
12 14 16
6 8 10
2 4

107 106 105 104 103 102 101 CC 2 4 6 8 10
107 106 105 104 103 102 101 BB 2 4 6
107 106 105 104 103 102 101 AA 2 4

Stage

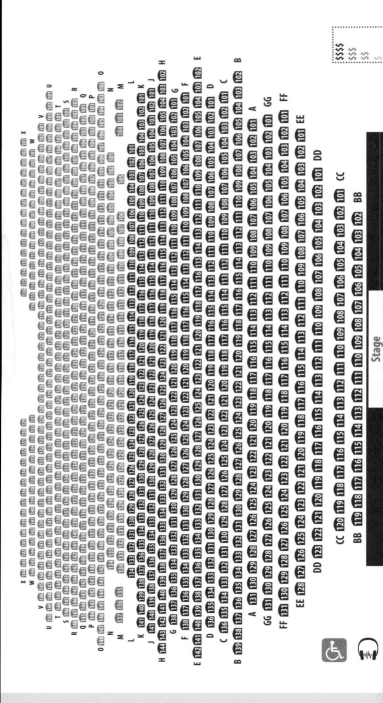

Stage

Main Stage

278

LIE [495] East to Exit 62: Take Nicolls Road **P** Parking Garage on Site // Meter Parking
[Rte. 97] North to Stony Brook

[www.staller.sunysb.edu]

Recital Hall

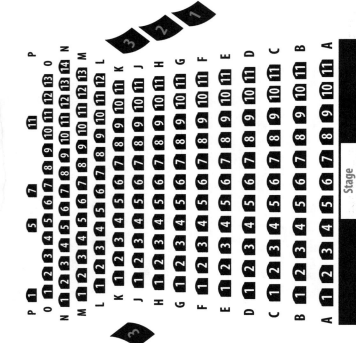

Leonard Nimoy Thalia

B, C, 1, 2, 3 to 96th St.

Kinney: 711 West End Ave. [entrance on 95th St.]
PAO: 214 West 95th St. [bet. Amsterdam & Broadway]

M7, M11, M96, M104, M106

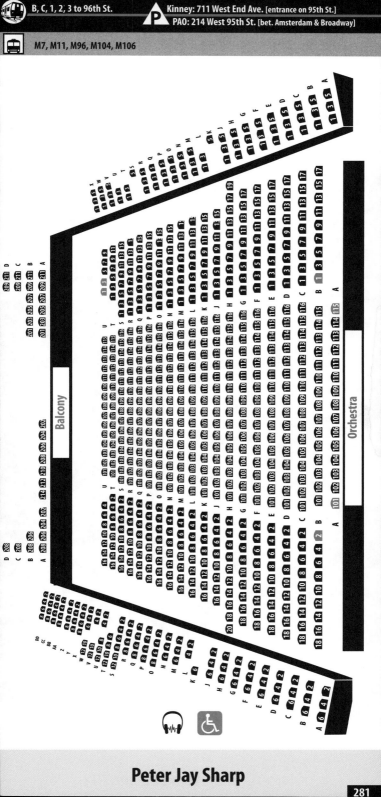

Peter Jay Sharp

Tilles Center For the Performing Arts (Mainstage)

Long Island University [C.W. Post Campus] // 720 Northern Blvd. Greenvale, NY

Tilles Charge: (516) 299-3100   [www.tillescenter.org]

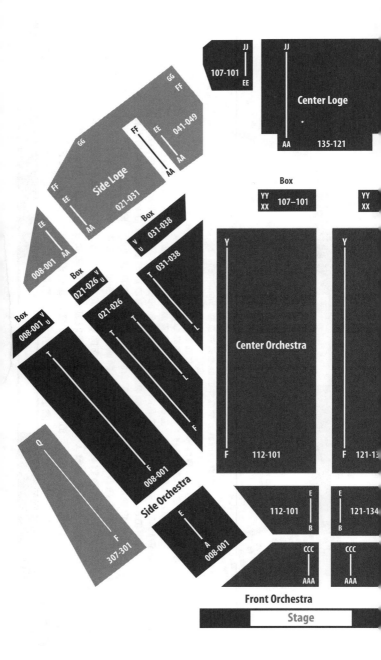

Concert/Orchestra Seating Plan

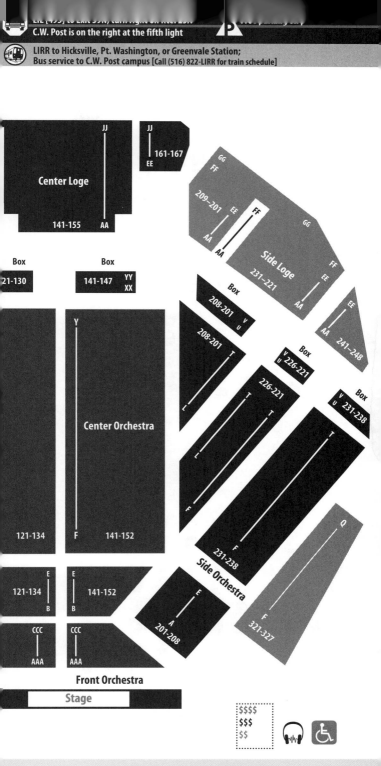

This is the seating plan for:
Concert Series, Orchestral Variations, & Grand Duo Miniseries

Tilles Center For the Performing Arts (Recital Hall)

Long Island University [C.W. Post Campus] // 720 Northern Blvd. Greenvale, NY

Tilles Charge: (516) 299-3100 [www.tillescenter.org]

EXL [495] to Exit 39N, turn right
C.W. Post is on the right at the fifth light

LIRR to Hicksville, Pt. Washington, or Greenvale Station;
Bus service to C.W. Post campus   [Call (516) 822-LIRR for train schedule]

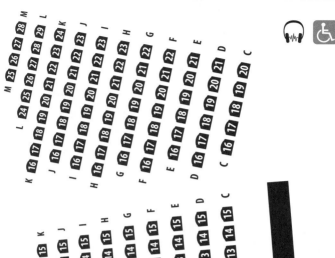

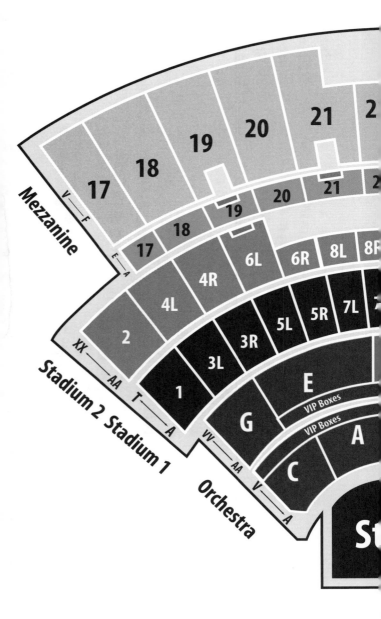

Mezzanine

17 18 19 20 21

17 18 19 20 21

Stadium 2 Stadium 1

2 4L 4R 6L 6R 8L 8R

3L 3R 5L 5R 7L

1 E

G VIP Boxes

VIP Boxes

C A

Orchestra

St

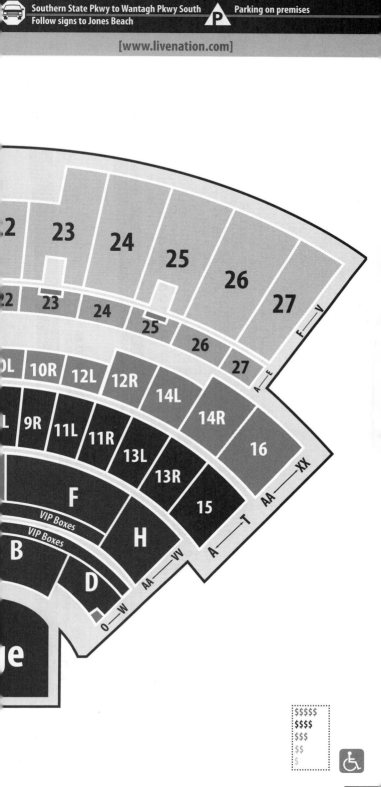

123 West 43rd Street // New York, NY [between Broadway & 6th Avenue]

Box Office: (212) 840-2824 [www.the-townhall-nyc.org]

Balcony
Loge
Loge overhangs Orchestra Row K

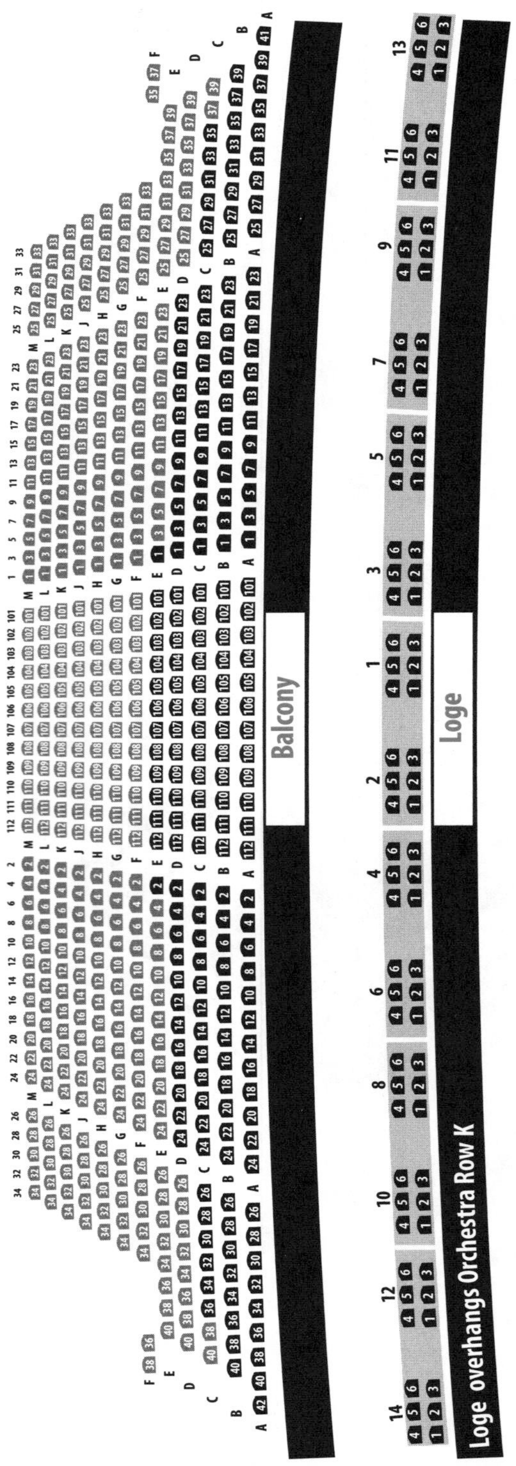

1,2,3,7,B,D,F to 42nd St. & 7th Ave.
4,5,6,A,C,E to 42nd St. & Grand Central

Edison: 1120 6th Ave. [bet. 43rd & 44th Sts.]
Manhattan: 120 W. 45th St. [bet. 6th & 7th]

M1, M2, M3, M4, M5, M6, M7, M27, M42, M104, Q32

Midtown Map #39

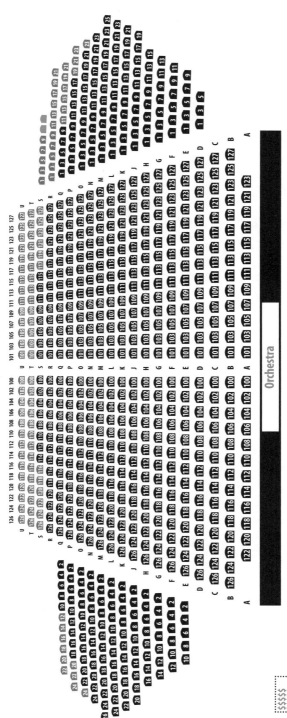

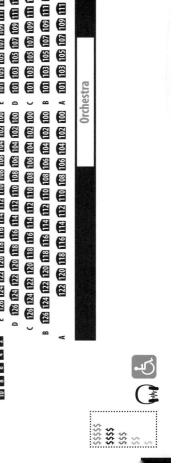

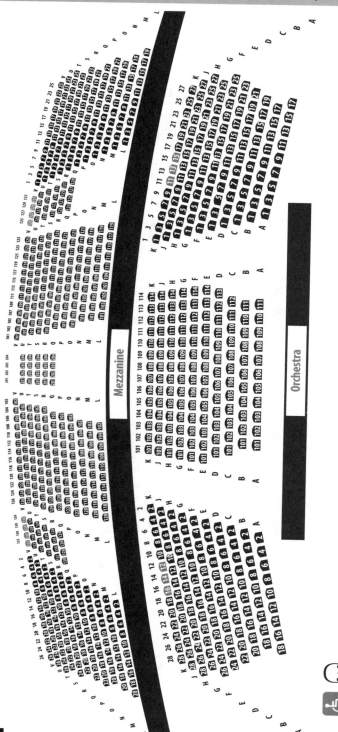

A, C, 1, 2, 3, 9 to Chambers St.   Kitchey: 56 N. Moore St. [bet. Greenwich & Houston St.]
4, 5, 6 to Brooklyn Bridge   Katz: 86 Warren St. [bet. Greenwich & W. Broadway]

M1, M6, M10, M20, M22

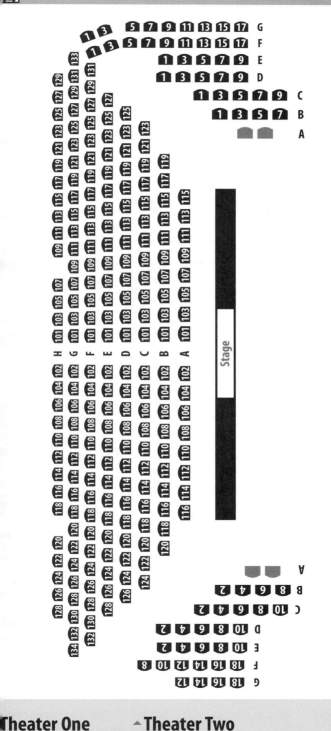

Theater One   ▲ **Theater Two**

4140 Broadway // New York, NY [between Broadway & 175th Street]

Box Office: (212) 568-0915 (Latin) // Box Office: (212) 568-5260 (Rock

[www.theunitedpalace.com]

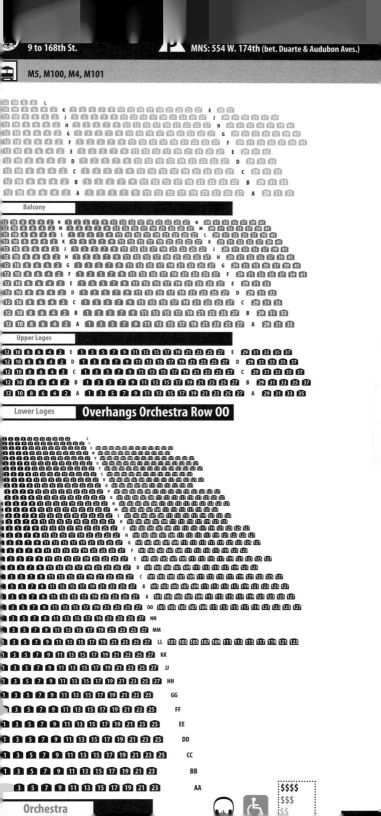

Capital One Bank Theatre at Westbury
960 Brush Hollow Road // Westbury, NY
Info Line: (516) 334-0800 // Group Sales: (516) 247-5210
Box Office: (631) 888-9000

[www.livenation.com]

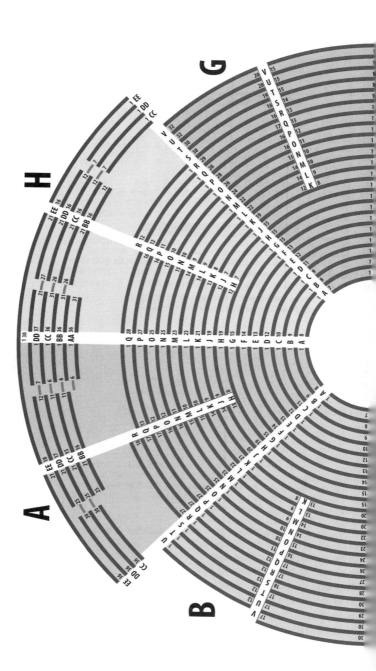

LIE [495] East to Exit 40W [Jericho/Westbury] — Parking on the
Turn right at light; left onto Brush Hollow Rd.   P   in ticket price

LIRR to Westbury Station; Cab to theater. [Call (516) 822-LIRR for train schedule]

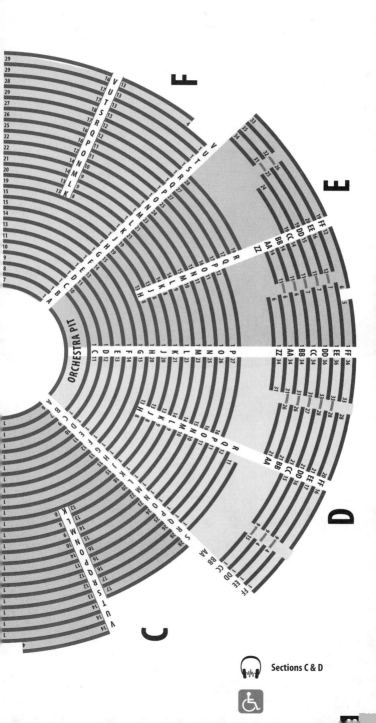

Sections C & D

CITI FIELD

The New Home of the New York Mets

stadiums

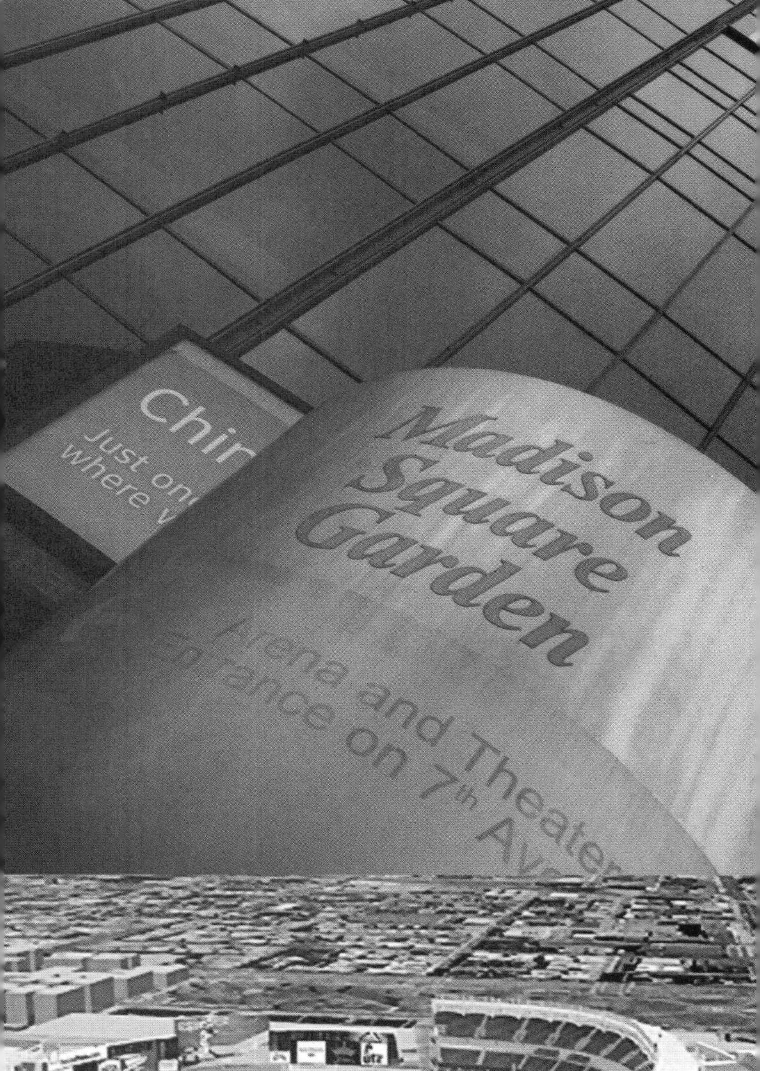

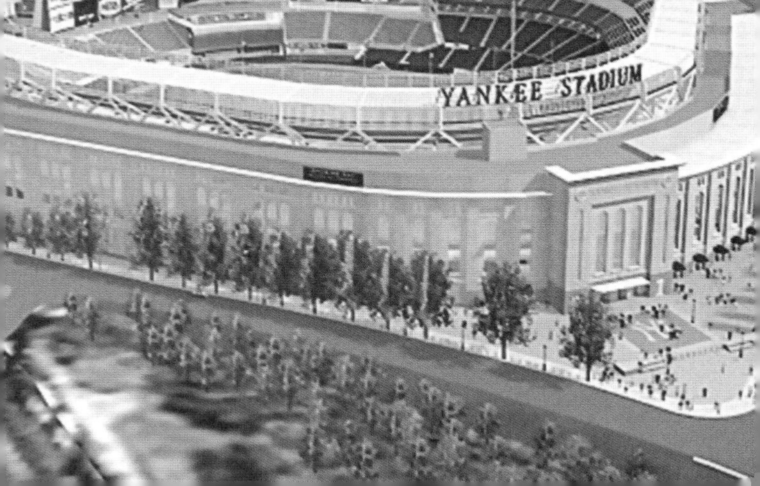

Madison Square Garden

4 Penn Plaza // New York, NY [7th Avenue between 31st & 33rd Streets]

Information: (212) 465-MSG1 // Ticketmaster: (212) 307-7171

Group Sales: (212) 465-6080 // Disabled Services: (212) 465-6034

Tower C

33rd St. & 8th Ave.

Boxing

31st St. & 8th Ave.

Tower B

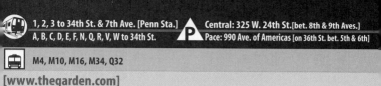

1, 2, 3 to 34th St. & 7th Ave. [Penn Sta.]
A, B, C, D, E, F, N, Q, R, V, W to 34th St.

Central: 325 W. 24th St.[bet. 8th & 9th Aves.]
Pace: 990 Ave. of Americas [on 36th St. bet. 5th & 6th]

M4, M10, M16, M34, Q32

[www.thegarden.com]

Madison Square Garden
4 Penn Plaza // New York, NY [7th Avenue between 31st & 33rd Streets]
Information: (212) 465-MSG1 // Ticketmaster: (212) 307-7171
Group Sales: (212) 465-6080 // Disabled Services: (212) 465-6034

Tower **C**

33rd St. & 8th Ave.

Concerts

31st St. & 8th Ave.

Tower **B**

STAGE

1, 2, 3 to 34th St. & 7th Ave. [Penn Sta.]
A, B, C, D, E, F, N, Q, R, V, W to 34th St.

Central: 325 W. 24th St.[bet. 8th & 9th Aves.]
Pace: 990 Ave. of Americas [on 36th St. bet. 5th & 6th]

M4, M10, M16, M34, Q32

[www.thegarden.com]

Tower **D**

33rd St. & 7th Ave.

Concerts

31st St. & 7th Ave.

Tower **A**

Floor level configurations are subject to change

Madison Square Garden

4 Penn Plaza // New York, NY [7th Avenue between 31st & 33rd Streets]

Knicks Info: (212) 465-JUMP // Liberty Info: (212) 564-WNBA

Ticketmaster: (212) 307-7171 // Disability Services: (212) 465-6034

Tower **C**

33rd St. & 8th Ave.
Gate 92

Tower **B**

31st St. & 8th Ave.
Gate 97

Knicks & Liberty Basketball

1, 2, 3 to 34th St. & 7th Ave. [Penn Sta.]   Central: 325 W. 24th St.[bet. 8th & 9th Aves.]
A, B, C, D, E, F, N, Q, R, V, W to 34th St.   Pace: 990 Ave. of Americas [on 36th St. bet. 5th & 6th]

M4, M10, M16, M34, Q32

www.nba.com/knicks] [www.wnba.com/liberty]

Tower **D**

33rd St. & 7th Ave.

Gate 93

Knicks & Liberty Basketball

Tower **A**

31st St. & 7th Ave.

Gate 90

Madison Square Garden

4 Penn Plaza // New York, NY [7th Avenue between 31st & 33rd Streets]

Information: (212) 465-6486 // **Ticketmaster:** (212) 307-7171

Group Sales: (212) 465-6080 // **Season Tickets:** (212) 465-6073

Disability Services: (212) 465-6034

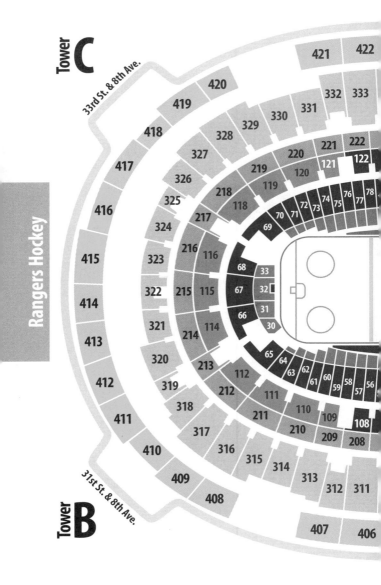

Tower **C**

33rd St. & 8th Ave.

Rangers Hockey

31st St. & 8th Ave.

Tower **B**

1, 2, 3 to 34th St. & 7th Ave. [Penn Sta.]
A, B, C, D, E, F, N, Q, R, V, W to 34th St.

M4, M10, M16, M34, Q32

Central: 325 W. 24th St.[bet. 8th & 9th Aves.]
Pace: 990 Ave. of Americas [on 36th St. bet. 5th & 6th]

[www. thegarden.com]

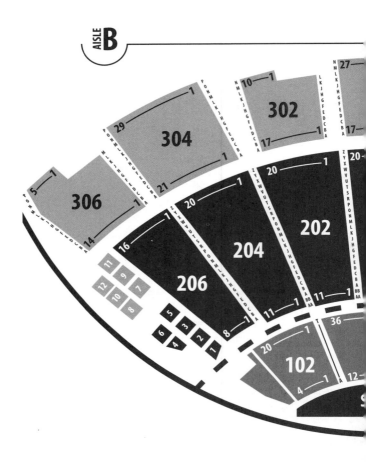

**WaMu theater at MSG
Boxing configuration**

306

1, 2, 3 to 34th St. & 7th Ave. [Penn Sta.]   Central: 325 W. 24th St.[bet. 8th & 9th Aves.]
A, B, C, D, E, F, N, Q, R, V, W to 34th St.   P   Pace: 990 Ave. of Americas [on 36th St. bet. 5th & 6th]

M4, M10, M16, M34, Q32

www.thegarden.com] [www.wamuatmsg.com]

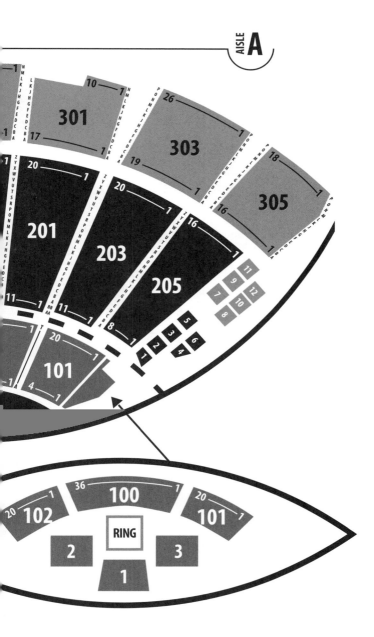

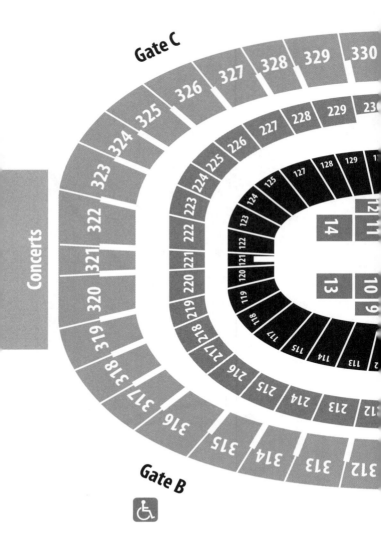

Meadowlands Sports Complex
50 Route 120 // East Rutherford, NJ

Information: (201) 935-3900 // Ticketmaster: (212) 307-7171

Group Sales: (201) 460-4370   [www.meadowlands.com]

Gate C

Concerts

330 329 328 327 326 325 324 323 322 321 320 319 318 317 316 315 314 313 312

230 229 228 227 226 225 224 223 222 221 220 219 218 217 216 215 214 213 212

129 128 127 125 124 123 122 121 120 119 118 117 115 114 113

14 13 12 11 10 9

Gate B

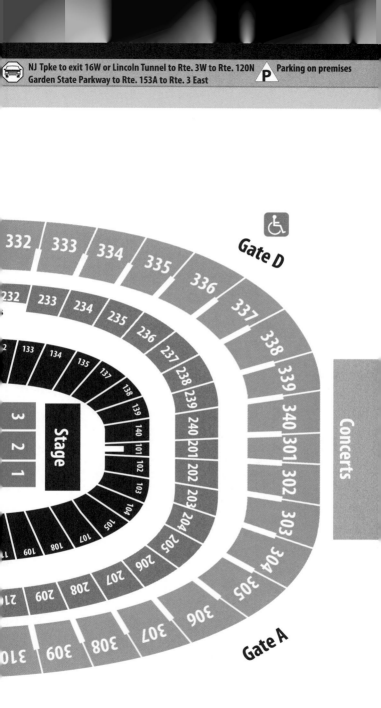

Gate D

Concerts

Gate A

Stage

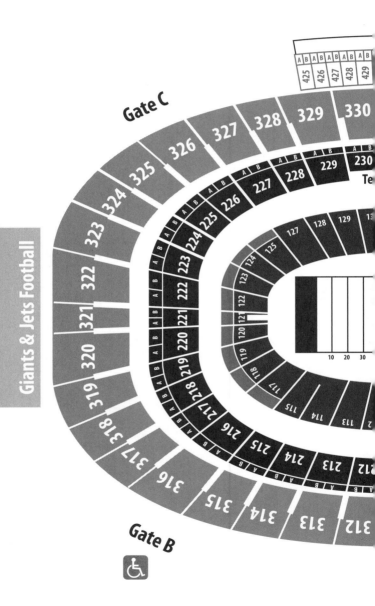

Meadowlands Sports Complex

50 Route 120 // East Rutherford, NJ
Information: (201) 935-3900 // Ticketmaster: (212) 307-7171
Giants Season Tickets: (201) 935-8222   [www.giants.com]
Jets Season Tickets: (516) 560-8200 [www.newyorkjets.com]

Gate C

Giants & Jets Football

Gate B

Giants Stadium

NJ Tpke to exit 16W or Lincoln Tunnel to Rte. 3W to Rte. 120N
Garden State Parkway to Rte. 153A to Rte. 3 East

Parking on premises

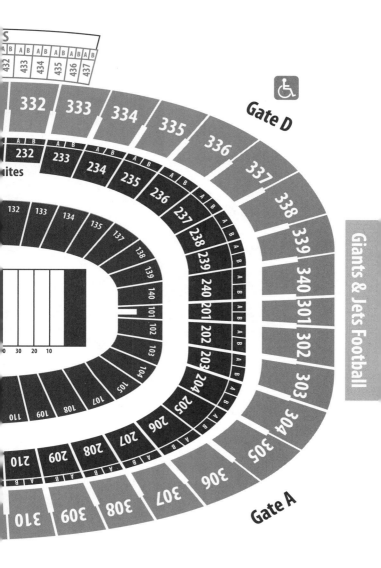

Gate D

Gate A

Giants & Jets Football

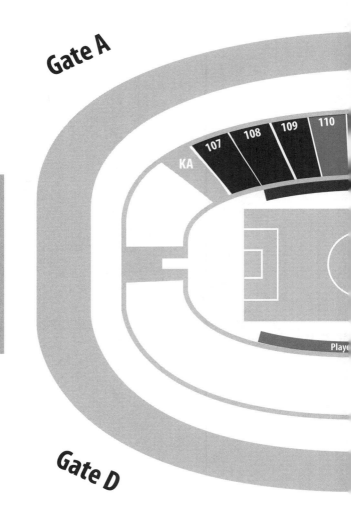

Gate A

Gate D

Red Bulls Soccer

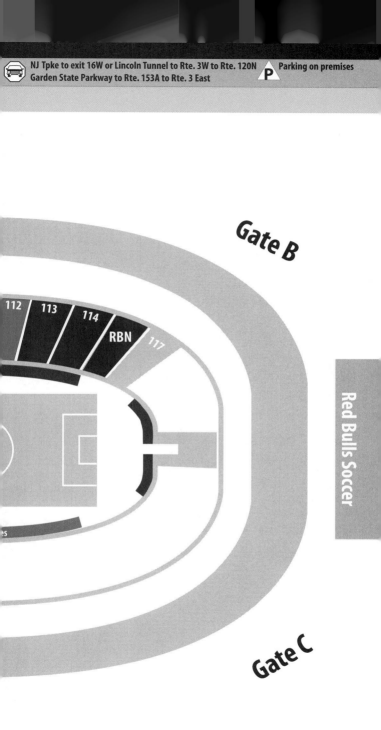

NJ Tpke to exit 16W or Lincoln Tunnel to Rte. 3W to Rte. 120N   Parking on premises
Garden State Parkway to Rte. 153A to Rte. 3 East

Gate B

112   113   114

RBN   117

Red Bulls Soccer

Gate C

Meadowlands Sports Complex

50 Route 120 // East Rutherford, NJ
Information: (201) 935-3900 // Ticketmaster: (212) 307-7171

[www.meadowlands.com]

NJ Tpke to exit 16W or Lincoln Tunnel to Rte. 3W to Rte. 120N   **P**   Parking on premises
Garden State Parkway to Rte. 153A to Rte. 3 East

Floor level configurations are subject to change

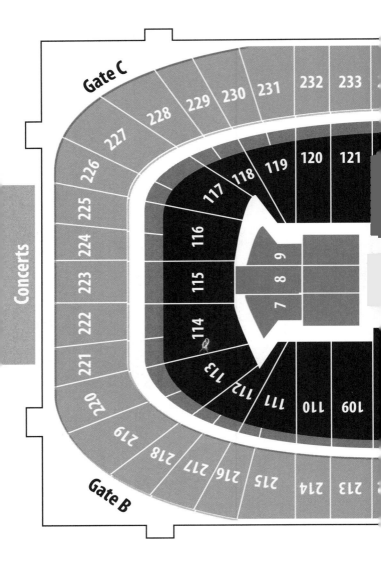

Floor level configurations are subject to change

Izod Center (Basketball)

NJ Tpke to exit 16W or Lincoln Tunnel to Rte. 3W to Rte. 120N
Garden State Parkway to Rte. 153A to Rte. 3 East

P Parking on premises

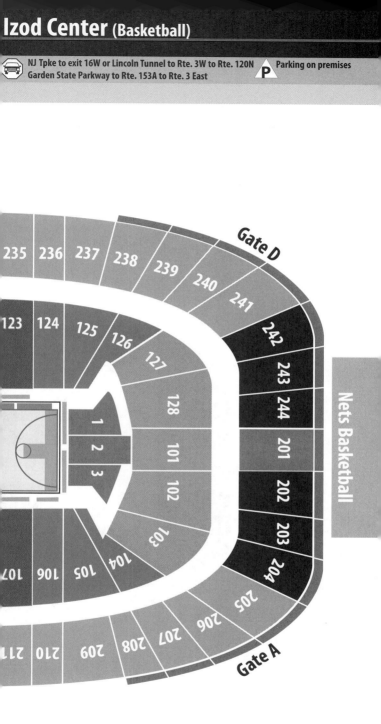

LIE [495] East to Exit 38 [Northern State Pkwy East] to Exit 31A [Meadowbrook Pkwy South] to Exit M4

Parking on premises

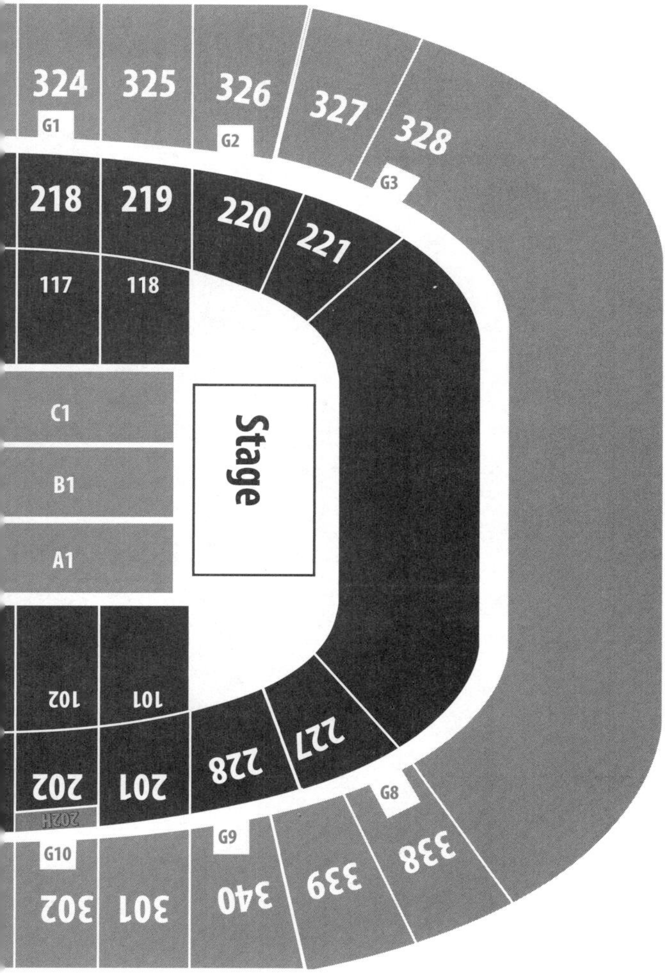

324	325	326	327	328
G1		G2		G3
218	219	220	221	
117	118			
C1				
B1	Stage			
A1				

Concerts

102	101		
202	201	228	227
G10		G9	G8
302	301	340	339	338

Floor level configurations are subject to change

Nassau Veterans Memorial Coliseum

1255 Hempstead Turnpike // Uniondale, NY

Information: (516) 794-9300 // Ticketmaster: (516) 888-9000

[www.nassaucoliseum.com]

LIE [495] East to Exit 38 [Northern State Pkwy East]
to Exit 31A [Meadowbrook Pkwy South] to Exit M4

Parking on Premises

Concert in the Round

Floor level configurations are subject to change

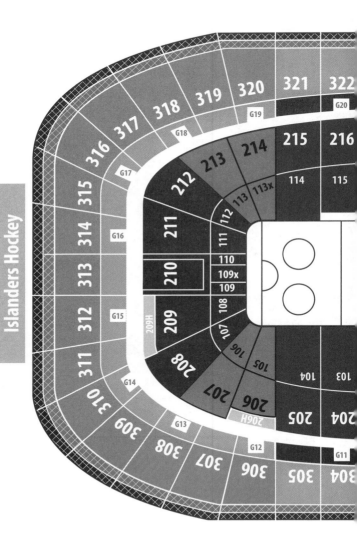

Islanders Hockey

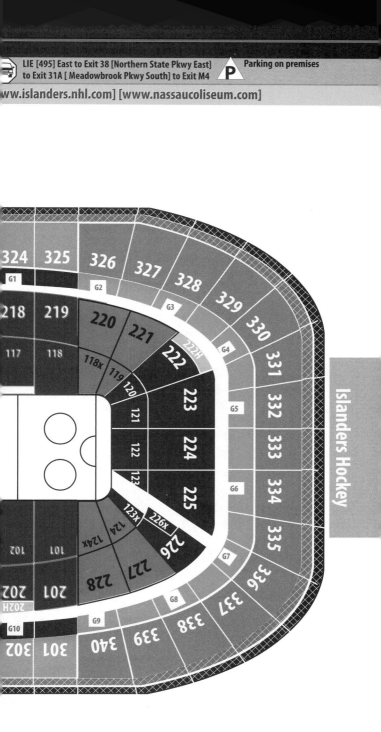

Islanders Hockey

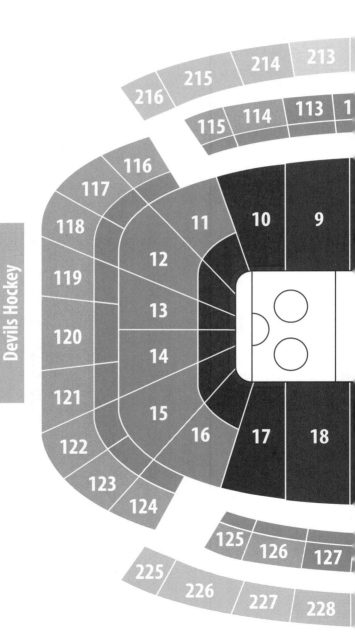

Prudential Center
195 Mulberry Street // Newark, NJ
Box Office: (973) 854-8760 // (201) 507-8900 // Info: 1 (800) NJ-DEVIL
Group Sales: (201) 939-6690

NJ Transit: Newark Broad Street Sta. [Free shuttle, two hours before and after event]

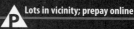 Lots in vicinity; prepay online

From NYC: G. Washington Bridge or Lincoln Tunnel to NJ Turnpike South to exit 15 Eeast. Right on Raymond Blvd., Left on Mulberry St.

www.prucenter.com] [www.devils.nhl.com]

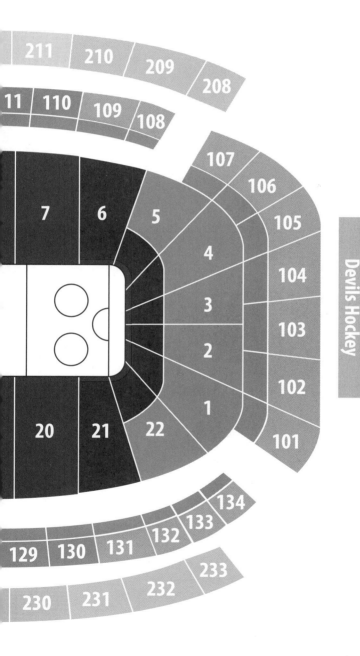

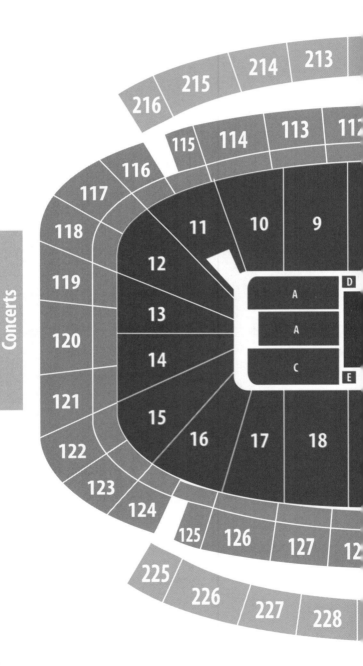

Concerts

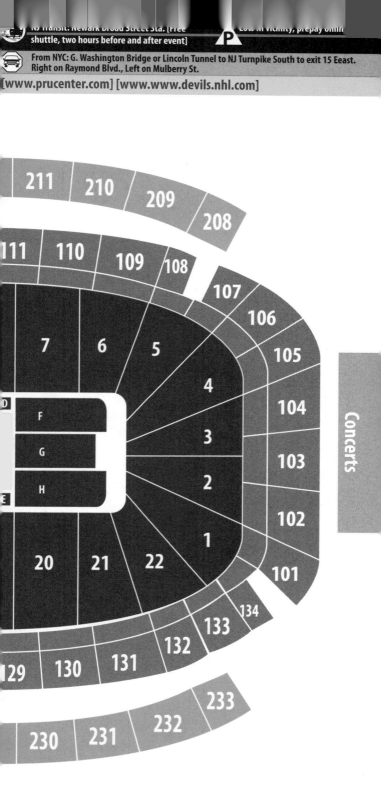

NJ Transit: Newark Broad Street Sta. [Free shuttle, two hours before and after event]

Lot in vicinity, prepay onlin

From NYC: G. Washington Bridge or Lincoln Tunnel to NJ Turnpike South to exit 15 Eeast. Right on Raymond Blvd., Left on Mulberry St.

[www.prucenter.com] [www.www.devils.nhl.com]

Concerts

Mets Baseball

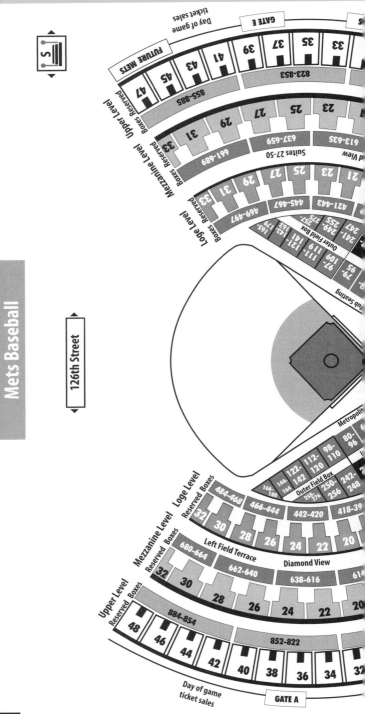

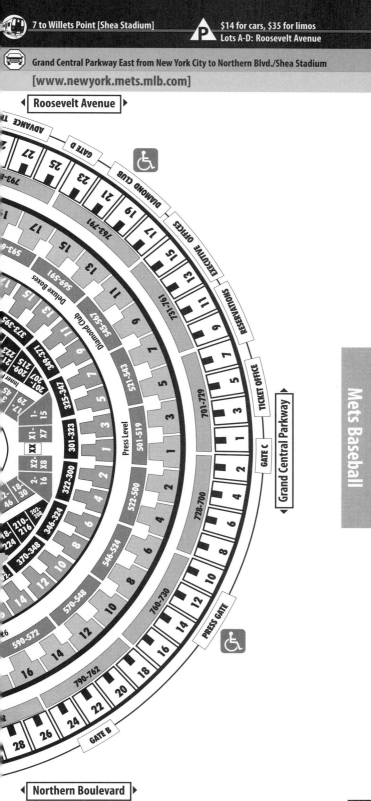

Roosevelt Avenue

ADVANCE T...

GATE D

DIAMOND CLUB

EXECUTIVE OFFICES

RESERVATIONS

TICKET OFFICE

GATE C

Grand Central Parkway

Deluxe Boxes

Diamond Club

Press Level

Inner

PRESS GATE

GATE B

Northern Boulevard

Mets Baseball

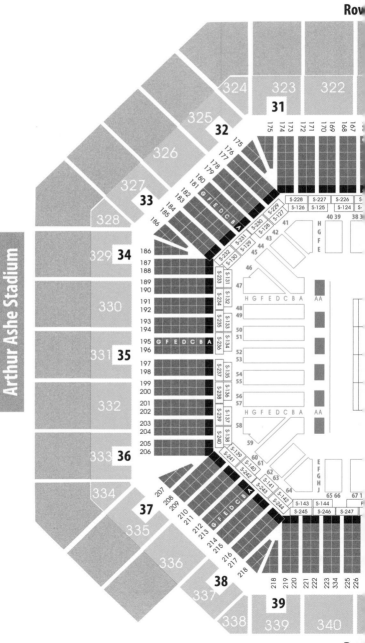

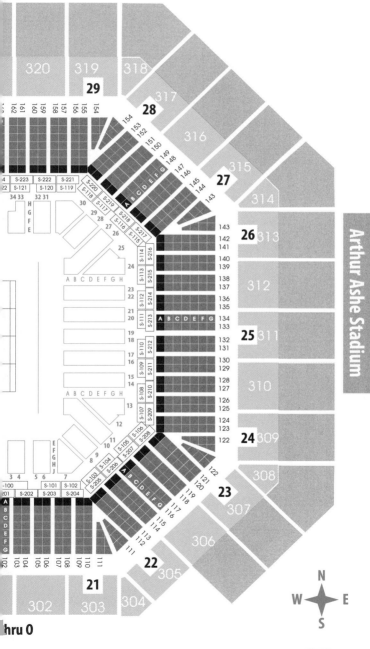

Shade: South, South West, and West sides of stadium

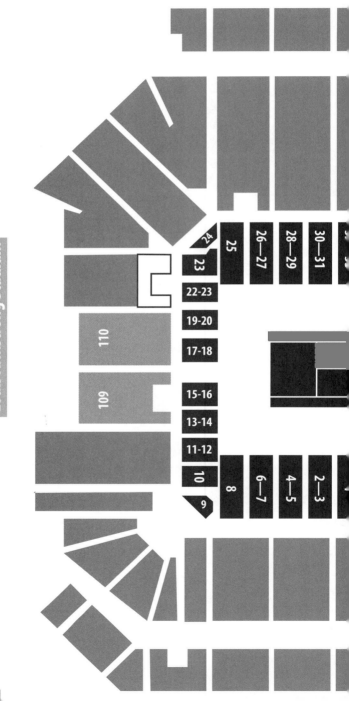

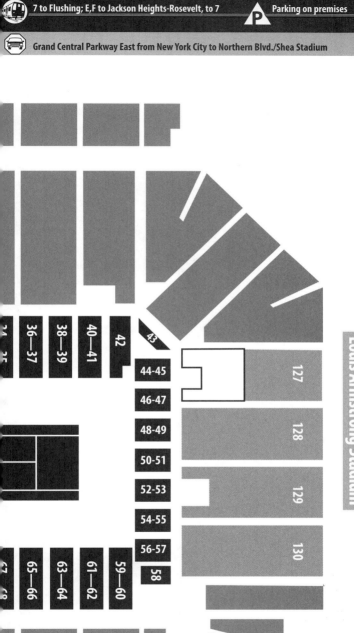

Louis Armstrong Stadium

36—37 · 38—39 · 40—41 · 42 · 43

44-45 · 46-47 · 48-49 · 50-51 · 52-53 · 54-55 · 56-57 · 58

59—60 · 61—62 · 63—64 · 65—66

127 · 128 · 129 · 130

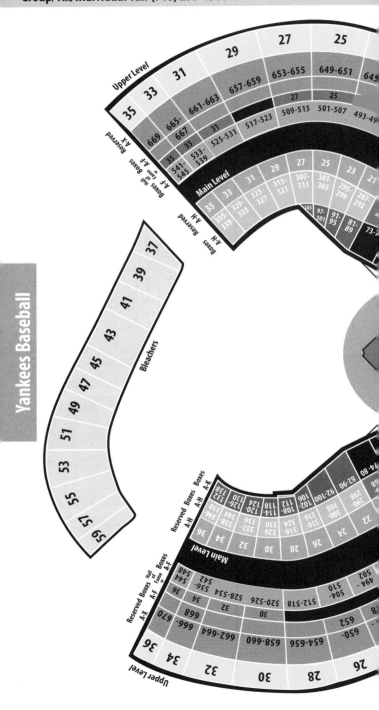

Yankees Baseball

Upper Level

35 33 31 29 27 25

649-651 649

653-655

657-659

661-663

665-667

669

27
25
509-515 501-507 493-49

517-523

525-531

533-539

541-545

31
33
35

Boxes Half A-F
of Fame
Reserved A-X

Main Level

35 33 31 29 27 25 23 21

335-339

329-333

323-327

315-321

307-313

301-305

295-299

287-293

103 97-101 91-95 81-89 73-

Boxes Reserved A-H

Bleachers

37 39 41 43 45 47 49 51 53 55 57 59

Reserved Boxes   Boxes
A-H   A-H   A-X

138 132 126-130 120-124 114-118 108-112 102-106 92-100 82-90 4-80

346-350 338-342 332-336 326-330 318-324 310-316 300-308 290-298 8

36 34 32 30 28 26 24 22

Main Level

Reserved Boxes   Boxes
A-F A-F   A-X
Half
of Fame

36 666-670 662-664 658-660 654-656 650-652 4

668

548 542 536-540 528-534 520-526 512-518 504-510 494-502 502

544

36 34 32 30 28 26

Upper Level

East 162st St. at Jerome & River Aves.

Major Deegan Expressway/I-87 North to Exit 4 [149th St.] or Exit 5 [155th St.]

[newyork.yankees.mlb.com]

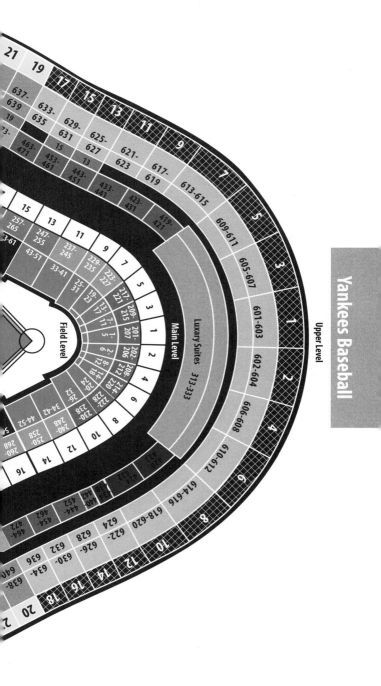

Yankees Baseball

Upper Level

Luxury Suites 313-333

Main Level

Field Level

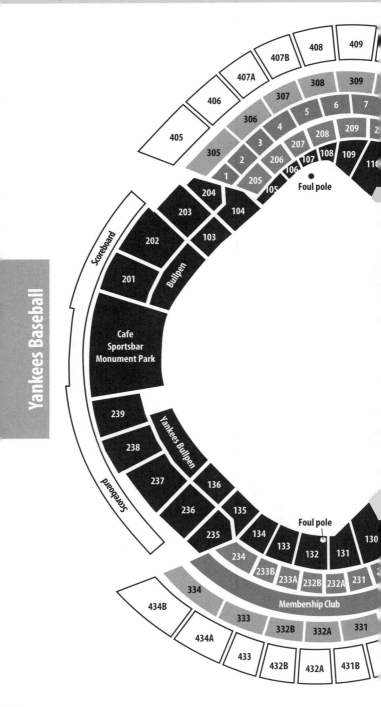

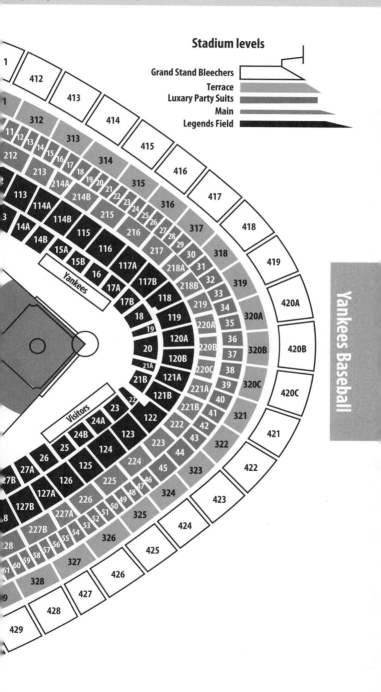

East 162st St. at Jerome & River Aves.

Major Deegan Expressway/I-87 North to Exit 4 [149th St.] or Exit 5 [155th St.]

ewyork.yankees.mlb.com]

Stadium levels

Grand Stand Bleechers
Terrace
Luxary Party Suits
Main
Legends Field

Yankees Baseball

Map Key

p icons

S Subway

Theatre

Information Services

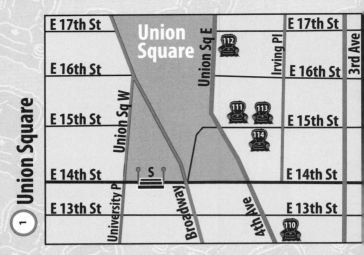

1 Union Square

E 17th St · Union Square · Union Sq E · E 17th St · 3rd Ave
112
E 16th St · Union Sq E · Irving Pl · E 16th St
111 · 113
E 15th St · Union Sq W · E 15th St
114
E 14th St · S · Broadway · E 14th St
University Pl · 4th Ave
E 13th St · E 13th St
110

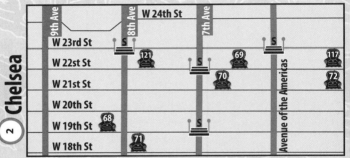

2 Chelsea

9th Ave · W 24th St · 8th Ave · 7th Ave
W 23rd St · S
W 22st St · 121 · S · 69 · S · 117
W 21st St · 70 · 72
W 20th St · Avenue of the Americas
W 19th St · 68 · S
W 18th St · 71

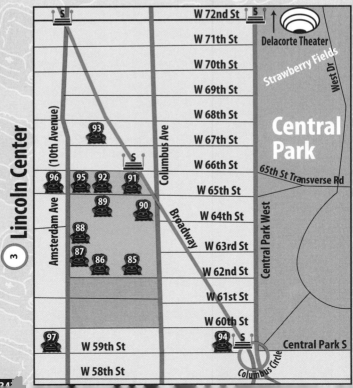

3 Lincoln Center

S · W 72nd St · S
Delacorte Theater
W 71st St
W 70th St · Strawberry Fields
W 69th St · West Dr
W 68th St
93 · W 67th St · Central Park
(10th Avenue) · Columbus Ave · W 66th St
S
96 · 95 · 92 · 91 · W 65th St · 65th St Transverse Rd
89 · 90 · W 64th St · Broadway · Central Park West
88 · W 63rd St
87 · 86 · 85 · W 62nd St
Amsterdam Ave · W 61st St
W 60th St
97 · W 59th St · 94 · S · Central Park S
W 58th St · Columbus Circle

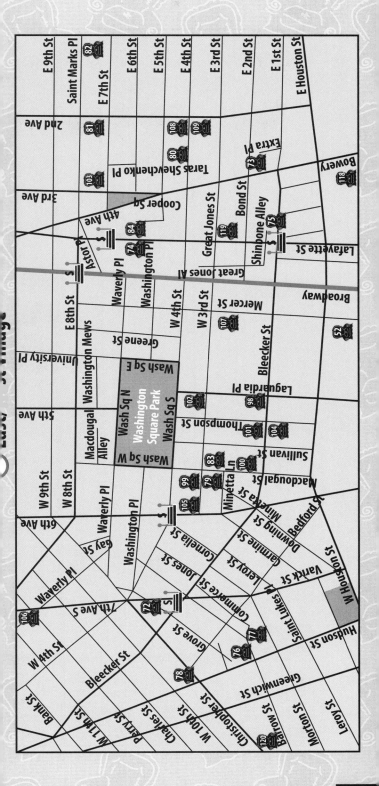

East Village
343

8th Ave

61
58
64
63
55
62
66
116

PORT AUTHORITY

9th Ave
54
115

57
60

Dyer Ave
65
67
59

10th Ave

11th Ave
56

W 47th St
W 46th St
W 45th St
W 44th St
W 43rd St
W 42nd St
W 41st St